THE HATEFUL AND THE OBSCENE:
STUDIES IN THE LIMITS OF FREE EXPRESSION

In a series of landmark decisions since 1990, Canadian courts have shaped a distinctive approach to the regulation of obscenity, hate literature, and child pornography. Missing from the debate, however, has been any attempt to determine whether the legal status quo can be justified by reference to a framework of moral/political principles. *The Hateful and the Obscene* is intended to fill that gap.

L.W. Sumner brings philosophical depth and theoretical rigour to some of the most important and difficult questions concerning free expression. Building on a framework set out by J.S. Mill – that a legal restriction of expression is justified only when the expression in question is harmful to others and when the benefits of the restriction will exceed its costs – Sumner shows how the Canadian courts have replicated Mill's framework in their interpretation of the Canadian Charter of Rights and Freedoms.

The Hateful and the Obscene is a compelling interpretation of freedom of expression that combines serious philosophical thought with a focus on Canadian law, thus offering the breadth capable of dealing with both obscenity and hate literature.

(Toronto Studies in Philosophy)

L.W. SUMNER is University Professor of Philosophy at the University of Toronto

The Hateful and the Obscene

Studies in the Limits of Free Expression

L. W. Sumner

UNIVERSITY OF TORONTO PRESS
Toronto Buffalo London

© University of Toronto Press Incorporated 2004
Toronto Buffalo London

Printed in Canada

ISBN 0-8020-4239-2 (cloth)
ISBN 0-8020-8083-9 (paper)

∞

Printed on acid-free paper

Toronto Studies in Philosophy
Editors: Donald Ainslie and Amy Mullin

National Library of Canada Cataloguing in Publication

Sumner, L.W. (Leonard Wayne), 1941–
    The hateful and the obscene : studies in the limits of free
    expression / L.W. Sumner.

    (Toronto studies in philosophy)
    Includes bibliographical references and index.
    ISBN 0-8020-4239-2 (bound)   ISBN 0-8020-8083-9 (pbk.)

    1. Freedom of speech – Canada.   2. Hate speech – Canada.
    3. Pornography – Law and legislation – Canada.   I. Title.
    II. Series.

    KE 4420.S93 2004   342.71'90853   C2004-900307-0
    KF4483.C522S93 2004

University of Toronto Press acknowledges the financial assistance to its
publishing program of the Canada Council for the Arts and the Ontario
Arts Council.

University of Toronto Press acknowledges the financial support for its
publishing activities of the Government of Canada through the Book
Publishing Industry Development Program (BPIDP).

This book has been published with the help of a grant from the Canadian
Federation for the Humanities and Social Sciences, through the Aid to
Scholarly Publications Programme, using funds provided by the Social
Sciences and Humanities Research Council of Canada.

For Herbert Hart and Joel Feinberg,
who established standards for writing
on philosophy and law
to which I continue to aspire

Contents

Preface

In 1990 I was invited by Wil Waluchow to participate in a conference on freedom of expression that he was hosting at McMaster University. Although I had written on general theoretical questions concerning rights, the more focused topic of speech rights was new territory for me. When I received Wil's invitation I was serving as department chair and finding it difficult to clear the large blocks of time I needed for the book-length project on well-being I had underway. A shorter piece on a cluster of intrinsically interesting issues seemed both feasible and attractive, and so I presented a paper at Wil's conference defending Canada's hate propaganda law. Little did I suspect on that occasion that this modest initial foray would evolve into its own book-length project. But once having begun to think about issues of expressive freedom I found it impossible to stop. This book is the (belated) outcome of that process.

Work on the project has been sustained by two mutually reinforcing interests on my part. The first is a strong belief in human rights in general and civil liberties in particular. I have long had a special concern with the issues raised by legal controls on obscenity and hate speech – the two main areas of focus in this book. My instinctive, not fully thought-out, stance was opposed to the former but in favour of the latter (thus my defence of the hate propaganda law at the McMaster conference). But I was never quite convinced in my own mind that these two commitments were mutually consistent. Why should I find censorship of the hateful easier to justify than censorship of the obscene? Continuing to work on this territory, and eventually deciding that nothing short of a book would suffice, provided me with the opportunity to scrutinize and test my own pretheoretical convictions.

My other reason for persisting with this project was theoretical rather than practical. In 1987 I published a book entitled *The Moral Foundation of Rights* which argued that both rights and their limits are best justified by an appeal to consequences. In the abstract that argument seemed compelling (to me at least), but it needed to be tested by working it out in detail for some particular constellation of important rights. Given my pre-existing interest in the right to free expression, this seemed the natural testing ground for the general theory. Working out its implications for expressive freedom would both enable me to see how well the theory fared in this domain and – ideally, anyway – provide my pretheoretical convictions with more of a principled foundation.

So this book tries to unite theory and practice by developing a principled framework for expressive rights and then applying it to the particular cases of obscenity and hate literature. Although it starts on a fairly philosophical plane, it ends with some quite practical conclusions about Canadian public policy in this area. Those conclusions are rather sweeping, and some readers may find some of them radical. Indeed, I still find some of them radical. One of the results of testing my own previous convictions by reference to a principled theory was that not all of them survived. In particular, I reached the conclusion that my earlier pair of commitments – in favour of legal controls on hate speech, against similar controls on obscenity – was indeed inconsistent. To render it consistent I was compelled to revise my view of Canada's hate propaganda law and therefore to repudiate the position I had defended at that McMaster conference. This was, for me, a bracing reminder of how awkward it can be to accept the philosophical discipline of following one's own arguments wherever they might lead.

During the course of articulating and defending my views on freedom of expression I have received a great deal of assistance from others. First off, I want to acknowledge the support I received from the Social Sciences and Humanities Research Council, which awarded me two Research Grants for the period from 1994–2000, and from the Connaught Fund of the University of Toronto, whose Research Fellowship provided valuable release time from teaching in 1998. I am also grateful for the encouragement I received from Ron Schoeffel and Len Husband, philosophy editors at University of Toronto Press. I apologize to them for having taken so long to deliver the finished product and thank them for their patience.

Along the way I have been helped enormously by a small army of research assistants. The three graduate assistants who worked with me were Sharon Kaye, Cheryl Cline, and Anthony Skelton. The undergraduates who signed on to the project through the University of Toronto's innovative Research Opportunities Program were Anita Chong, Jacob Glick, Maira Hassan, Olivia Leung, Mai Phan, Shahmeen Sadiq, and Darren Yuen, and the high school student who participated through the university's Mentorship Program was Bernadette Chung. In addition, in the latter stages of the book's development most of its chapters were workshopped in undergraduate and graduate seminars, from whose members I received much valuable feedback. The impassioned dissenters from my general line of approach were particularly helpful in forcing me to improve my arguments and rethink my conclusions.

Academic colleagues were equally generous with their time. Particular chapters were read by Hilliard Aronovitch, Brian Barry, Raphael Cohen-Almagor, David Dyzenhaus, Richard Moon, Kevin O'Rourke, Jonathan Riley, Hillel Steiner, and Scott Woodcock. I received detailed comments on the manuscript as a whole from Donald Ainslie, David Braybrooke, and Anthony Skelton, all of whom were instrumental in improving the argument in countless ways. I owe a particular debt of gratitude to Tom Hurka, with whom I had very fruitful chapter-by-chapter discussions. The finished product is much the better for his acute comments and criticisms.

Finally, I wish to thank my wife, Heather Wright, for her many contributions to the development of this book, not least her suggestion of its title.

Toronto
October 2003

THE HATEFUL AND THE OBSCENE

So we are confronted with a situation in which many liberals and radicals are deeply angered and shocked by racist remarks and want to use the law to suppress them, whereas many politically conservative people argue against such suppression by invoking the general right to free speech. On the other hand, these same liberals and radicals are against the censorship of obscenity and blasphemy. If there is an inconsistency in their attitudes, this inconsistency is equally evident in the views of those who firmly believe that blasphemy should be a crime, while at the same time preaching the right of people to express racist views. Both sides seem to have been carried away by the strength of their respective feelings, and to have abandoned all firm principles.

C.L. Ten, *Mill on Liberty*

Chapter 1

A Theory of Free Expression?

We all agree that the right to free expression has limits, but we do not agree on where those limits are to be drawn. Issues of the extent and boundaries of the right confront us every day, in the media, in the courts, in the classroom, in our workplaces, in our neighbourhoods. If our convictions on these issues are to reflect more than just the strength of our feelings, then it seems that we must follow C.L. Ten's exhortation to ground them on 'firm principles'. But why not raise our sights even higher, by trying to construct (what we may grandly call) a *theory* of free expression: a coherent set of principles capable of answering the most important conceptual, moral, and political questions about expressive freedom and its limits? These questions would include (but not be limited to) the following: Why do we regard expression as important enough to be protected by a right? What values are served by a right to free expression? What counts as expression for the purpose of such a right? Are different kinds of expression protected equally by this right? What are the limits of the right? What values can come into conflict with the exercise of the right to free expression? Are these values also protected by rights? If so, how do we adjudicate conflicts between these rights? Does the right to free expression always trump competing rights? If not, when must it give way to them? What are the costs of limiting or abridging the right to free expression?

The project of this book is twofold: to develop a theoretical framework for answering these questions and to apply that framework to the challenges to free speech rights raised by two problematic forms of expression: hate speech and pornography. Most of that work will be done in subsequent chapters. The task of this chapter is both general and preliminary: to explore some of the key concepts and issues which will recur through the later discussions. Since our topic is the right to free expression, we open with an inquiry into the concept of a right.

1.1 An Anatomy of Rights

We can begin this inquiry by trying to identify the distinctive kind of normative work rights are best equipped to do. Let us say that one part of our ethical thinking has to do with the promotion of social goals which we deem to be valuable for their own sake: the general welfare, equality of opportunity, the eradication of poverty, the achievement of peace, or whatever. It is this part of our thinking which is well captured by the broad family of consequentialist ethical theories. On the other hand, we also tend to think that some means societies might employ to achieve these goals are unjustifiable because they exploit or victimize particular individuals or groups. One natural way of expressing this thought is that these parties have rights which constrain or limit the pursuit of social goals, rights which must (at least sometimes) be respected even though a valuable goal would be better promoted by ignoring or infringing them. This is the part of our ethical thinking that deontological theories aim to accommodate. On this way of thinking, rights function normatively as safeguards for vulnerable individuals or groups in the face of collective social action.

This characterization takes us some way toward identifying the moral/political function of rights, and also begins to explain their perennial appeal. But it is not yet sufficient to show how rights are distinctive or unique. Duties and obligations impose similar constraints on the pursuit of collective goals: if I have an obligation to pay my income tax then that is what I must do, even though more good would result from my donating the money to Oxfam. So what is the particular way in which rights limit our promotion of valuable states of affairs? And what exactly is the relationship between rights and duties? We need to look more closely at the anatomy of rights.[1]

A simple example will serve to get us started. Suppose that you have lent me your chainsaw, so that I can cut up some fallen tree branches for firewood, on condition that I return it by Tuesday. You now have the right to have your chainsaw returned by Tuesday. Note that there are three distinct elements to this right. First, it has a *subject*: the holder or bearer of the right (in this case, you). Second, it has an *object*: the person against whom the right is held (in this case, me). Third, it has a *content*: what it is the right to do or to have done (in this case, to have the chainsaw returned by me). Every right has these three elements, though they may not always be spelled out fully in the specification of the right. The paradigm subjects of rights are competent adult humans, though nothing in this analysis prevents them from being attributed as well to other beings, such as children, persons with serious cognitive disabilities, animals, corporations, collectivities, and so on. The object of a right must be an agent capable of having duties or obligations, since your right that I return your chainsaw on Tuesday entails my obligation to return it on Tuesday. The class of objects of rights may therefore be narrower than the class of subjects (it may be true, for instance, that animals have rights, but it cannot be true that we have rights against them). The object of your right is a specific assignable person (me), since it is I who have borrowed your chainsaw and am duty-bound to return it. However, the objects of a right may also be an unassignable group; some rights, such as the right not to be assaulted or killed, may hold against everyone in general.

Finally, the content of a right is always some action on the part of either the subject or the object of the right. This fact is obscured by the shorthand way in which we refer to many rights, where it may appear that the content of the right is a thing or state of affairs. We may speak, for instance, of the right to an education or to health care or to life itself. But in all such cases the full specification of the right will reveal the actions which constitute its content: that the state provide subsidized public education or health care, or that others not act in such a way as to endanger life, or whatever. The contents of many rights are intricate and complex actions on the part of (assignable or unassignable) others, actions which must be fully spelled out before we know exactly what the right amounts to. In the case of your right, the action in question is simple and specific: my returning your chainsaw by Tuesday. You therefore have the right that something be done (by the person against whom your right is held). This kind of normative advantage on your part is usually described as a *claim*: you have a claim *against me* that I return your chainsaw which is logically equivalent to my duty *to you* to return the chainsaw. In general, A's claim against B that B do X is equivalent to B's duty toward A to do X: claims and duties are in this way correlative. Claims are always of the form that something be done: the actions which make up their content must be those of another, never those of the right-holder herself. Since the content of your right against me has the form of a claim, we may call it a *claim-right*. Claim-rights constitute an important class of rights, one which includes contractual rights (held against assignable parties) and rights to security of the person (held against everyone in general).

However, not all rights are claim-rights. Another example will make this clear. Because you own your chainsaw, you have the right to use it (when you want to). This right has the same subject (you) as your claim-right, but a different content and a different object. Its content is once again an action, but this time an action by you rather than someone else: it is a right *to do* (yourself) rather than *to have done* (by someone else). The content of the right therefore does not have the form of a claim; it is common instead to refer to it as a *liberty*. To say that you have the liberty to use your chainsaw is to say that you are under no obligation not to use it or, alternatively, that your use of it is permissible. Actually, it is implicitly to say more than this, since your right to use your chainsaw (when you want to) includes the right not to use it (when you don't want to). You therefore have two distinct liberties: to use the chainsaw (which means that you have no duty not to use it) and not to use it (which means that you have no duty to use it). We normally treat these as the two sides of one (complex) liberty: to use or not to use the chainsaw, as you wish. In general, A's liberty to do X (or not) is logically equivalent to the absence both of A's duty to do X and A's duty not to do X. Your ownership right over the chainsaw therefore entails your freedom to choose whether or not to use it; how this is to go is up to you. Since the content of your right has the form of a liberty, we may call it a *liberty-right*. Liberty-rights constitute another important class of rights, exemplified *inter alia* by property rights and by rights to various freedoms (of thought, belief, conscience, expression, etc.).

So far we have located a subject and a content for your liberty-right, but not an object. Against whom is this right held? In the case of claim-rights the answer to this question is straightforward: whoever bears the duty which is equivalent to the claim. Because claim-rights specify obligations, and because these obligations are assigned to particular parties (or to everyone in general), claim-rights enable us to easily locate their objects. But your liberty-right to use your chainsaw involves on the face of it no claim (or duty); the liberty in question just consists in the absence of duties on your part. It is therefore not so obviously held *against* anyone. And indeed if we restrict ourselves just to its stipulated content, that is true: it is a right which imposes no duties. However, we know that property rights are typically protected by duties imposed on others: for instance, duties not to interfere with the use or enjoyment of the property in question. By virtue of your property right you have more than just the bare unprotected liberty to use (or not use) your chainsaw as you please; this liberty is safeguarded by what H.L.A. Hart has usefully called a 'protective perimeter' of duties imposed on others.[2] I therefore have the duty not to interfere with your use of your chainsaw (by stealing it, damaging it, using it without permission, etc.), and so does everyone else. We learn therefore the lesson that liberty-rights are not as simple as they seem: they involve a complex bundle of liberties (held by the subject) and duties (imposed on others). The others who bear these duties are the (implicit) objects of the right.

Even claim-rights are not as simple as they seem. Let us return to your right that I return your chainsaw by Tuesday. Your claim against me is, as we have seen, logically equivalent to my duty to you. Now suppose that I need the chainsaw for an additional day and ask to return it on Wednesday instead. You can, of course, refuse my request and insist on the performance of my duty. But you can also agree to it, in which case you waive your right to have the chainsaw returned by Tuesday and release me from my original obligation. You now have a new right (to have the chainsaw returned by Wednesday) and I have a new correlative obligation. In waiving your original right you have exercised a *power* which enables you to alter my obligation. Indeed, in entering into the agreement about the chainsaw in the first place, both of us have exercised powers which resulted in the creation of your claim-right against me and my liberty-right to use your chainsaw. Contractual rights, which constitute one important class of claim-rights, therefore involve more than just claims; they also involve powers (and liberties to exercise those powers, and duties imposed on others not to interfere with those liberties, and immunities against being deprived of the powers, and so on). Even relatively simple-seeming claim-rights are therefore typically quite complex bundles of different elements. The core of the right is still a claim, but this core is surrounded by a periphery made up of other elements (claims, liberties, powers, etc.).[3] This periphery may be quite different for different claim-rights. Contractual rights typically confer on their subjects considerable discretion about the exercise of the right, including the power to waive it or to annul it entirely. Other claim-rights, such as the right not to be harmed or killed, may impose more limits on the subject's liberty (or power) to waive or annul the right. The full specification of a claim-right, including all of its periphery, can therefore be a very complex matter.

The same complexity, and the same relation of core to periphery, can be found in the case of liberty-rights. Your liberty-right to use your chainsaw (or not, as you please) is not accompanied only by a protective perimeter of duties imposed on others. It also includes your power to annul your liberty to use the chainsaw, either temporarily (by lending the chainsaw to me) or permanently (by selling it), plus your liberty to exercise this power, plus further duties imposed on others not to interfere with your exercise of this power, plus ... Like claim-rights, libertyrights are typically complex bundles of different elements. The core of the right is still a liberty, but it too is surrounded by a periphery made up of other elements (claims, liberties, powers, etc.).

A full exploration of the intricate anatomy of rights can be a complicated affair.[4] Fortunately, we have revealed enough of this anatomy to be able to answer our questions about the distinctive normative function of rights. First, the relationship between rights and duties. Although these two concepts are clearly connected, the connections between them are more complex than they first appear. There is a simple relationship between claims and their correlative duties: A's claim against B that B do X is logically equivalent to B's duty toward A to do X. Exclusive attention to claim-rights might lead one to think that rights are just duties seen, as it were, from the perspective of the patient rather than the agent. But this is not the case. There is more to a right, even a claimright, than just a claim against some correlative duty-bearer. Claimrights, like liberty-rights, are typically complex clusters of different kinds of elements (duties, liberties, powers, immunities, etc.). Every such right will include some duties, either in its core or in its periphery (or both). But no right of either kind can just be reduced to a duty, or a set of duties. Rights also contain elements which are not duties and are not definable in terms of duties. Furthermore, they have a structure, an internal logic, which is distinctively different from that of duties.

This brings us to our other question: how is it that rights limit the pursuit of valuable social goals? The complex structure of rights reveals two answers to this question. First, by containing duties imposed on their objects, rights limit the freedom of others to pursue such goals; they must (at least sometimes) fulfil their duty even when a worthwhile goal would be better promoted by not doing so. Second, by containing liberties conferred on their subjects, rights secure the freedom of right-holders not to pursue such goals; they may (at least sometimes) choose to exercise their right even when a worthwhile goal would be better promoted by not doing so. Rights therefore impose restrictions on others (who must not promote the collectively best outcome) and confer prerogatives on their holders (who need not do so).[5] By these means, rights define protected spaces in which individuals are able to pursue their own personal projects or have their personal interests safeguarded, free from the demands of larger collective enterprises.

The qualifiers 'at least sometimes' in the preceding paragraph deserve some brief attention. They signal that neither the liberties that rights confer on their holders nor the duties they impose on others need be absolute. And this brings us to a fourth dimension of a right (besides its subject, object, and content), namely its *strength*. The strength of a right is its level of resistance to rival normative considerations, such as competing rights or the promotion of worthwhile goals. A right will insulate its holder to some extent against the necessity of taking these considerations into account, but it will also typically have a threshold above which they dominate or override the right. Should it turn out, for instance, that I need your chainsaw in order to protect myself against serious property damage (a tree limb is about to fall on my house) or against serious personal injury (a gang of terrorists is trying to kidnap me), then my duty to return it on time (and your claim that it be returned) may be overridden even without your permission. Likewise, the same degree of urgency may override your liberty-right to use the chainsaw when you please. Rights raise thresholds against considerations of social utility, but these thresholds are seldom insurmountable. Some particularly important rights (against torture, perhaps, or slavery, or genocide) may be absolute, but most are not.

1.2 Concepts and Issues

Having gained some sense of the structure and function of rights in general, we can now begin to focus on the right to free expression in particular. In the abstract, a right is typically identified or individuated by its content – what it is a right *to*. At least on the surface, the content of this right appears to be the freedom to engage in a particular form of conduct, namely expression. However, that appearance is slightly misleading. While some kind of freedom is clearly guaranteed or protected by the right to free expression, that freedom is entailed by the fact that we are clearly dealing here with a liberty-right. We know that a liberty-right is in question because the core of the right is the subject's liberty to do (express) something. And we know that the function of a liberty-right to engage in a particular form of conduct is to safeguard the right-holder's freedom of choice over that conduct (to engage in it or not, as s/he wishes). Strictly speaking, therefore, it is redundant to speak of the right to *freedom of expression*, instead of simply the liberty-right to expression.[6] What is distinctive about the right – what differentiates it from other liberty-rights – is that its content consists in expression rather than some other form of conduct.

To specify the right more precisely, therefore, we need to ask what is to count, for its purposes, as expression.[7] When it is a legal right which is in question, the ultimate authorities on the interpretation of its content are the legislature and courts. In a later chapter we will note the gloss that the Supreme Court of Canada has put on 'expression' for the purpose of interpreting and applying the guarantee of free expression in the Charter of Rights and Freedoms.[8] However, we can anticipate that exercise by construing expression very broadly so as to include any act of communicating a meaning or content by any means whatever. The paradigm instances of expression are those in which the medium of communication is language and the content communicated is a belief or idea. But communication can also take non-linguistic forms, including gestures or body language, visual images, sounds, symbolic objects, and actions. Communicative content also need not be strictly cognitive or propositional but can instead consist of feelings, attitudes, emotions, desires, requests, or other (wholly or partially) non-cognitive states. In general, the test of whether or not some action counts as expressive is whether it is intended by the agent to convey a meaning. On this interpretation, even acts of violence (such as those carried out by the Unabomber or the terrorists who destroyed the World Trade Center) may qualify as expressive if they are meant by their perpetrators to send a message. The conclusion which follows immediately is that the right to (free) expression cannot be unlimited: no society can afford to protect people's right to communicate whatever content they wish by whatever means they choose. The question must be not whether to limit expressive freedom, but which expression to limit (and when and how).

Now that we have some sense (however preliminary) of the content of a right to free expression, let us return for a moment to the freedom issue. Despite the fact that the freedom to communicate some meaning or other is implicit in the liberty-right, it is none the less worth some separate attention. It is common in political philosophy to distinguish two types or concepts of freedom (or liberty): negative and positive.[9] Negative freedom is the absence of external restrictions or constraints on action, especially those imposed by the agency of others. Whatever its particular formulation, the liberty-right of expression is clearly intended to protect the subject's freedom of choice against such constraints.

Where the constraints are normative (whether legal or moral), this protection is logically implied by the liberty-right itself, since the liberty to express some content (or not, as the subject wishes) is incompatible with being under an obligation not to do so (or, for that matter, to do so). At a bare minimum, therefore, the legal right to engage in some particular form of expression must preclude both a legal requirement and a legal prohibition with respect to that expression. But the absence of normative constraints is only the beginning of the story about negative freedom. Having the normative liberty to communicate is of little use if others are preventing one from doing so (by means of force, or threats, or any other form of interference). Securing the subject's freedom against constraints of this sort is one of the functions of the 'protective perimeter' around the core liberty which will impose duties on others not to interfere (thereby conferring on the subject a claim-right not to be interfered with). These duties will be negative in form: *not to do* this, that, or the other which will hamper or restrict the subject in the exercise of her expressive freedom. But freedom may need more than protection against externally imposed constraints: it may also need enhancement, or development, or facilitation. Just as the normative liberty to communicate is of little value in the face of adverse constraints, it may also be nugatory if the subject lacks the means or resources to exercise it. Those means or resources can include a venue or medium where one can connect with an audience (a hall, a public space, a publication), or the material wherewithal necessary for circulating one's opinions (a computer, funds to run a newspaper advertisement or to start up a newsletter), or an interpreter to bridge a language gap between speaker and audience, or a tutor to develop linguistic skills, or ... Whatever the precise form of the goods or services in question, the periphery surrounding the core liberty can also include duties imposed on others (or on the state) to provide them (thereby conferring on the subject claim-rights to be so provided). Because these duties will be positive (duties *to do* this, that, and the other), the freedom they enhance is itself positive in nature.

The bare concept of a right of free expression does not determine the nature and extent of the duties imposed on others which constitute its periphery. They can be confined to negative duties of non-interference, in which case the freedom protected will itself be merely negative, or they can also include positive duties of assistance or facilitation. Particular articulations of the liberty-right will have to specify just which duties, and therefore which claim-rights, are included in its periphery, thus how normatively demanding it is. They will also have to specify any limits on the content of the right – that is, on the forms of expression in which the subject is at liberty to engage. Limits on expressive freedom may be either externally or internally imposed. The limit is external if it results from conflict between the right and some other normative consideration (such as a competing right) of equal or greater strength. In that case, the rival consideration can be said to override or trump the expressive right, whose content is internally unlimited.[10] The limit is internal if it imposes a restriction on the forms of expression protected by the right, so that the content of the right is now interpreted as *any form of expression, except the following* ... We noted above that the concept of expression is extremely expansive, encompassing any meaning communicated by any means. Not all forms of expression need be included within the scope of a right to free expression. Historically, the chief candidates for exclusion have been blasphemy, obscenity, and defamation. In religiously pluralistic societies we are less likely nowadays to be overly upset about blasphemy (unless it also takes the form of defamation). But we remain concerned about obscenity (in the form of pornography) and about defamation (in the form of hate propaganda).[11] To better understand possible limits to expressive rights, we need to take a preliminary look at both of these forms of expression.

What is pornography? The first step toward answering this question is to underline the difference between pornography and obscenity. Pornography is a kind of representation, using media such as words and pictures, which is presumably to be distinguished from other kinds of representation by some peculiar features of content or context (yet to be identified). Obscenity, by contrast, can mean either of two things, neither of them identical with pornography. In ordinary language, the obscene is whatever we find disgusting or repugnant or shocking; it thus marks a particular modality of response to something by the viewer or audience. The thing in question may be found to be obscene on grounds of sexual content, but it need not. It also need not be a representation of anything; instead, it may be an event or state of affairs, such as an obscene display of wealth in the face of abject poverty. If some (or even all) pornography is obscene in this sense then this is clearly an added (and culturally and historically conditioned) feature of it, rather than part of its very definition. In the language of the law, on the other hand, the obscene is whatever is defined as such for the purpose of legal regulation. In Canadian law the statutory definition of obscenity picks out publications 'a dominant characteristic of which is the undue exploitation of sex'.[12] This definition confines the scope of obscenity to representations with sexual content, but leaves it an open question whether all pornography is obscene (and also, for that matter, whether all obscenity is pornographic).[13] Since the question whether pornography should be regulated, by an obscenity law or any other means, is one we want to explore, we clearly cannot identify the pornographic with the obscene from the outset.

So we are seeking a definition of pornography, not obscenity. Since pornography is a kind of representation, the natural way to proceed is to identify it in terms of its content – what it represents. And it seems clear that in order for a representation to count as pornographic its content must be sexual: either the depiction of sexual scenes or activities, or the display of bodies as sexually attractive, or the representation of other scenes (such as violence) in a sexualized way. But non-pornographic representations (including novels, films, advertisements, etc.) can also have sexual content: what distinguishes the pornographic representation from the sexual or erotic? In answering this question, we have two ways to go. One is exemplified by the distinction between pornography and erotica which has been advocated by a number of feminist writers.[14] While both have sexual content, erotica is confined to material which depicts women under conditions of equality and mutuality. Pornography, on the other hand, is defined as representations of sex in which women are subordinated, degraded, and/or exploited.[15] This definition of pornography is heavily moralized or politicized: erotica is nice, good, to be tolerated or even celebrated; pornography is nasty, bad, to be regulated or suppressed entirely. For our purposes in this discussion the definition is badly flawed. For one thing, it applies only with considerable strain to entire subcategories of the genre: gay male pornography, for instance, in which women do not figure at all, and lesbian pornography in which men do not figure at all. Its moral/political content also makes it difficult to apply without controversy, since standards of equality and mutuality (and therefore of subordination, degradation, and exploitation) vary widely, even among feminists.[16] Erotica inevitably turns out to be *our* preferred sexual material, while pornography is *theirs*.[17] But its fatal defect for present purposes is that it threatens to close by definitional fiat a question which we need to have open for exploration – namely, should pornography be subject to regulation or suppression? If pornography is defined in advance as that-which-is-fit-for-suppression then there can be no intelligent debate about the justifiability of the law of obscenity (at least as it applies to pornography). In order to make sense both of our ordinary concept of pornography and of the inquiry to follow, we must find a definition of the genre which is not morally and politically loaded.

So we are back to the question what makes a representation with sexual or erotic content pornographic. Were we to seek a full-blown philosophical answer to this question, setting out necessary and sufficient conditions for the application of the property 'pornographic,' then our inquiry would likely be both long and convoluted.[18] On the other hand, in reaction to the probable futility of such an exercise, it would be tempting to take refuge in the analogue of the oft-quoted admission by Justice Potter Stewart of the U.S. Supreme Court concerning (not pornography but) obscenity: 'I shall not today attempt further to define [obscenity] ...; and perhaps I could never succeed in intelligibly doing so. But I know it when I see it.'[19] Fortunately, we can find a middle path here between philosophical rigour and judicial abdication. We do know pornography when we see it, and an account of its nature will suffice for our purposes if it succeeds in capturing the central, paradigmatic instances of the genre, even though it may inevitably leave plenty of room for uncertainty and dispute around the edges. (Pornography is just not the sort of concept which admits of clear and definite boundaries.) So far we know that pornography is a form of representation with erotic content; its paradigm instances include 'adult' magazines such as *Penthouse* and *Hustler*, hard-core videos, sexually explicit websites, and the like. What distinguishes pornography from other materials with erotic content – literary, artistic, educational, medical, or whatever – is its primary purpose or function: the sexual arousal of its audience. This function pornography shares with other sexual stimulants, such as vibrators or dildos, which tend to be marketed alongside pornography in specialized sex shops. Unlike these purely mechanical devices, however, pornography arouses by means of representing a content.[20] We can understand the unique character of pornography only if we take into account both its erotic content and its erotic function.[21] Its nearest analogue would be something like food magazines or television shows whose mouth-watering depictions of exotic dishes have the function of arousing a desire to eat (which is why it makes only slightly metaphorical sense to speak of food porn).

It is a virtue of a functional definition of pornography that it extrapolates readily to the case of hate propaganda. Again we can begin by identifying the distinctive content of this form of expression, which we will take to be a derogatory opinion about or attitude toward some group identified by a marker such as race, religion, ethnicity, or sexual orientation, or toward an individual qua member of such a group. In this case the content may be either cognitive (e.g., a belief in the inferiority of the group) or non-cognitive (e.g., a feeling of hostility or antipathy toward the group). Whatever the content, it can be communicated by a variety of means: a pamphlet circulated or posted on a website, graffiti scrawled in a public place, anonymous threats over the telephone, face-to-face insults, and so on. But once again the content alone is not sufficient to identify the expression as hateful, since a negative view of a particular group may be communicated as a contribution to a scientific or historical or political debate. In order to qualify as hateful, the expression must have the primary purpose or function of arousing hatred or hostility toward the group in question; that is, the arousal of such an attitude or feeling must be what the material in question is *for*.[22]

These accounts of the nature of pornography and hate propaganda are doubtless far from airtight, but they will suffice to identify two important challenges to freedom of expression. Does the right to free expression include the production, distribution, and consumption of pornographic or hateful materials or do these forms of expression constitute a limit to the right (whether external or internal)? More importantly, whichever side one takes on these questions, how is that position to be defended? How might we develop a theory of free expression which would be capable of justifying both the right itself and its limits?

1.3 Things to Come

We have defined expression as a communicative act, and it is important to keep in mind that such acts are typically, if not invariably, relational, involving the conveying of some message from a speaker to an audience. Since the form, content, participants, and occasions of such communicative acts are infinite in their variety, the landscape of free expression is very broad indeed. We have already narrowed it somewhat by focusing attention on two particular categories of message: the pornographic and the hateful. We are still left, however, with a bewildering variety of possible restrictions on the communication of these messages. The communicative relationship between speaker and audience is blocked or interfered with whenever the speaker is prevented from transmitting a message or the audience is prevented from receiving it. The interfering agent can be anyone (individuals, groups, institutions, the state), and the means employed can be anything that will work (physical force, threat, social pressure, economic sanctions, the law). In order to keep the ensuing discussion manageable, we need to impose further boundaries on it.

My boundaries will be the following. First, I will confine attention to one particular jurisdiction: with the exception of the occasional glance south of the border, the focus of my discussion will be squarely on Canadian law and public policy. Second, I will deal with only one agent in the business of imposing restrictions on pornography and hate speech, namely the state. Third, out of the many ways in which the state might enforce such restrictions, I will explore only one in depth: the use of criminal law. The chapters to follow therefore provide a detailed treatment of two particular limits to expressive freedom: the Canadian criminal statutes concerning obscenity and hate propaganda and the adjudication which they have generated. Largely absent from the discussion, except for occasional appearances, will be limits which target other forms of expression or which employ other means of regulation or which are imposed by other agencies. There will therefore be little or no treatment of a wide range of important issues, including laws governing commercial expression, broadcast standards for radio or television, speech codes in schools or universities, prohibitions by school boards on the classroom use of controversial books, the refusal by libraries or bookstores to stock certain titles, publication bans imposed by courts during criminal trials, the concentration of media ownership, and many others. My reason for excluding coverage of these topics is not that I judge them to be less pressing, or less interesting, than the ones on which I have chosen to focus, but only that I am unable to give them the attention they deserve within the very finite confines of this book.

Each of the remaining chapters addresses a particular dimension of the selected landscape, chosen for its philosophical interest or practical importance (and sometimes both). Chapter 2 undertakes the task of constructing (or, rather, adapting from John Stuart Mill) a normative framework for determining when, and how, restrictions on free expression can be justified. Chapter 3 turns its attention primarily to hate propaganda, using it as a model case of a conflict between the right of free expression and competing rights belonging to target minorities and exploring how such conflicts are conceptualized and resolved by the Canadian courts. The outcome of this exploration is a convergence between the normative framework of chapter 2 and current judicial practice concerning free expression. In chapter 4 the focus shifts to the law of obscenity and the central role played in the adjudication of obscenity cases by community standards of tolerance. This role is problematic for a variety of practical and legal reasons, but additionally because it appears to threaten the core case for individual liberty articulated by Mill. Chapter 5 then addresses the harm issue, which is highlighted both by Mill's framework and by current judicial orthodoxy in free expression cases. The chapter reviews the available evidence of the harms that can be attributed to pornography (including child pornography) and hate literature.

Each of these chapters is written so as to be more or less intelligible on its own; as advertised in the book's subtitle, they are a series of 'studies in the limits of free expression'. However, there are numerous cross-references between them, and later chapters do return to and elaborate on some of the themes in the earlier ones. These four chapters do not, however, on their own provide conclusions about when, if ever, the limits to free expression which they explore can be justified. Since it would be rather deflationary and anticlimactic to end the book without some such conclusions, the final chapter attempts to draw together the threads of the earlier discussions and extract some lessons from them. It begins with a brief look at some of the forms of regulation of pornography or hate speech which fall outside the very narrow focus of the preceding chapters and ends with some concrete proposals for the shape of Canadian law in this controversial area.

Chapter 2

Mill's Framework

Liberals aiming to construct a theory of free expression have two methodologies from which to choose. The *foundational* approach involves appealing to some more comprehensive moral/political theory from which principles applicable to this particular issue may be derived. The background theory invoked may be broadly ethical (utilitarian or deontological or contractarian) or more specifically political (a theory of democracy, say, or of justice). Whatever the favoured theory, it is claimed to be capable of both justifying a right to free expression and defining the limits of that right. Most of the major figures in the liberal tradition have employed one or another version of the foundational strategy, taking advantage of the fact that every mainstream moral/political theory will make some sort of case for freedom of expression. The weakness of the approach, however, is that any particular justification is only as persuasive as the underlying theory on which it rests, and there is no consensus, either popular or philosophical, on the question of which theory is the one to invoke. The desire to bypass this arena of perennial controversy has led some contemporary liberals, chiefly John Rawls, to try a less theoretically demanding strategy. Rawls works with the assumption that citizens of modern pluralistic democracies will continue for the foreseeable future to hold a variety of mutually incompatible moral and political doctrines, few of which can be ruled out of consideration as unreasonable. Because it must be possible to justify the core elements of a liberal polity – such as freedom of expression – to the adherents of all such doctrines, it is inappropriate to argue for it exclusively on the basis of any one of them. Rawls therefore aims to provide a *freestanding* justification for liberalism, one which appeals not to any comprehensive theory but only to an 'overlapping consensus' among all reasonable theories.[1]

The freestanding approach has its obvious attractions, since it holds out the tantalizing prospect of making significant progress in politics without having to engage in the messy business of defending a favoured moral theory. However, it has equally obvious limitations. Rawls insists that an overlapping consensus is not a mere *modus vivendi* among competing interest groups, since each group must genuinely endorse the political principles in question on the basis of its own comprehensive doctrine. This implies that freedom of expression can be justified only by reference to a consensus among doctrines all of which share some prior commitment to it as an ideal, thus that no case can be made for it to illiberal societies (or illiberal groups within liberal societies). The strength of the freestanding justification is its shallowness, since it does not require citizens, or theorists, to take sides in long-standing controversies over rival comprehensive theories. But the price it pays for this advantage is a corresponding narrowness: it is applicable only to societies and groups who already situate themselves within the liberal tradition. By contrast, the foundational approach, as the label suggests, aims to provide a deeper and potentially more universal justification which, however, may presuppose commitment to a particular ethical world view. Parochialism or sectarianism – these appear to be the available argumentative options.

The freestanding approach is very much in fashion now, driven in part by declining confidence in the power of philosophy to resolve disputes among rival comprehensive moral theories. However, one of my aims in this book is to explore the potential of the foundational strategy by appropriating and building on the work of its most famous exponent. John Stuart Mill's classic essay *On Liberty* defends freedom of expression within the broader context of a general theory of liberty which is grounded in turn in a utilitarian ethical theory. At least in Mill's conception of his overall project, this is as overt a commitment to the foundational option as one could imagine. Although Mill's essay has been very influential within the liberal tradition, few political philosophers now work explicitly within its argumentative framework.[2] I want to see where that framework is capable of taking us, with respect both to freedom of expression in general and to the hard cases of hate literature and pornography in particular. Much of the argument of this book, therefore, attempts to adapt and apply Mill's framework to the various moral, political, and legal issues raised by these forms of expression. In the course of carrying out this project we will, of course, need to keep in mind that, of all comprehensive moral theories, the utilitarianism which is the avowed foundation of Mill's liberalism is undoubtedly one of the most controversial and sectarian. One question we will need to face, therefore, is the extent to which it can be modified or weakened so as to have wider appeal. But that question can be postponed for later consideration. We must first set out the framework Mill uses to defend freedom of expression, and draw from that framework such lessons as we can for our own treatment of the issues.

2.1 The Harm Principle

Although *On Liberty* remains alive today largely because of its trenchant defence of freedom of expression, its principal theme, Mill tells us at the outset, is much broader: 'the nature and limits of the power which can be legitimately exercised by society over the individual'.[3] What Mill is seeking is a general principle which will define the limits of social interference with the activities of individual citizens or, what comes to the same thing, the limits of individual liberty of action. The kinds of social interference he has in mind include not only the formal mechanisms available to the state through its legal system, but also the more informal ways in which dissident minorities can be oppressed or silenced by dominant social groups – what Mill calls 'the tyranny of the majority'. Among the activities susceptible to these forms of interference, it is clear that Mill attached a special importance to the expression or discussion of opinions, since he allocated the longest chapter of his essay (ch. 2) exclusively to this case. However, it is but one example of the freedoms Mill defended, which is why its treatment is embedded within the larger theme of liberty of action in general. Furthermore, for reasons which will shortly become clear, freedom of expression is somewhat anomalous within Mill's overall argumentative framework. We will therefore begin with Mill's general theory of liberty and then work our way back to the special case.

Mill's statement of his principle of liberty is well known: 'the only purpose for which power can be rightfully exercised over any member of a civilized community, against his will, is to prevent harm to others. His own good, either physical or moral, is not a sufficient warrant.'[4] Because this principle defines the limits of individual liberty in terms of harm to others, it has come to be known as the Harm Principle. The Harm Principle states that where harm to others is involved, individuals may rightfully be subject to coercion or control, while in their purely personal conduct, where no such harm is involved, their liberty must be protected. Exactly how the boundary between the personal and the social parts of life is to be drawn and, in particular, how harm to others is to be understood, have been the subject of much discussion both by Mill and by his critics.[5] Although these issues are important, indeed crucial, for the application of Mill's argumentative framework, for the time being I will sidestep them and focus instead on the function of the personal/social distinction – however it is to be drawn – within that framework.[6]

One striking feature of Mill's Harm Principle is its absolutism. At the beginning of the paragraph in which he introduces the principle, Mill says that it is to 'govern absolutely the dealings of society with the individual in the way of compulsion and control'. Then, toward the end of the same paragraph, Mill reasserts its stringency: 'in the part [of his conduct] which merely concerns himself, [the individual's] independence is, of right, absolute.' Mill clearly intends the limits the principle sets to social 'compulsion and control' to trump all competing arguments in favour of such interference. Once it has been determined, therefore, that someone's conduct belongs to the personal part of her life, there can be no further question as to whether she should be at liberty to engage in it. In particular, whether she has a right to such liberty is not to be decided by any calculation of the costs and benefits of social interference in that particular instance. The Harm Principle states that if the conduct is personal then it is protected from interference – period.

In a perfectly ordinary sense, then, Mill offers individuals a principled defence of liberty in their personal lives – one which excludes case-by-case utilitarian calculation. At the same time, however, the justification Mill offers for the Harm Principle itself is utilitarian: 'It is proper to state that I forego any advantage which could be derived to my argument from the idea of abstract right, as a thing independent of utility. I regard utility as the ultimate appeal on all ethical questions; but it must be utility in the largest sense, grounded on the permanent interests of man as a progressive being.'[7] The argument *to* the Harm Principle (from Mill's general ethical theory) is therefore utilitarian, while arguments *from* that principle (to particular cases) are deontological. Mill defends a policy of respecting an absolute right to liberty in the personal sphere of life on the basis of a cost-benefit calculation: such a policy will have better consequences than any alternative, including the alternative of determining, by means of a cost-benefit calculation, whether to respect individual liberty on each particular occasion. He therefore offers a utilitarian argument for excluding further utilitarian arguments about whether to interfere in people's personal lives. An

absolute right to liberty – one which trumps social utility – is justified on
the ground of social utility.

Mill's argument for his Harm Principle foreshadows more recent
indirect consequentialist justifications of strong, even absolute, rights.[8]
In order to appreciate the structure of that argument properly, it is
important to distinguish two possible consequentialist claims about
interference in the personal sphere: (1) the general policy of absolutely
prohibiting such interference will be optimal, and (2) following this
general policy will be optimal on every particular occasion. Mill certainly accepted the first of these claims: it is the burden of much of the
argument in *On Liberty* to establish it. However, there is no reason to
think that he also accepted the second – the view that interference in an
individual's personal affairs (for her own good, let us suppose) will
never be for the best. Mill certainly believed that people are generally
the best judges of their own interests and that any overruling of that
judgment by others is likely to be mistaken.[9] However, as far as I am
aware he never claimed that paternalistic interference is misguided or
counterproductive in every instance. Such a claim would in any case be
very implausible. However, it is not implausible (though it may be false)
that the best policy is to act as though interference were always wrong,
on the ground that things will turn out for the best that way in the long
run. One of the implications of defending such a policy is that it will
sometimes lead to mistakes – it will prohibit interference in some cases
in which it would have been the optimal course of action. But Mill's
argument must be that the alternative policy of deciding whether to
interfere on the basis of a case-by-case calculation of consequences will
in the long run have worse consequences.

A utilitarian justification of any social policy is obviously dependent
on the facts of the matter. The hypothesis which Mill uses to defend his
Harm Principle must be that, as matters stand and taking full account of
'utility in the largest sense', guaranteeing individuals an absolute right
to liberty in the personal sector of their lives is the best policy. But that
immediately raises a question: the best policy where and when (and
under what circumstances)? Utilitarian arguments for social policies are
notoriously context-dependent: what is best for a society at one time
may not be best at another time; what is best for one society might not
be best for another. Mill might, of course, have thought that the utilitarian case for the Harm Principle holds equally in all societies at all stages
of their evolution. But we know that he did not believe this. Just after
the paragraph in which he introduces his general principle of liberty,

Mill tells us that it 'has no application to any state of things anterior to the time when mankind have become capable of being improved by free and equal discussion'.[10] Now Mill thought that this time had been reached in all of the civilized societies of his day, thus that his arguments for the Harm Principle applied equally to them all, regardless of local circumstances. In this he was doubtless driven by the conviction that 'the permanent interests of man as a progressive being' were the same for Italians or Americans as they were for the English. But he is not really entitled to assume that the utility calculation will favour liberty equally, or underwrite exactly the same right to liberty, in all 'civilized' countries at all times and under all conditions. Under different social circumstances it is possible for Mill's utilitarian methodology to generate a less absolute principle concerning liberty in the personal sphere.

If Mill's utilitarian arguments for the Harm Principle are context-dependent, so also is the whole problematic of *On Liberty*. Mill's subject – the nature and limits of the power which can be legitimately exercised by society over the individual – he takes to be as old as society itself; but, he says, it now 'presents itself under new conditions, and requires a different and more fundamental treatment'.[11] The 'new conditions' he has in mind have to do with the attainment of a reasonable degree of democracy in many of the nations of Europe and North America which made it both harder for governments to oppress the majority of their peoples and easier for the majority, through the mechanisms of government, to oppress internal minorities. This 'tyranny of the majority' which so concerned Mill might operate either through the official sanctions of public law or through the unofficial sanctions of public opinion. In either case, Mill considered it to constitute the principal threat to liberty and individuality in the developed nations of his day, and it was with that threat in mind that he set out to define the limits of the authority of society over its individual members.

What is interesting here is Mill's idea that, while the abstract question of the relationship between the individual and society is perennial, it can assume different concrete forms in different epochs and under different sociopolitical conditions. The arguments of *On Liberty*, as well as the issues which it foregrounds, are clearly shaped by Mill's analysis of the direction from which liberty was most likely to be imperilled in the England of his own age. Might they then take a different shape in a different age, such as ours? It is easy to be as pessimistic now as Mill was then about the prospects of resisting the suffocating power of conformity. Many of the political, economic, and technological developments since Mill's day provide more efficient and pervasive means for public opinion to stifle independent thought: public education systems, mass communication, multinational corporations, highly concentrated ownership of the media, the global hegemony of American culture, and so on. In that case the tyranny of the majority might still be regarded as the pre-eminent threat to individuality, a threat which needs to be resisted by erecting high, perhaps insurmountable, barriers against collective interference in individual self-expression. However, we might equally be impressed by the heightened danger to personal safety posed by other modern technologies – cars, motorcycles, snowmobiles, and so on – and by the need to protect individuals against their own risky behaviour (by means of seat-belt or helmet laws, for instance). In that case we might endorse a Paternalism Principle which would permit restrictions on people's personal conduct for their own good. Or we might feel that individualism has now gone too far and that societies suffer corrosion or fragmentation from the lack of social consensus on a set of core moral values. In that case we might be tempted by a Moralism Principle which would sanction the regulation of some forms of personal conduct which cause harm to no one, on the ground that they are contrary to public morals. As forms of social interference, both paternalism and moralism are, of course, strictly prohibited by the Harm Principle. However, while that principle is absolute in its nature, in its justification it is contingent on both a diagnosis of the main threat to 'the permanent interests of man as a progressive being' and a prescription of the best means of protecting those interests.

2.2 Liberty of Thought and Discussion

Whatever lies within the personal part of people's lives is protected by the Harm Principle. So what does lie therein? According to Mill, three things:[12] (1) the 'inward domain of consciousness', comprising conscience, thought, feeling, opinion, and the like; (2) living out our own plan of life (as long we do not thereby harm others); and (3) voluntary association with others (again for purposes which do not harm third parties). These 'parts of life' are to be protected against social interference by means of rights to such things as freedom of conscience, privacy (as we would now put it), and freedom of association. What is noteworthy about this list for our purposes is what it does not include: the activity of 'expressing and publishing opinions'. Mill clearly does not mean to exclude this activity from the protected region of liberty. But he does flag its special status by recognizing that 'it belongs to that part of the conduct of an individual which concerns other people'.[13] In other words, while Mill argues for an extensive freedom to express and publish opinions, he does not base his argument for that freedom on the claim that these activities belong to the personal domain by virtue of posing no risk of harm to others. He therefore acknowledges that expression is a form of conduct capable of causing harm. But this means that Mill's treatment of freedom of expression (or discussion) is anomalous within the overall argumentative scheme of *On Liberty*: it is the only activity falling within the social (rather than the personal) sphere to which Mill allocates an extended discussion (in ch. 2) and also the only one for which he urges (nearly) absolute protection against social interference. His reason for giving expression this privileged status is that liberty of discussion 'being almost of as much importance as the liberty of thought itself, and resting in great part on the same reasons, is practically inseparable from it'.[14]

Mill's point is obvious, and impeccable: the freedom to hold any opinion you wish is worth little without the companion freedom to advocate, discuss, and circulate it. However, his recognition that these latter activities are, by virtue of their capacity for harming others, social rather than personal has far-reaching implications for his defence of freedom of discussion. Whatever falls within the personal realm receives principled protection: social interference, whether by official or unofficial means, is here absolutely prohibited. The case is quite different for social acts: 'As soon as any part of a person's conduct affects prejudicially the interests of others, society has jurisdiction over it, and the question whether the general welfare will or will not be promoted by interfering with it, becomes open to discussion. But there is no room for entertaining any such question when a person's conduct affects the interests of no persons besides himself ...'[15] Mill is not of course suggesting that interference with an activity is warranted just because it falls within this social realm; on the contrary, 'it must by no means be supposed, because damage, or probability of damage, to the interests of others, can alone justify the interference of society, that therefore it always does justify such interference. In many cases, an individual, in pursuing a legitimate object, necessarily and therefore legitimately causes pain or loss to others ...'[16] Under the Harm Principle harm to others is a necessary, but not a sufficient, condition for social interference with an activity.

Mill mentions trade as an example of another activity which, because it 'affects the interest of other persons', comes 'within the jurisdiction of society'.[17] Where trade is concerned, Mill's default presumption is *laissez-faire*. But because he regards trade as a social act, he cannot base his defence of the free market on the Harm Principle: 'Restrictions on trade, or on production for purposes of trade, are indeed restraints; and all restraint, *qua* restraint, is an evil: but the restraints in question affect only that part of conduct which society is competent to restrain, and are wrong solely because they do not really produce the results which it is desired to produce by them.'[18] Like his defence of free expression, Mill's case for free trade therefore 'rests on grounds different from, though equally solid with, the principle of individual liberty'.[19] For Mill, those grounds are utilitarian: interference in the free market tends to be wrong because it tends to be inefficient and counterproductive.[20] However, there is room in Mill's view for some restraints on trade, such as regulations prohibiting fraud or enforcing workplace safety; whether or not a particular restraint can be justified depends on whether the general welfare will or will not be promoted by it.

Since, like trade, the expression of opinions falls within the social and not the personal realm, the question whether it should be interfered with in any way should also be 'open to discussion' and settled by reference to the general welfare. If we assume that this is the way Mill sees the question, then it becomes possible to understand what he is trying to do in chapter 2 of *On Liberty*.[21] There are two things he is *not* trying to do: he is not arguing for the Harm Principle (that argument begins with the defence of the value of individuality in ch. 3), and he is not arguing that the expression of an opinion can have no adverse effects on the interests of others (Mill has already conceded that expressing an opinion, unlike merely holding it, 'belongs to that part of the conduct of an individual which concerns other people'). What he *is* arguing is that, while the expression of opinion is indeed a social act, a policy of interference with it will none the less be inimical to the general welfare. His reasons for thinking this are well known: censorship will cause valuable truths to be suppressed, will discourage inquiry on the part of promising intellects, will lead dominant or orthodox opinions to be held as dead letters, and in general will disserve 'the mental well-being of mankind (on which all their other well-being depends)'.[22]

Of the liberties defended in Mill's essay, free expression (along with free trade) occupies a special position, by virtue of being more immediately subject to utilitarian argument. For Mill, utility plays a role at two different levels in the arguments of *On Liberty*. On the one hand, it is appealed to as the justificatory foundation of the Harm Principle itself;

this argument largely occurs in chapter 3 and appeals to the pre-eminent value of individuality. Since the Harm Principle affords individuals absolute protection against (paternalistic or moralistic) interference in their personal conduct, no further appeals to utility are permitted within this domain. With the significant exception of chapter 2, the burden of most of Mill's argument in the essay is to condemn the use of coercion or compulsion against individuals (of sound mind and adult years) for their own good. However, this leaves open the question when interference with social conduct may be justified. This question is settled, on a case-by-case basis, by considerations of utility: some social acts may be exempt from interference, others not, and the same act may be exempt from some forms of interference and not from others. Furthermore, the optimal policy under one set of social circumstances may be sub-optimal under another. Mill's case in favour of freedom of expression falls within this territory. I suggested earlier that the context-dependence of Mill's utilitarian argument for his Harm Principle might require its reconsideration or revision under different social conditions. Mill's defence of freedom of expression, though also absolute (or nearly so) in its nature, has the same contingent status.

For Mill, therefore, whether a policy of interfering with expression, or with a particular category of expression, is justified or not is to be determined by the outcome of a utilitarian cost-benefit calculation. For those who tend to regard Mill as a free speech absolutist this may be a surprising result, but only if they conflate two different aspects of his doctrine. The liberty of discussion Mill advocates is indeed (nearly) absolute; however, it is also the conclusion of an extended cost-benefit argument. Furthermore, it appears to be quite narrowly defined. For us the term 'expression' has a very broad connotation, extending as it does well beyond the articulation of opinions or beliefs to include non-verbal means of communication such as body language, symbolic acts, and artistic works. However, when Mill speaks of expression he seems to have in mind strictly the expression of opinions.[23] Indeed, he rarely uses the term 'expression' at all, more frequently referring to speaking, writing, or discussion.[24] Furthermore, the kinds of opinions whose discussion Mill was particularly concerned to safeguard were those concerning 'morals, religion, politics, social relations, and the business of life'.[25] In other words, Mill's primary focus is on what we would now consider to be political expression (or political speech): the advocacy of ideas concerning public affairs or matters of public life.

For those who would wish to situate freedom of expression beyond the reach of consequentialist calculation, Mill's arguments may be disappointing. After all, appeals to utility are notoriously susceptible to interpretation and manipulation; they may seem, therefore, shaky ground for the defence of a core political freedom. In fairness to Mill, he does not leave us entirely without guidance when we are attempting to decide whether, and when, interference in social acts would be justified. Mill outlines two kinds of conduct which he thinks society has the right to demand from its members: 'This conduct consists first, in not injuring the interests of one another; or rather certain interests, which, either by express legal provision or by tacit understanding, ought to be considered as rights; and secondly, in each person's bearing his share (to be fixed on some equitable principle) of the labours and sacrifices incurred for defending the society or its members from injury and molestation.'[26] What is chiefly interesting in this general formula is the reference to violating the rights of others. Mill returns to this theme a number of times, arguing that encroachment on others' rights is a fit object of 'moral reprobation, and, in grave cases, of moral retribution and punishment'.[27]

The right of free expression can therefore be justifiably restricted when its exercise threatens to violate the rights of others. But what are these competing rights? Mill does not offer us the resources in *On Liberty* to answer this question, since he does not there sketch any general account of (individual or collective) rights. For that we need to turn instead to chapter 5 of his *Utilitarianism*. The account we find there leads us in the first instance straight back to utility: 'To have a right, then, is, I conceive, to have something which society ought to defend me in the possession of. If the objector goes on to ask why it ought, I can give him no other reason than general utility.'[28] But Mill in this instance does go on to give us some idea of the kinds of interests which considerations of social utility will lead us to protect by means of rights: 'The most marked cases of injustice ... are acts of wrongful aggression, or wrongful exercise of power over some one; the next are those which consist in wrongfully withholding from him something which is his due; in both cases, inflicting on him a positive hurt, either in the form of direct suffering, or of the privation of some good which he had reasonable ground, either of a physical or of a social kind, for counting upon.'[29] Mill adds that hurting another may include hindering him 'in his freedom of pursuing his own good'.[30]

As most liberals and feminists see things now, one of the core social values threatened by some forms of expression (such as hate literature and pornography) is equality: the equal status of minorities or women within the social fabric, their equal opportunities to live their lives free of fear or intimidation and to pursue their own conceptions of the good, and their right to equal consideration and respect. So we can ask: was Mill committed to this value? If so, did he attribute to it an importance similar to that of liberty? The answer to both questions appears to be yes. The principal context in which he addresses equality issues is *The Subjection of Women*, where he opens the essay by endorsing 'a principle of perfect equality, admitting no power or privilege on the one side, nor disability on the other'.[31] Here Mill is of course referring to gender, and not racial or ethnic, equality. But most of what he has to say in the essay about the corrupting influence of inequalities of power and privilege would translate readily to the racial arena, where members of oppressed groups may be as unable as the women of Mill's day to pursue their own good, or even to form an autonomous conception of it. In any case, we know from some of Mill's other writings that he abominated the forms of racism with which he was familiar, above all the social and political inequality of blacks in America.[32] It seems safe to say that Mill thought utility, as he understood that notion, required (some form or other of) social equality just as much as individual liberty.[33] But in that case only a social cost-benefit analysis will determine what utility requires when some people's liberty threatens other people's equality.

There is one further aspect of Mill's treatment of freedom of discussion relevant to this issue. After defending the freedom to form and express opinions, Mill turns to the further question whether men 'should be free to act upon their opinions – to carry these out in their lives, without hindrance, either physical or moral, from their fellowmen, so long as it is at their own risk and peril'.[34] This latter proviso refers, of course, to Mill's distinction between social acts which may adversely affect the interests of others and personal acts whose potential harms are confined to the individual. He then continues, in a well-known passage: 'No one pretends that actions should be as free as opinions. On the contrary, even opinions lose their immunity, when the circumstances in which they are expressed are such as to constitute their expression a positive instigation to some mischievous act. An opinion that corn-dealers are starvers of the poor, or that private property is robbery, ought to be unmolested when simply circulated through the press, but may justly incur punishment when delivered orally to an excited mob assembled before the house of a corn-dealer, or when handed about among the same mob in the form of a placard.'

Elsewhere, Mill says that 'the case of a person who solicits another to do an act, is not strictly a case of self-regarding conduct. To give advice or offer inducements to any one, is a social act, and may, therefore, like actions in general which affect others, be supposed amenable to social control.'[35] In this context he is discussing cases of counselling or abetting another to do something which itself falls into the personal, rather than the social, sphere, and he finds these cases to 'lie on the exact boundary line between two principles' (the personal and the social) with 'arguments on both sides'.[36] But how do matters stand when someone counsels or solicits another to commit an act harmful to others? Mill addresses this issue briefly in a footnote in which he discusses the case of a prosecution for 'circulating what was deemed to be an immoral doctrine, the lawfulness of Tyrannicide'.[37] Mill allows that circulating this opinion through the press might constitute an instigation to the act and thus 'a proper subject of punishment, but only if an overt act has followed, and at least a probable connexion can be established between the act and the instigation'.

Mill's treatment of the corn-dealer case suggests that, while restrictions of time, manner, and circumstance might be justified for the expression of opinions, no opinion is to be completely prohibited from circulation on grounds of its content. However, his brief reference to the tyrannicide case seems to allow that, under the appropriate circumstances, the mere advocacy of an opinion in the press could constitute incitement to the commission of a crime and thus be subject to prosecution on that ground. It is by no means clear when advocacy crosses over into incitement (or instigation) for Mill, thus when the expression of even political opinions might be properly subject to content restrictions.[38] What is clear is that while for Mill the right to free expression has very considerable weight in the scales, even against competing rights, it is not quite absolute.

2.3 The Lessons of Mill's Framework

We have seen that Mill appeals to utility as the foundation of rights, including the right to free expression. However, it will be useful to distinguish different claims, of different degrees of strength, that are run together in Mill's utilitarian arguments. First, he holds that the justification of rights must be *instrumental*: rights are devices – instruments – for the protection of important values, such as freedom or equality. Rights are therefore not the ultimate premisses of moral/political argument;

that role is played by the foundational values which they protect or promote. Second, the justification of rights must be *consequentialist*, requiring an exercise of cost-benefit balancing. As Mill fully appreciates, one person's right is another person's obligation. Recognizing a right therefore simultaneously confers a benefit on the rightholder – consisting of whatever value the right protects – and imposes a burden on those who bear the correlative duty. It follows that every liberty-right both enhances and restricts liberty; if you are free to express your opinions then I am not free to prevent you from doing so. Furthermore, the exercise of liberty-rights may impose further – non-liberty – costs on others; if you exercise your right of free expression by broadcasting your opinions over loudspeakers just outside my bedroom then you will disturb my peace and rest. Deciding when a particular right is justified therefore requires determining when the benefits it confers sufficiently outweigh the burdens it imposes. For Mill this is a consequentialist exercise in which we seek to maximize the overall balance of benefits over burdens.[39] Third, for Mill the justification of rights must be *welfarist*: the values involved are all interests ultimately belonging to individuals.[40] Mill's own account of the nature of interests, or well-being, is a form of hedonism: well-being consists in happiness, which in turn consists in 'pleasure, and the absence of pain'.[41] However, his distinction of different qualities of pleasure enables him to privilege the more intellectual pleasures and ultimately leads to his reliance on 'the permanent interests of man as a progressive being' in *On Liberty* – interests which give pride of place to what Mill calls individuality and what we nowadays would be more likely to call autonomy. If we abstract again from the particularities of Mill's own views, we may say that, whatever one takes them to consist in, the interests of individuals are the values which need to be balanced when deciding whether a particular right should be recognized. Fourth, for Mill the justification of rights must be *aggregative*: a right is justified when its recognition will maximize the sum total of welfare. Mill's utilitarianism therefore assigns no independent significance to the distribution of welfare; it favours neither an equal distribution nor a greater weight for those who are worse off, except where these distributive policies will increase total welfare.

It is worth distinguishing these four elements in Mill's justificatory scheme for rights, because it is entirely possible to accept some of them and reject others. One could be an instrumentalist about rights without accepting any of Mill's further commitments, or one could follow Mill as far as his consequentialism while still rejecting welfarism (by acknowl-

edging a plurality of independent and equally basic values) or aggregation (by accepting distributive constraints). Since we are seeking a
foundational, rather than freestanding, justification for free expression,
there is much to be said for keeping our commitments as weak as possible, so as to ensure their wider acceptability and avoid the problem of
conflict among rival comprehensive theories. On the other hand, the
commitments must still be strong enough to yield fairly determinate
results – including results for the hard cases. The former pressure will
tend to push us back to the basic platform of Mill's instrumentalism,
which may be widely – though not universally – endorsed, while the latter pressure may pull us all the way forward to his full-blown utilitarianism. Since it is difficult at this early stage to predict where the balance
point between acceptability and determinacy might lie, the best practice
as we proceed will be to make assumptions no stronger than are needed
for the argument to move forward.

The fact that we can distinguish stronger and weaker forms of Mill's
background moral theory tends to narrow the gap somewhat between
foundational and freestanding justifications of free expression. Recall
that the aim of the freestanding strategy was to appeal to principles on
which all reasonable comprehensive doctrines could converge. If a
foundational approach wishes to avoid sectarianism then it too will do
well to broaden its appeal, by making the ethical theory which it invokes
no stronger than is necessary to support the right in question. While
utilitarianism is a very sectarian doctrine indeed, consequentialism
(with no commitment to either welfarism or aggregation) is much less
so, especially in the arena of public policy. If it could be shown that the
parties to public debates about rights in general, or the right to free
expression in particular, share a commitment – whether implicit or
explicit – to a consequentialist framework, then the risk of merely sectarian appeal is minimized. Whether something like this can be shown is
a question to be explored later. Meanwhile, we note only that, like their
freestanding counterparts, foundational strategies can also be more
broadly or narrowly based, and that inclusiveness is here too a virtue (as
long as it is not purchased at the cost of underdetermining a specific
result). The two methodologies still differ, since the foundational
approach aims to derive political rights from a (broadly defined) ethical
framework while the freestanding strategy seeks a consensus on such
rights among competing frameworks. But the gap between them is less
wide than it might seem.

Besides the broadly consequentialist justification of rights, the other principal lesson to be drawn from Mill's framework is the centrality of the harm question. On Mill's view, coercive interference with some particular form of expression (hate literature, pornography, or anything else) can be justified only if both of the following conditions are satisfied:

Harm Principle: the expression in question must cause harm to others, and

Consequentialist Principle: interference with the expression must yield a better balance of benefits over costs than non-interference.

Both conditions impose argumentative burdens on any agency, such as the state, that would restrict expression. The first burden is that of showing that the expression in question poses a significant risk of harm to parties other than those who are voluntary consumers of it.[42] Because liberty is a benefit for those who possess it, every restraint (as Mill puts it), qua restraint, is an evil. Especially where forms of expressions are concerned, we begin with an initial presumption of freedom, against which it is the burden of the state to make a convincing case by providing convincing evidence of the link between the expression in question and the harm it causes. It follows immediately that if there are forms of expression which pose no risk (or no significant risk) of harm to others then the freedom to engage in them must be inviolable. Much work still remains to be done, of course, to determine what constitutes harm, when one individual's actions pose a risk of harm to others, and when that risk should be deemed to be significant. But once that work is done, a finding that some form of expression is harmless (in the relevant sense) is a guarantee of the right to circulate it.

The more difficult cases, and surely the majority of cases, will be those in which the risk of harm is a factor and in which it must therefore be decided whether that risk justifies (some form of) social interference. The second, consequentialist, condition does not provide a simple algorithm for deciding whether, and when, the state is entitled to enforce restrictions on forms of expression in those cases in which the Harm Principle is satisfied. However, it does suggest the kinds of factors which will be relevant. First, the restriction must have some reasonable expectation of success. While it may be thought desirable to inhibit or suppress some form of expression by legal means, it is a further question whether doing so is possible. To the extent that the restrictions can be readily circumvented, by an underground market or by technological innovations such as the Internet, the case for them is weakened. Second, there must be no less costly policy available for securing the same results. Even when it promises to be effective in preventing some significant social harm, censorship abridges personal liberty and deprives consumers of whatever benefits they may derive from the prohibited forms of expression. It should therefore be the last, not the first, resort of government for preventing the harm in question. Where less coercive measures (education, counterspeech, etc.) promise similar results, they should be preferred. Where a narrower infringement of freedom of expression will be equally effective, it too should be preferred. Third, the expected benefits of the restriction must, on balance, justify its costs. Censorship can compromise other important social values, such as vigorous engagement in public debate. It can have a 'chilling effect' on legitimate forms of expression (literary, artistic, etc.). However well intended the restriction might be, in practice it will be administered by police, prosecutors, judges, or bureaucrats who may use it to justify targeting unpopular, marginal forms of literature with no significant capacity for social harm. Given the inevitable gap between the *de jure* and the *de facto* policy, the additional protection of vulnerable groups provided by legal restraints on expression must be great enough to justify the collateral costs.

These conditions raise a high justificatory threshold for restrictions on freedom of expression. Whether a policy of imposing content restrictions on hate literature or pornography can surmount this threshold remains to be determined. Mill's argumentative framework in *On Liberty* does not answer this question for us, but it does help us to get the question right. Besides the centrality of the harm question, it teaches us two important general lessons. The first is not just the wisdom but the inevitability of eschewing appeals to 'abstract right' in favour of considerations of the social good. One need not travel all the way here to Mill's utilitarianism as a comprehensive moral theory, but the unavoidable balancing of conflicting social values – such as liberty and equality – is what motivates a broadly consequentialist approach to the delineation of basic political rights. The second lesson – the context-dependence of those basic rights – follows from the first: if the question every liberal society must ask is how to strike the optimal balance between two of its core values, then different circumstances may dictate different answers to that question. Working out the right answer for any society will be a complex matter requiring evidence and argument, and will consequently be perpetually open to re-examination and revision. No one therefore should ever be too certain they have got it right. Even if a particular balance turns out to be clearly indicated for a particular social structure, there will be no simple extrapolation of that result to other liberal jurisdictions. There may be a consequentialist case for certain abstract and universal human rights, and rights to freedom of expression and to social equality may be among them, but the appropriate balance to be struck when these rights conflict may be a very parochial matter indeed.

2.4 Excluded Harms

Mill's framework dictates that the justification of restrictions on free expression must be harm-based. But what is to count as harm, for the purposes of the framework? Mill's own treatment of this important question is less complete and explicit than could be wished. His welfarism takes us a certain distance by suggesting a quite general account of harm, one in which someone is harmed just in case she is (somehow or other) made worse off. However, without further elaboration this account does not tell us just which kinds of worsenings are to qualify as harms. The aim of this section is to provide a partial answer to this question by excluding from the scope of Mill's framework two alleged kinds of harm – moral harm and moral distress – both of which have played an important role in justifying limits to free expression.

A moral harm is one whose characterization requires the use of moral concepts. Most harms can be described in morally neutral ways, involving only physical or psychological terms: this quantity of pain or suffering, the loss of this object or opportunity, and so on. We can be said to have suffered a moral harm only when someone or something has made us worse off in a distinctively moral way. It is essential to the idea of moral harm both that the worsening be specifically moral in character and that we be its site. We could say that we are put into a worse situation, from a moral standpoint, whenever we are the victim of a wrong – for instance, when we are robbed or cheated by another. But the notion of harm involved in that case has no special moral quality: it is just the familiar non-moral harm of losing or being deprived of something valuable to us. In this case the (negative) moral quality belongs to the agent of our misfortune: it is he who is bad or evil, not us. For a harm to us to count as distinctively moral, its negative quality must somehow adhere to us: we must be made morally worse, by comparison with our antecedent condition.

There may be many varieties of moral harm. We will be concerned here only with two of them – moral corruption and moral degradation – both of which have frequently been associated with pornography. You have been morally corrupted when your character has been changed for the worse – when, for instance, you have become more inclined to do bad or evil things, such as cheating on exams or accepting bribes from criminals. Where moral corruption is in question your rating as a moral agent has declined; you have become a more vicious (less decent or honourable) person. You have been morally degraded when something has been done to you that is not only wrong but also leaves you demeaned or devalued, such as being treated as a slave or a plaything. Unlike moral corruption, moral degradation does not make you a morally worse person; instead, it compromises your status as a subject, as opposed to an object.[43] The evil resides not in you, but in the agent who has degraded you. You are victim, not perpetrator, but the loss you have suffered is still of a specifically moral kind.

The law of obscenity has been a particularly fertile terrain for the notion of moral corruption. For nearly a century the test of obscenity in Canadian law was the one formulated by Lord Cockburn in the 1868 *Hicklin* case in England: 'whether the tendency of the matter charged as obscenity is to deprave and corrupt those whose minds are open to such immoral influences, and into whose hands a publication of this sort may fall'.[44] By contrast with the more recent reliance on the Harm Principle as a rationale for restricting (at least some forms of) pornography, the more traditional rationale, the one emanating from *Hicklin*, is usually taken to be an example of the Moralism Principle: either pornography is itself immoral or indecent or it encourages thoughts or actions which are immoral or indecent, and that is the primary and best reason for trying to reduce or eliminate its circulation. Through the remainder of the nineteenth and well into the twentieth century, the language of the courts when dealing with obscenity was overtly and unmistakably moralistic. Pornography was denounced and dismissed as trash, filth, or dirt, and its effect on the mind of the consumer was to contaminate, corrupt, or pollute. Finding no redeeming social value in sexually explicit materials, judges pretty clearly thought that ridding the country of them was necessary in order to protect the purity of public morals. Thus far, it seems that their justification for criminalizing obscenity must have been the Moralism Principle, which authorizes restrictions on forms of expression thought to be indecent or immoral, even if they cannot be shown to cause harm.

All of this is true, but it is also true that they had another connected thought. Let us return to the *Hicklin* case and Lord Cockburn, who complained that as a result of the circulation of the material in question (a pamphlet intended to discredit the Roman Catholic church) 'the minds of those hitherto pure are exposed to the danger of contamination and pollution from the impurity it contains'.[45] This language of 'contamination and pollution' is borrowed from the realm of health or hygiene: to have one's body contaminated or polluted by some foreign substance is to suffer a kind of harm protection against which is the legitimate business of the law. Lord Cockburn seems to be suggesting that those who consume pornography are thereby exposed to contamination and pollution of their minds, and this too is a kind of harm which the law may legitimately seek to prevent. This line of thought, implicit in *Hicklin*, was nicely articulated in a 1909 prosecution in Ontario for possession of 'a quantity of obscene books, printed matter, pictures and photographs tending to corrupt morals', where the trial judge expressed his regret that

> only two years' imprisonment can be inflicted for this heinous offence. One who administers physical poison so as to inflict upon another grievous bodily harm is liable to 14 years' imprisonment; one who administers mental and moral poison, and thereby inflicts grievous harm upon the mind and soul, even if this is not possibly, indeed probably, accompanied by bodily harm as well, is let off with two years – rather a reversal of the injunction not to fear them that kill the body and after that have no more that they can do.[46]

This judgment merely makes unusually explicit a current of thought that runs through obscenity cases in common-law jurisdictions right up to (and probably beyond) the 1950s. At its core is the idea that thinking impure – that is, lustful – thoughts is a harm to the thinker, and acting on them – through masturbation, for instance – is a harm to the actor. This judicial mindset had its roots in a sexual morality that regarded sex as having an inherent tendency toward vice unless carried on in the right circumstances (within heterosexual marriage) and for the right purpose (procreation). The pornography market has always been sustained largely by randy post-pubertal males for whom sexually explicit materials – especially visual ones – are essentially masturbation aids.[47] Needless to say, the sexual fantasies which these materials encourage, and the sexual acts which they stimulate, fall well outside the officially sanctioned zone of purity. If the thoughts and deeds are immoral, then it is but a short step to regarding their encouragement and stimulation as likewise immoral. Taken no farther, this line of argument emanates in the traditional moralistic justification for the regulation of pornography. The added thought is that such regulation is necessary in order to protect innocent adolescent boys (and adult men) from a particular kind of harm to themselves.

In this way the justification of censorship is relocated from the Moralism Principle to the Paternalism Principle. The conceptual shift requires the notion of moral harm – more particularly, the notion of moral corruption. The key idea here is that the corruption of a person's morals is a harm to that person – in other words, that the person is made (prudentially) worse off by being made (morally) worse. For Canadian legislators and judges this idea provided the underlying rationale for the law of obscenity over the better part of a century. It is therefore entirely apt to say that the prevention of harm (whether to self or to others) has always provided the official justification for criminalizing the production and distribution of pornography.[48] That has not changed from *Hicklin* to now; what has changed is our conception of what the harm of pornography might consist in and who might be its victims. Whereas now it is assumed to take the form of sexual violence against, or degradation of, women, in the older way of thinking it was a kind of moral corruption or contamination to which men (especially working-class men) and boys were particularly susceptible. It is only relatively recently that the accepted rationale for obscenity laws has had anything to do with the protection of women (or children) against the (male) consumers of pornography, as opposed to the protection of those consumers against themselves and against pornographers.

This application of the idea of moral harm can of course be challenged by questioning the particular sexual morality on which it rests. Most of us are now disinclined to take seriously the condemnation of lustful thoughts (or masturbatory deeds) as inherently immoral. But this is too easy a way with the line of thought in question, since it can readily be adapted to a more progressive outlook. Let us therefore imagine Adam, an impressionable young man whose immersion in the world of pornography has gradually led him to a taste for scenarios not of fully consenting and egalitarian sex but of women being raped or otherwise brutalized. Even those of us who embrace a liberal sexual morality might agree that finding solitary sexual stimulation in these scenarios is evil, manifesting a corrupt mind. In that case, it might be true that

Adam has been morally corrupted by violent and misogynistic pornography – at least if we suppose that the pornography was the cause of the corruption, rather than merely a symptom of it. The force of this example does not rest on any fear that Adam will act out his fantasies in real life – in fact, quite the contrary. The risk that exposure to this type of pornography might lead to sexual violence against women is frequently used to justify its regulation.[49] But in that case the rationale for intervention is to prevent harm to unwilling female victims, not to willing male consumers. So in order to make this example work we need to control (perhaps unrealistically) for this spillover into real life; Adam's enjoyment of sexual violence, we must stipulate, remains strictly at the level of fantasy. It is still (we are assuming) morally corrupt, though it results in harm to no one else.

Let us concede, for the sake of the argument, that Adam has been corrupted by pornography. Has he thereby been harmed? There are two quite different ways we could go about answering this question.[50] On the one hand, we could presuppose a particular normative framework (such as Mill's) and ask whether the notion of moral harm coheres with the point or spirit of that framework or helps to articulate it in its best, most defensible, form. Alternatively, we could prescind from all prior normative commitments and ask instead whether the notion of moral harm makes sense within the best descriptive account of the nature of harm. The two approaches might, of course, converge: the normatively best account might also be descriptively best. But they also might not. The conception of harm needed by Mill's framework should not stray too far from our linguistic intuitions, lest it become a mere term of art, but it need not be completely congruent with them either – it might be narrower (excluding some conditions which we would ordinarily recognize as harms) or broader (including some conditions we would not so recognize) or both.[51]

On the surface at least, the notion of moral harm seems at odds with the spirit of the Harm Principle, since it enables an essentially moralistic objection to pornography to be recast as a harm-based one. Acknowledging the legitimacy of moral harm might therefore provide a quick and easy way of justifying censorship which is consistent with the Harm Principle.[52] That would be a surprising result of Mill's framework, one which would be deeply disturbing to liberals. The point of the framework is to protect individuals against state interference in the personal sphere, and consumption of pornography seems to belong in that sphere. It would therefore seem a perversion of the framework to use it to make a case for interference. However, the implications for the framework of recognizing moral corruption as a harm would not be as serious as they might seem. The key point is that even if we agree that Adam is harmed by virtue of being corrupted, it is a harm in which he has been a willing, indeed eager, collaborator. For the purposes of the Harm Principle, consensual harm does not count as harm to others. That is why, as we noted earlier, counting moral corruption as a harm would have the effect of relocating the case for censorship of pornography from the Moralism Principle to the Paternalism Principle: access to pornography would be restricted in order to protect vulnerable male consumers like Adam against themselves. Since the Harm Principle condemns both moralism and paternalism, this shift need have no fundamental effect on Mill's framework.

Leaving the framework aside for a moment, it is true that recognizing moral corruption as a harm might make it easier to justify restrictions on pornography to liberals. Because the Moralism Principle countenances legal restraint of harmless (though immoral) activities, it is largely out of favour as a justificatory ground for public policy in liberal democracies. By contrast, there is strong support in those societies for a broad range of paternalistic policies, even when directed at competent adults. Redefining censorship as a case of paternalism rather than moralism might therefore have the effect of making it more palatable to liberals.[53] However this might be, the acceptance of moral harm as a category would have no fundamental implications for Mill's framework, since it would not relocate the consumption of pornography from the personal to the social realm.[54] It might still be thought a bad thing to blur the distinction between moralism and paternalism by what seems little more than conceptual sleight of hand, but that by itself would not give us sufficient reason to reject moral harm on strictly normative grounds.

However, there is a much stronger descriptive ground for rejecting it, since it is inconsistent with the straightforward welfarist account of harm in which we say that a person is benefited if she is made better off, harmed if she is made worse off. As noted earlier, this account situates the concept of harm within that of welfare or well-being. Welfarist notions like benefit and harm pertain to the prudential value of a life, which is its value *for the person whose life it is.*[55] Prudential value is perspectival: it measures the value of a life from a particular standpoint (that of the subject). Other dimensions of value for lives (aesthetic, perfectionist, moral), while perfectly legitimate in their own right, lack this distinctive subject-relativity. I have argued elsewhere that because welfare is subject-relative, it is also subjective, where this means, roughly, that whether something is good or bad for a person depends ultimately on that person's desires, preferences, aims, tastes, or values – what I call generically her (pro- or con-) attitudes.[56] The fatal flaw in the notion of moral harm is that it lacks this grounding. It is essential to the idea of moral harm that the sufferer is made worse off simply by virtue of being put into a morally worse condition, regardless of any negative attitude toward this condition (regretting it, being distressed by it, wishing to be rid of it, etc.). For the subjectivist about well-being this is impossible. It is in general a fallacy to make inferences across different dimensions of value for a person or a life; in particular, it is a mistake to infer that someone is badly off (prudentially) from the fact that he is bad (morally), or that a person is made worse off (prudentially) by being made worse (morally). The concept of moral harm is therefore a category mistake – a confusion of the moral with the prudential, of someone's *goodness* with her *good*. The moral corruption we are supposing to have been induced by Adam's indulgence in violent pornography does him no harm unless it impedes or frustrates some interest or concern of his. But we may hypothesize that the very process of moral corruption undercuts this possibility: by virtue of coming to enjoy depictions of sexual violence against women, Adam becomes morally calloused about that violence or blinded to the evil of enjoying it. He is not conflicted, feels no guilt or shame at his misogynistic thoughts and feelings, and so the notion of harm can obtain no grip on him. He has been corrupted, but he has not thereby been harmed.[57]

It appears, therefore, that there is no room for moral corruption within a general welfarist account of the nature of harm. It remains to consider the other variety of (so-called) moral harm, namely moral degradation. Whereas the notion of moral corruption was the centrepiece of the traditional conservative objection to pornography, moral degradation has been an important theme in more recent feminist thinking. The site of the alleged harm, however, has shifted from men (the consumers of pornography) to women. The claim that pornography harms women by degrading them can be understood in either of two ways: (1) pornography harms women in general by portraying them in a degrading manner, or (2) it harms the women who participate in its production by subjecting them to degrading treatment. The first claim looks to the content of pornography, the second to the process of its production. In general it would be a mistake to argue from either claim to the other.

A degrading portrayal of women need not degrade anyone in the making of it (for instance, if it is a story or a cartoon), and women can be degraded (for instance, by being used or manipulated) in the making of a portrayal which is not itself degrading. The gap between the two claims is admittedly narrowed in the case of hard-core video pornography, where the sexual activity being portrayed is also being performed. Even in this case, however, the two claims have a different focus, the first on what the pornographic product *shows*, the second on what the production process *does*. For this reason they raise rather different issues concerning possible harms to women. Our immediate concern is with the degradation of the women who participate in the making of pornography, since it more clearly implicates moral degradation as a variety of moral harm. We will therefore postpone until later the broader issue of the harm that might be done to women in general by the circulation of degrading portrayals of them.[58]

Are women degraded by performing in hard-core videos? The short way with this question is to point out that they are exchanging sex for money and to claim that any such exchange is intrinsically degrading. This approach, however, would require drawing a moral line between erotic labour (in all of its forms) and non-erotic labour, and it is difficult to see how this could be done without again invoking an outmoded sexual morality. In any case, it is not the line of argument that has been favoured by most feminists or supported by the courts. Many feminists have wished to draw a distinction, among explicit depictions of sex, between pornography (bad) and erotica (good), and for them degradation (along with violence and aggression) has served as one of the crucial markers separating the two genres.[59] This distinction obviously leaves conceptual space for non-degrading sexually explicit performances in films and videos, but it also requires a different conception of degradation.

Feminists who have addressed this question have tended to associate the degradation of women involved in the making of mainstream, male-oriented pornography with their sexual subordination.[60] Men are the primary consumers of pornography, which thrives by feeding male sexual fantasies. In those fantasies the role of women is to provide sexual services, and sexual gratification, for men. In this respect, women are depicted in pornography as subservient to male needs. The fantasy scenario typically begins with the male participant's arousal (erection) and continues to feature primarily those activities (fellatio, vaginal and anal penetration) which maximize male pleasure; any servicing of the woman's sexual needs is a sideline to the main plot. Throughout the scenario he is in control, frequently directing the action by telling her what to do next. She assumes postures of submission (kneeling, presenting herself for penetration), he of domination (standing, thrusting). The plot ends with his orgasm, whether or not she has achieved any comparable state of completion.

Does this subordination degrade the female performers in these scenarios? If we think of degradation as the reduction of a subject to the status of object or accessory, then it is tempting to say that it does. Women in pornography are there not for their own fulfilment but for that of the male viewer; they are in that respect vehicles or instruments of someone else's purposes. However, as long as their participation is voluntary, this yields only a relatively weak sense of degradation, since it applies with equal force to actors in Hollywood films – or, indeed, in any performance medium – who are paid to satisfy the audience's interests. Pornography is merely a genre which appeals to one particular kind of audience interest. If appearing on screen in a way which serves an audience interest counts as degradation, it carries little moral baggage with it.

Perhaps what matters are the particular sexual scenarios in which female performers are asked to participate. For some years the Ontario Film Review Board, the agency charged with the responsibility of reviewing and classifying all films and videos exhibited in Ontario, had a checklist of forbidden activities which included the insertion of objects (other than penises) into the anus, double penetration, fisting, and ejaculation on a woman's face. But these restrictions have all been relaxed, with the result that videos available for rent throughout Ontario are full of depictions of just such scenarios (which seem to attract an especially high level of male interest, judging by the shelf space allotted to them). So now these depictions as well are judged, at least by one authority, not to degrade the women in the film. There are still limits, excluding such sexual tastes as coprophilia, necrophilia, and bestiality, but they are currently drawn pretty broadly.

Fortunately, for our present purposes we need not determine what *really* counts as a degrading scenario. It should be obvious by now that any distinction between the degrading and the non-degrading will necessarily be a moral one. We deem a sexual activity to be degrading when we consider it to lower a person's agency or subjectivity below what we take to be an acceptable level. On that ground we think it an activity no one ought to engage in, or be depicted as engaging in, even with full consent. Where we locate the critical level will inevitably depend on the particular sexual morality to which we subscribe. One extreme view would regard all sexual performances before the camera as degrading, while another would happily countenance depictions of the activities on the Film Review Board's current prohibited list. Most of us would probably seek some middle ground.

Our interest, however, lies not in degradation *per se* but in harm. So let us assume that Eve, a performer in hard-core videos, engages in consensual sexual activities before the camera which all of us agree are degrading. Is Eve thereby harmed? The case parallels that of moral corruption in every important respect. Recognizing Eve's degradation as a harm will shift the case for coercive interference in her activities from the realm of moralism to that of paternalism; there will still be no case for such interference under the Harm Principle. There is therefore no conclusive reason for refusing to countenance moral degradation as a harm for the purposes of Mill's framework. However, like moral corruption, degradation has no claim to status as a kind of harm in the strictly descriptive sense, for it too lacks the necessary anchoring in the interests or concerns of the 'victim'. While some women have undoubtedly found their performances in hard-core videos degrading or humiliating, many report enjoying their work or even experiencing it as liberating.[61] How can women be harmed by freely engaging in, and even enjoying, activities which (by some moral standard) degrade them?

There is, of course, a possible feminist answer to this question – namely, that women who enjoy performing in male-oriented pornography, or in any kind of sex work, have been brainwashed by patriarchy and consequently their responses can be discounted or ignored. The claim that these women do not experience their treatment as degrading because their autonomy has already been compromised is one which we have to take seriously. I have argued elsewhere that self-reports of enjoyment or satisfaction are not reliable indicators of well-being unless they are autonomous.[62] If it can be shown that a woman's enjoyment of treatment which has been determined (by some moral standard or other) to be degrading invariably fails to be autonomous, then it might be possible to make the case that she is being harmed, despite her view to the contrary. But the chance of showing this seems slight. The case for heteronomy is undermined by the women in the pornography industry who by all appearances are as strong, independent, articulate, well-educated, even as feminist, as one could reasonably wish and who claim to have made a free choice to pursue this line of work.[63] If they fail to qualify as autonomous, it is unclear who among us will.

We have therefore reached a mixed result for the notion of moral harm: while it may cohere with Mill's framework, there is no room for it in (what is to my mind) the most plausible descriptive account of the nature of harm. However, it is important to distinguish moral harm (whether corruption or degradation) from the quite distinct phenomenon of moral distress,[64] which consists in the discomfort or disturbance you experience in the face of actions or events which transgress your moral standards. Unlike moral harm, which requires that something genuinely bad occur, moral distress requires only the belief that this is so.[65] However justified or unjustified your moral standards might be, you can still be distressed by the persistent failure of others to live up to them. Of course, you can also be distressed by your own persistent failure to live up to them, in which case moral distress may take the form of guilt or remorse or shame. But the perceived failure more commonly lies in others: whereas you have a firm fix on what is morally right, the world stubbornly persists in sin and error. Moral distress also differs from moral harm in the location of the (alleged) wrong. For you to suffer moral harm, something must alter your moral condition; you must be the site of the loss of value. By contrast, you can be morally distressed by the (supposedly) deplorable state of any part of the world; the site in question need not have anything directly to do with you (though you are, of course, the location of the distress).

Moral distress is similar, but not quite identical, to moral offence. Offence, like distress, can be experienced as the result of a wide variety of stimuli, many of which have nothing to do with one's moral standards.[66] However, the common element in all cases of offence is some level of disgust or revulsion at the stimulus in question. The offence is moral when the revulsion is a reaction to conduct or character which one deems to be bad or evil – in other words, when one's moral standards are essential ingredients in the explanation of the reaction. Moral offence can be, but need not be, a response to something within one's immediate experience. Those who believe homosexuality to be immoral will be offended by the sight of a same-sex couple holding hands or otherwise expressing affection in public, but they may equally be offended by the very thought of what the couple might be getting up to in private. All of this is true of moral distress as well, but the latter is a broader notion because it need not include the element of disgust or revulsion. One can be distressed by a situation simply because one wishes that it were better and is pained by the shortfall; the further element of repugnance is not an essential component. Offence retains an element of taste – of finding the situation distasteful – which may not be present in the more thoughtful and reflective instances of distress. Moral distress includes moral offence, but much else besides.

What moral offence and moral distress have in common is that they are states which the subject experiences as disagreeable. As such, it is not difficult to make the case that they can constitute harms within a subjective account.[67] Moral distress has the reference back to the concerns of the subject which was conspicuously lacking in the case of moral harm: the distress is experienced precisely because one of the subject's (moral) concerns is not being adequately satisfied. Like physical discomfort, emotional distress in general is readily recognizable as a kind, or source, of harm for the subject: it is the kind of thing which, just in itself, makes one's life go less well and which the subject would prefer not to experience. If distress is in general a kind of harm, there is no reason to exclude moral distress as a particular species of it; it is just one possible source or ground of the experience. It is true, of course, that moral distress involves an element of choice on the part of the subject: the distress would not occur but for the acceptance of the moral standard in question. But that is true of many, indeed most, kinds of distress: the distress I feel at the loss of a loved one is dependent on the choice I made to love her in the first place. If we excluded moral distress as a kind of harm on this choice-dependent ground, we would be compelled to exclude most non-moral distress as well. The simpler way to go is just to say that distress *tout court* is at least typically a bad thing for those who experience it, and moral distress no less bad than the other kinds.

Unlike moral harm, moral distress therefore fits comfortably within a descriptively adequate (welfarist) account of harm. We therefore face a different normative question this time around: given this result, should moral distress also be recognized as a kind of harm for the purposes of the Harm Principle? It is easy to see why it should not. The point of the Harm Principle is to secure for individuals a sphere of liberty in which they will be protected against interference by others, whether these others are individuals (singly or collectively) or institutions (such as the state). This security takes the form of immunity against the outcome of a cost-benefit calculation: within the protected sphere, liberty is guaranteed even if, on particular occasions, its costs exceed its benefits. It is obvious that the Harm Principle can fulfil this normative function only if it establishes a fairly high threshold against cost-benefit reasoning. Allowing moral distress to count as harm would lower that threshold and open up the possibility of intolerable degrees of intrusiveness into individuals' personal lives. Moral distress can, though it need not, result from the violation of moral standards regarding other people's private affairs. Imagine then a situation in which a homophobic majority is deeply distressed by the very thought that same-sex couples might be having sex with one another in the privacy of their own bedrooms. If this distress counts as harm, within the meaning of the Harm Principle, then the question of intervention will be decided by a cost-benefit calculation. If the homophobic majority is large enough, and if the distress they feel is intense enough, and if the gay minority is small enough, then that might tip the balance toward licensing the state to police the bedrooms of the nation (or at least of the gay community).

The objection to extending the Harm Principle to countenance moral distress has been best articulated by H.L.A. Hart:

> a right to be protected from the distress which is inseparable from the bare knowledge that others are acting in ways you think wrong, cannot be acknowledged by anyone who recognises individual liberty as a value. For the extension of the utilitarian principle that coercion may be used to protect men from harm, so as to include their protection from this form of distress, cannot stop there. If distress incident to the belief that others are doing wrong is harm, so also is distress incident to the belief that others are doing what you do not want them to do. To punish people for causing this form of distress would be tantamount to punishing them simply because others object to what they do; and the only liberty that could coexist with this extension of the utilitarian principle is liberty to do those things to which no one seriously objects. Such liberty plainly is quite nugatory. Recognition of individual liberty as a value involves, as a minimum, acceptance of the principle that the individual may do what he wants, even if others are distressed when they learn what it is that he does – unless, of course, there are other good grounds for forbidding it. No social order which accords to individual liberty any value could also accord the right to be protected from distress thus occasioned.[68]

There may be good harm-based reasons for restricting or prohibiting some kinds of pornography (child pornography, violent pornography, or whatever). But the fact that these kinds of pornography cause many, or most, people moral distress cannot be one of them. Let us put the matter this way. Suppose that the distress is based on the apprehension that consumption of these materials will increase the incidence of sexual violence or abuse. Either this belief is true or it is not. If it is true then the unamended Harm Principle may provide grounds for the restriction (depending on the other values and interests at stake), and so any reference to moral distress is redundant. On the other hand, if the belief is false then the moral distress deserves no weight on its own. In either case it is irrelevant and should be excluded from the conception of harm incorporated into the Harm Principle.

This conclusion can be generalized to all cases of moral distress.[69] Remember that we are not questioning the reality, as a natural fact, of the harm constituted by moral distress. Nor must we assume that moral distress always, or typically, arises from moral standards which are themselves repugnant. The moral distress suffered by homophobes as a result of coexisting with their gay and lesbian fellow citizens is doubly suspect: it is nosy to begin with, since it has to do with how others behave in private, and it is grounded in a conviction about the immorality of homosexual conduct which is utterly without rational foundation. But moral distress need suffer from neither of these defects. Imagine, for instance, the situation of a particularly sensitive person deeply committed to ideals of social justice who is distressed by the ample evidence of injustice in the world: vast disparities of wealth, racial prejudice, ethnic cleansing, the sexual subordination of women, and so on. These are grounds of distress with which we can, and should, sympathize; we should therefore also sympathize with the pain she feels at the apprehension of so much global injustice. But her distress gives us no further reason for intervention to remedy these injustices: either they are already objectionable (because of the harm they do), in which case Mill's framework may already give us grounds for intervention, or they are not (because harmless), in which case there are no grounds for intervention. In either case, her moral distress by itself adds nothing to the case.

Moral distress, therefore, should not be counted as harm for the purposes of Mill's framework. This may seem, however, an overly sweeping conclusion, for it appears to threaten one common, and popular, way of thinking about the regulation of pornography (and other sexual activities as well). Many anti-censorship advocates who oppose any outright prohibition on pornographic materials are none the less prepared to countenance regulation of their public display.[70] Such regulations are in place in many localities, where sexually explicit magazines and videos are sold or rented in discreet premises with posted warnings about their contents. This distinction between prohibition and regulation was defended forcefully in the 1979 Report of the Committee on Obscenity and Film Censorship chaired by Bernard Williams. The Williams Committee argued as follows:

> Laws against public sex would generally be thought to be consistent with the harm condition, in the sense that if members of the public are upset, distressed, disgusted, outraged or put out by witnessing some class of acts, then that constitutes a respect in which the public performance of those acts harms their interests and gives them a reason to object ... The offensiveness of publicly displayed pornography seems to us ... to be in line with traditionally accepted rules protecting the interest in public decency. Restrictions on the open sale of these publications, and analogous arrangements for films, thus seem to us to be justified.[71]

Many people, including me, find this distinction between outright prohibition of sexually explicit materials (a content restriction) and regulation of their public display (a time, manner, or circumstance restriction) perfectly acceptable. However, the distinction seems to rest, and does so explicitly in the Williams Committee's rationale for it, on treating (a certain kind of) moral distress as a harm. So isn't the absolute exclusion of moral distress from the ambit of Mill's framework too extreme?

The most promising approach to this problem seems to be that of Joel Feinberg, who falls back on the model of nuisance law.[72] Something is a nuisance if it not only annoys or irritates us but also intrudes or imposes on us in a way which is difficult or inconvenient for us to avoid. Standard cases of nuisances include your neighbour's loud music which intrudes on your peaceful enjoyment of your own home, the call from the telemarketer which disturbs your family's mealtime, and the spam messages which clog up your e-mail inbox. 'We demand protection from nuisances,' Feinberg writes, 'when we think of ourselves as *trapped* by them, and we think it unfair that we should pay the cost in inconvenience that is required to escape them.'[73] Feinberg handles the particular case of public displays of obscene materials in the following way:

> the offended and otherwise unpleasant states caused by these ... activities are objectionable for roughly the same kind of reason as the evils combatted by nuisance law. Even when they are not harms, they are annoying distractions, unwelcome demands on one's attention, a bother that must be coped with however inconvenient it may be at the time to do so. They are,

in short, themselves nuisances in a perfectly ordinary sense ... If they are to be the concern of the criminal law at all, it should be only when they occur in open places and thereby inconvenience elements of the general public, in the manner of 'public' or 'common' nuisances.[74]

Feinberg's solution to the problem of regulating the public display of pornography seems to be on the right track, but it still leaves open the question whether a particular kind of moral distress – namely, distress *at the public display* – is not being recognized as a harm.[75] It would be if the distress stemmed from moral disapproval of the sexual content of the display (or of the mere fact that it is advertising pornography). No doubt most people who object to such displays do so because pornography offends their moral sensibilities. But this need not be the case. Your objection to an intrusive nuisance may be purely one of context (occasion) rather than content (message). You may find your neighbour's loud music just as disturbing even when you think it is in excellent taste and the telemarketer's call just as disruptive even when it is soliciting donations for your favourite charity. I find spam a nuisance because of the effort needed to delete it from my inbox every day, but the sexually explicit messages bother me no more than the offers to buy cheap Viagra or to share in unclaimed millions in a Nigerian bank account. Restrictions on public display that are specific to pornography and do not apply to the equally intrusive advertising of other products and services may indeed require acknowledging the distress felt by those who find pornography morally objectionable. But more content-neutral time, manner, and circumstance restrictions need appeal only to such values as autonomy, privacy, and peace of mind. They can be justified without assigning any weight to moral distress.

2.5 Conclusion

Mill's framework for justifying a restriction on liberty consists of two tests: (1) Does the conduct in question cause harm to others? (2) If so, will the restriction yield a better overall balance of benefits over costs than an unrestricted liberty? The first test is given by Mill's Harm Principle, the second by his Consequentialist Principle. A limitation of liberty is justified only when both questions can be answered affirmatively. These tests are as applicable to expression as to any other form of conduct (and are so applied by Mill). The justification Mill offers for this framework is itself consequentialist, indeed utilitarian, which is enough to show that his political morality is foundationalist rather than free-standing in its methodology. However, the sectarian nature of his overall approach can be neutralized somewhat by prescinding from some of the more specific tenets of utilitarianism (such as its welfarism and aggregation) and embracing instead a broader commitment to consequentialism. As embodied in the second of the foregoing tests, this commitment will seem even less parochial and divisive if it turns out to capture the standard form of public and judicial debate about the justification of policies imposing limits on freedom of expression.

Using Mill's framework to determine when any such policies are justified foregrounds the issue of the harm done by the forms of expression – such as pornography and hate speech – which are the traditional candidates for regulation. However, if we are to work within the framework then we must from the outset discount two kinds of (alleged) harm. Moral harm (in the form of corruption or degradation) fails an essential condition for harmfulness because it lacks a reference back to the interests or concerns of its subject. Moral distress, on the other hand, is intelligible as a kind of harm but cannot be acknowledged as such for the purposes of the framework without threatening to annihilate the personal sphere of liberty in whose defence Mill was so passionate.

Chapter 3

The Balancing Act

Hate propaganda is a difficult issue for liberals because it seems to reveal a conflict between their two most cherished values. A liberal society prides itself on its acceptance, even celebration, of cultural pluralism and on its fostering of a climate of equal respect for members of minority communities. It therefore rejects all forms of discrimination on grounds such as race, ethnicity, national origin, religious affiliation, gender, age, disability, and sexual orientation. At the same time, commitment to freedom of expression requires liberals to tolerate the advocacy of opinions which they regard as abhorrent. Hate propaganda therefore threatens to expose a contradiction between liberal equality and liberal freedom. Hate groups decisively reject the liberal ideal of pluralism and equality, and the public advocacy of their views arguably serves to undermine the equal social status of their favoured targets. However, as a form of political expression, that advocacy seems to call for particularly robust protection in a liberal society. Liberals must therefore decide how far they are prepared to tolerate the expression of opinions which are themselves intolerant. However this issue is resolved, it looks as though it must be at the cost of limiting one of the values that liberals hold most dear. Are they to side with liberty at the cost of threatening equality, or equality at the cost of restraining liberty?

This dilemma for liberals presents itself as a conflict of rights: on the one side a liberty-right (to express opinions), on the other a claim-right (to equal protection or consideration).[1] When the conflicting rights are legal, and especially when both are constitutionally protected, the courts inevitably become the ultimate site for resolving the tensions between them. In Canada the right to 'freedom of thought, belief, opinion and expression' finds its constitutional protection in section 2(b) of the Charter of Rights and Freedoms, while section 15 guarantees members of minority groups the right to 'the equal protection and equal benefit of the law'.[2] These two rights come into apparent conflict whenever restrictions are imposed on expression in order to promote or protect equality. One such restriction is contained in the hate propaganda statute in the Criminal Code prohibiting communication which 'wilfully promotes hatred against any identifiable group'.[3] Since the *prima facie* conflict between this statute and the Charter guarantee of freedom of expression is pretty obvious, it is scarcely surprising that the law was challenged in the post-Charter era on constitutional grounds. The court's handling of that challenge – in *Keegstra* (1990) – will serve as our model for the adjudicative resolution of conflicts of rights.

3.1 When Rights Collide

Before taking a closer look at the *Keegstra* case, however, we need to get clear about why it features a conflict of rights at all. At least on the face of it, the conflict confronting the court in *Keegstra* was between a section of the Criminal Code and a section of the Charter. Even these two items do not conflict unless the statute limits or infringes the constitutionally protected right. In order for this to be the case, two conditions must be satisfied: (1) the statute must restrict expression, and (2) the expression which it restricts must fall within the protection of section 2(b) of the Charter. Since, as we will see later, the court held that both of these conditions are satisfied, we may take the conflict between the statute and the Charter to be real and not merely apparent. The trouble is that this is not (yet) a conflict of *rights*. There is only one (constitutional) right in play which is being infringed by legislative action. So the question remains: how can this legal situation be construed as a conflict of rights?

There is both a technical (and less interesting) and a non-technical (and more interesting) way of securing this result. The technical way involves interpreting the right conferred on individuals by section 2(b) of the Charter not as a liberty but as an immunity – one which denies the legislature the power to enact legislation restricting expression.[4] The immunity, belonging to individuals, against legislative restrictions is logically incompatible with the power, belonging to the legislature, to impose such restrictions. So in deciding whether to uphold or strike down the hate propaganda statute, the court is after all adjudicating a conflict between rights.

As far as it goes, this is a perfectly legitimate way of conceptualizing the conflicting rights at stake in cases like *Keegstra*. Certainly the idea that the competing rights belong to individuals on the one hand and the legislature on the other resonates nicely with the worries of civil libertarians about the intrusion of the state into the protected domain of individual expression. But there is none the less something lacking in it. For one thing, it seems an incomplete analysis of the constitutionally protected right. As we saw in chapter 1, if we ask ourselves what the content of that right is (what it is a right *to*), the obvious answer seems to be 'expression' or 'freedom of expression', which is not an immunity but a liberty. The immunity against legislative restriction conferred by the Charter then becomes part of the 'protective perimeter' around that liberty, one of a number of ways of safeguarding its exercise. The immunity is, of course, logically incompatible with the aforementioned power of the legislature, but the liberty is not. The liberty is incompatible only with a duty, imposed on individuals, not to express certain opinions. The impugned statute does, of course, impose just such a duty by prohibiting the expression of opinions judged to promote hatred against an identifiable group. So there is still just one right in play here – a liberty – and a conflict between it and the legislation. We still lack a competing right on the other side of the conflict.

The element missing so far in this picture is the rationale behind the legislation. For the purpose of the hate propaganda statute an identifiable group is 'any section of the public distinguished by colour, race, religion or ethnic origin'.[5] The objective discerned by the Supreme Court for the statute was the protection of such groups against the harms to which they were likely to be exposed by the circulation of defamatory slurs. Such protection is arguably required by the claim-right of members of such minorities to 'the equal protection and equal benefit of the law' guaranteed by section 15 of the Charter. If the right to free expression is used to vilify minorities, thereby threatening their equality, then we have a conflict in which both items are the rights of individuals: the liberty-right of hate groups on the one hand, the claim-right of the target minorities on the other. To be sure, the conflict is now contingent and empirical rather than logical: the contention is that, as a matter of fact, the exercise of the right to promote hatred will lead to infringement of the right to equal protection and benefit, and therefore that if we wish to protect the latter we will need to limit the former (and vice versa).

This interpretation of the conflict restores our initial picture of an incompatibility between rights to liberty and to equality. It also suggests that a resolution of this conflict will take the form of limiting one or the other of these rights. Let us therefore look more closely at what is involved in limiting a right. The process seems to involve what Judith Thomson has called 'specification'.[6] Rights are most likely to come into conflict when their content is characterized in very general terms: Thomson's examples are the right to life and the right to self-defence. So described, a conflict between these rights will occur whenever someone must kill an attacker in order to defend her life. But perhaps the conflict disappears if we specify at least one of the rights in question more carefully. The needed specification, Thomson says, may be either normative or factual. It is normative if we redefine the right to life as, say, the right to not be *wrongly* or *unjustly* killed. Since killing in self-defence is arguably not wrong or unjust, then the right of self-defence no longer conflicts with the right to life. The specification is factual if the right to life is redefined as, say, the right not to be killed unless one is trying to kill someone else who can defend herself in no non-lethal way. So specified, once again the conflict vanishes.

Factual specification is one of the techniques available to courts in the face of conflicts between broadly defined rights: one (or both) of the rights is limited so that the overlap between them disappears. Where hate propaganda is concerned, limitation by specification can lead to either of two outcomes. On the one hand, the right of free expression can be internally limited by excluding expression intended to promote hatred: its content then becomes the liberty to express any opinions *except* hateful ones.[7] On the other hand, the right to equal protection can be internally limited by excluding protection against hateful expression. Both outcomes yield specified rights which no longer conflict, but they locate the boundary between these rights in different places. The first outcome contracts the expressive right so as to preserve the full equality right, while the second outcome does just the opposite.

If the conflict is to be resolved by limiting one of the rights in question, how are courts to decide which right is to yield to the other? Answering this question takes us back to the Charter, not to section 2(b) or section 15, which stipulate the conflicting rights, but to section 1, which guarantees the various rights set out in the Charter 'subject only to such reasonable limits prescribed by law as can be demonstrably justified in a free and democratic society'. It is an interesting and important feature of the Charter that it contains an explicit limitation clause; in this respect it differs markedly from the American Bill of Rights. When Canadian courts deliberate about whether (and which) rights are to be limited, they do so within the terms of section 1. The Supreme Court first defined these terms in its 1986 *Oakes* decision.[8] In order for a limit on a Charter right to be found 'demonstrably justified', the legislation imposing it must pass two tests, one concerning its end and the other concerning the means it employs to achieve that end:[9]

1 *Legislative objective.* The purpose of the legislation must be sufficiently 'pressing and substantial' to justify limiting the right.
2 *Proportionality.* The means employed by the legislation must be proportional to the objective to be achieved. The proportionality test subdivides in turn into three parts:

   (a) *Rational connection.* There must be reasonable grounds for expecting the legislation to be effective in achieving its objective.

   (b) *Minimal impairment.* The legislation must limit the right no more than is necessary in order to achieve its objective.

   (c) *Proportional effects.* The costs of the limitation must not exceed the benefits to be gained from achieving the objective.

Section 1 of the Charter and the *Oakes* tests which give it an operational meaning enable the Canadian courts to distinguish (in Judith Thomson's terminology) between an infringement of a right and an unjustified infringement (or violation).[10] They therefore open up the possibility that legislation which infringes the section 2(b) right of free expression might none the less be constitutionally valid. When the Supreme Court considers a free expression challenge to legislation, it engages in a two-step inquiry: (1) Does the legislation infringe section 2(b)? (2) If so, is the infringement justified within the terms of section 1? This procedure has enabled the court to be generous in conceding infringements of section 2(b), since the really difficult issues will be faced in the course of the subsequent section 1 analysis. The court has therefore adopted an expansive definition of expression – as any activity which 'conveys or attempts to convey a meaning' – and it has included all such expression within the scope of the section 2(b) protection unless it takes a physically violent form.[11] It has also taken the view that any legislation whose purpose is to impose a content restriction on expression automatically infringes section 2(b).[12] Since the purpose of the hate propaganda statute is to impose just such a restriction, the issue of its constitutional validity comes down to the question whether its infringement of section 2(b) is justified under the terms of section 1. That was the central issue in the *Keegstra* case, to which we now turn.

3.2 Hate Promotion on Trial

James Keegstra was a secondary school teacher in Eckville, Alberta, who used his classroom to advocate anti-Semitic views depicting Jews as treacherous, subversive, barbaric, sadistic, money-loving, power-hungry, and child killers. He taught his students that Jewish people seek to destroy Christianity and are responsible for depressions, wars, anarchy, and revolution. According to Keesgtra, Jews created the myth of the Holocaust to gain sympathy and, in contrast to the open and honest Christians, are deceptive, secretive, and inherently evil. He expected his students to reproduce his teachings in class, in essays, and on exams; if they failed to do so, their marks suffered.[13]

When Keegtra's classroom practices came to light he was dismissed from his teaching position and later charged with the wilful promotion of hatred. He applied to the trial court for an order quashing the charge, primarily on the ground that the hate propaganda statute was an unjustifiable infringement of section 2(b) of the Charter. The application was dismissed, and Keegstra was subsequently convicted.[14] He then appealed his conviction to the Alberta Court of Appeal, raising the same Charter issue. The Court of Appeal unanimously accepted his argument and quashed his conviction,[15] whereupon the crown appealed this result in turn to the Supreme Court. By a majority of 4 to 3, the court upheld the constitutionality of the hate propaganda statute and ordered a new trial for Keegstra, at which he was once again convicted.

The workings of a section 1 analysis are nicely illustrated in the *Keegstra* case. The constitutional issue before the Supreme Court was the seeming inconsistency of the hate propaganda law with the Charter protection of freedom of expression. Both the majority and the minority on the court agreed that hateful expression fell within the scope of this protection, thus that the law did indeed limit the Charter right. The issue therefore was whether this limitation was justifiable under the terms of section 1. In applying the *Oakes* tests, the majority and the minority also agreed that the objective of the law – which they saw as the protection of racial, ethnic, and religious minorities against the harms likely to result from the spread of contempt or enmity directed toward them – is sufficiently pressing and substantial to justify the limitation. Here the court was guided in part by section 15 of the Charter as well as section 27, which gives constitutional recognition to Canadian multiculturalism.[16] The main points of contention, therefore, were the first two parts of the proportionality test.

Writing for the dissenting minority, Justice McLachlin argued that the hate propaganda law failed both the rational connection and minimal impairment conditions. The law could not reasonably be expected to achieve its own objective since the criminal prosecution of hatemongers provides them with a public platform for the advocacy of their opinions and may also make them objects of public sympathy. In these ways the enforcement of the law may actually be self-defeating. McLachlin also pointed out how ineffective similar legal restrictions had been at combating racism in other cultures, such as Germany during the Weimar Republic. As far as minimal impairment was concerned, she contended that the law was overbroad, largely because of the potentially wide scope of the key notion of hatred, and that it therefore could have a substantial chilling effect on legitimate forms of expression. She also claimed that alternatives to criminalization (such as human rights legislation) available to the legislature as means of combating racial intolerance would be more protective of freedom of expression. For these reasons, she concluded, Parliament had not employed the least intrusive measure for achieving its objective.

Chief Justice Dickson, writing for the majority, defended the hate propaganda law on both counts. On the issue of rational connection, he argued that the prosecution of hatemongers can have the beneficial effect of endorsing the values of tolerance and equality and of expressing social condemnation of hate propaganda. He also disputed the relevance of the parallel with Weimar and pointed out the existence of analogues to the hate propaganda law in many other liberal democracies. As for minimal impairment, Dickson urged a strict interpretation of hatred, which confined it to the most intense and extreme feelings of antipathy toward the target groups. He also pointed to the legislation's *mens rea* requirement that the promotion of hatred be 'wilful' (i.e., either desired or foreseen as substantially certain) and to the array of defences which it makes available to the accused.[17] In these respects, Dickson argued, the legislation was crafted so as to minimize its impact on freedom of expression. Finally, he contended that the availability of non-criminal measures for combating racist speech did not preclude Parliament from utilizing the mechanism of criminal law for the same purpose.

The foregoing is the merest sketch of the extended dialogue concerning proportionality between the majority and minority on the *Keegstra* court. Keep in mind that the final outcome was very close: had just one judge switched sides, the hate propaganda law would have been struck down.[18] My focus for this chapter, however, is not on what divided the two sides – their substantive conclusions – but on the ground they shared – the methodology they used to reach those conclusions. Ignoring for a moment the particular components of the proportionality test, what it requires is some sort of balancing of the expected benefits of the hate propaganda law against its expected costs. In *Keegstra* both the majority and the minority helped themselves freely to this rhetoric of balancing. For the majority, Dickson wrote that 'the inquiry as to proportionality attempts to guide the balancing of individual and group interests',[19] but the most elaborate and developed account of what is involved in this process was provided by McLachlin, writing for the minority:

> The task which judges are required to perform under s. 1 is essentially one of balancing. On the one hand lies a violation or limitation of a fundamental right or freedom. On the other lies a conflicting objective which the state asserts is of greater importance than the full exercise of the right or freedom, of sufficient importance that it is reasonable and 'demonstrably justified' that the limitation should be imposed. The exercise is one of great difficulty, requiring the judge to make value judgments. In this task logic and precedent are but of limited assistance. What must be determinative in the end is the court's judgment, based on an understanding of the values our society is built on and the interests at stake in the particular case. As Wilson J. has pointed out in *Edmonton Journal, supra,* this judgment cannot be made in the abstract. Rather than speak of values as though they were Platonic ideals, the judge must situate the analysis in the facts of the particular case, weighing the different values represented in that context. Thus it cannot be said that freedom of expression will always prevail over the objective of individual dignity and social harmony, or vice versa. The result in a particular case will depend on weighing the significance of the infringement on freedom of expression represented by the law in question, against the importance of the countervailing objectives, the likelihood the law will achieve those objectives, and the proportionality of the scope of the law to those objectives.[20]

When the proportionality test was first devised in *Oakes,* the court recognized that it would require some form of balancing.[21] But what are the items to be balanced? Ultimately, as we have seen, they are rights: in *Keegstra* the right of free expression (which is infringed by the hate propaganda law) and the right to equal protection and benefit (which it is the object of the law to preserve and protect). The outcome of the balancing exercise will determine which of these rights is to be limited in favour of the other. The court majority was willing to limit the right to expressive freedom by upholding the hate propaganda law; the minority would have limited the right to equality by striking the law down. Presumably, the metaphor of balancing rights presupposes that we can compare their relative weights on some scale. But how is that to be done? The court suggests an answer to this question by speaking of balancing (not rights but) *values* or *interests*. It seems therefore to take the view that we can balance rights only by looking behind them to the interests they are meant to enhance or protect. Rights 'in the abstract' have no weight; they are weightless. But competing (individual and collective) interests can have weights, and it is only by weighing those interests that an appropriate balance can be struck between the rights which protect them.[22]

The balancing procedure which the court uses therefore seems to presuppose an instrumentalist view of rights. The instrumentalist sees rights as devices for advancing or protecting certain important values or interests.[23] In the case of expressive rights it is common to collect these interests into three main groups.[24] The first group consists of *speaker interests*, which include the many ways in which being able to express ideas, or indeed to engage in any form of communication, can be a benefit for the person who exercises this freedom. Speaker interests include, but are not restricted to, the self-fulfilment or self-esteem that may flow from being a participant in a public forum or being recognized as a citizen with a voice in the affairs of one's society. Correlative with speaker interests are *audience interests*, which consist of the many benefits realized by being the recipient of others' speech. Like speaker interests, these are impossible to enumerate exhaustively, but they typically consist of being better informed, being exposed to novel or mind-expanding ideas, being facilitated in the pursuit of one's tastes or values, and so on. Communication is a relationship between one or more speakers and one or more listeners (or viewers or readers), and the first two groups of interests served by free speech underscore the ways in which this relationship can be mutually profitable. The third group, *bystander interests*, points to a further dimension of the communicative relationship, namely its spillover effects for those who are not directly parties to it. Those effects can, of course, be negative, but we are here focusing, for the moment at least, on the positive payoffs of free expression. The most important of these consist of the many benefits we derive as citizens from living in a society in which our fellow citizens are open-minded, inquisitive, and well-informed. In addition to benefiting those directly involved in particular communicative exchanges, the free flow of information can be a public good by contributing to an atmosphere in which the general level of inquiry and debate is raised. This atmosphere is particularly important in a functioning democracy, where we expect at least a loose correlation between the quality of government and the degree of participation in the political system by informed citizens.

A similar account can be given of the important interests served by equality rights. Consider the impact that hate speech can have on the minorities it targets.[25] The immediate emotional distress which can result from exposure to racial insults or abuse includes feelings of humiliation, exclusion, and self-hatred. Racial labelling and stigmatization can seriously impair the individual's pursuit of education or a career. Minority children may come to question their competence, intelligence, or self-worth. Entire communities may come to feel that they have no legitimate place, and no reasonable prospects, in the social fabric, leading them to withdraw into quietism or apathy. Socially marginalized and relatively powerless groups are at genuine risk of harm from the racist attitudes of employers, landlords, police, bureaucrats, and the thugs whom hate groups use their propaganda to recruit. Equality rights are intended to protect minorities against the harms resulting from discriminatory treatment, to foster their self-esteem, to underline their equal social status, and to encourage their full participation in social and political life.

These two constellations of interests, served by the two kinds of rights in conflict, were the very ones the Supreme Court attempted to balance in the *Keegstra* case. The principal values the court identified as served by freedom of expression were individual self-fulfilment, the pursuit of truth, and the fostering of a participatory democracy.[26] On the other side of the ledger, the harms which the court attributed to hate speech, and which the hate propaganda law was intended to combat, included the immediate emotional damage to members of minority groups, especially feelings of humiliation and degradation, and the fostering of a social climate of discrimination, exclusion, or even violence aimed at these groups.[27] That these were the conflicting interests which needed to be balanced was a matter of broad agreement between the majority and the minority on the *Keegstra* court (though, of course, they reached opposing conclusions on how the balance between them was to be struck).

The Supreme Court's commitment to an instrumentalist view of rights extends beyond the arena of free expression. Early in the era of Charter adjudication the court adopted the view that the rights and freedoms guaranteed therein were to be interpreted purposively: 'The meaning of a right or freedom guaranteed by the Charter was to be ascertained by an analysis of the *purpose* of such a guarantee; it was to be understood, in other words, in the light of the interests it was meant to protect.'[28] The court's use of the term 'purpose' here may suggest a reference to the intentions of the framers of the Charter, or of the legislature in enacting it. But it is clear that what the Court primarily had in mind was a reading of the Charter in the context of the larger social and political values which define Canadian society. As Chief Justice Dickson put it in *Oakes*:

> The Court must be guided by the values and principles essential to a free and democratic society which I believe embody, to name but a few, respect for the inherent dignity of the human person, commitment to social justice and equality, accommodation of a wide variety of beliefs, respect for cultural and group identity, and faith in social and political institutions which enhance the participation of individuals and groups in society. The underlying values and principles of a free and democratic society are the genesis of the rights and freedoms guaranteed by the *Charter* and the ultimate standard against which a limit on a right or freedom must be shown, despite its effect, to be reasonable and demonstrably justified.[29]

A purposive interpretation of Charter rights is therefore equivalent to a functionalist or, as I have called it, an instrumentalist one. Both the rights themselves and their limitation are justified by reference to the appropriate underlying values or interests which they enhance or protect.[30]

It follows that in cases of conflict the court must look behind the rights in question to those values or interests. It is here that the language of balancing comes into play. However, the court's commitment to balancing as the means of conflict resolution appears to presuppose not just an instrumentalist justification of rights, and of their limitation, but something stronger. When two important social values (such as liberty and equality) conflict, the optimal tradeoff or balance between them is that point at which further gains in one of the values would be outweighed by greater losses in the other. Freedom of expression would be better protected were there no legal constraints whatever on hate propaganda, while the equal status of minority groups would (arguably) be better safeguarded by legislation more restrictive than the hate propaganda law, hedged round as it is by its various safeguards. Somewhere between these extremes lies a balance point at which the greater protection for these groups afforded by more restrictive legislation would be outweighed by the greater impairment of expression, while the greater protection for expression afforded by more permissive legislation would be outweighed by the greater risk of discrimination. Whether the existing hate propaganda statute properly locates that balance point is, of course, the issue on which the majority and the minority on the *Keegstra* court took opposing sides.

We have located the optimal balance between conflicting interests when the costs of a departure in either direction exceed its benefits. But in that case the optimal balance is that point any departure from which will result in a net loss of value – that is, the point at which the balance of benefits over costs is maximized. Consequentialism is the name for the kind of moral/political theory which tells us always to prefer the outcome which maximizes this balance. Although consequentialism about rights implies instrumentalism, the reverse is not the case. Someone could think that rights are justified by reference to the interests they protect without also thinking that their contours are to be determined by some overall cost-benefit calculation. It is an interesting feature of section 1 of the Charter, and of its operationalization in the *Oakes* tests, that it seems to require courts to engage in just this kind of calculation.

This is the appropriate place to take a closer look at the tests themselves, as they apply to the particular rights in play in *Keegstra*. The first test looks to the objective of the hate propaganda law, which must be sufficiently 'pressing and substantial' to justify limiting the Charter right of free expression. Since the legislation aims to protect or enhance the competing right of equality, the effect of this test is to determine the importance of the values or interests underlying that right. (It is not necessary that the competing right also enjoy Charter status, though in this case it does.) In the cost-benefit analysis of the legislation we are here on the benefit side: the protection of vulnerable minorities against the harms they might suffer as a result of hate speech. Only if the legislation aims to secure significant benefits – benefits comparable to the costs it inflicts on expressive freedom – will it be deemed to pass the first test.[31]

But aiming to secure benefits is one thing; actually securing them at an acceptable cost is the other. Thus we move to the proportionality test, which looks not to the legislation's objective but to the means it employs in order to achieve it. Here is where the cost-benefit balancing occurs. The rational connection requirement is intended to ensure that the benefits promised by the legislation will actually be delivered. It must therefore be shown at this stage that criminalizing hate speech will succeed in reducing its circulation, with corresponding gains in self-esteem and other important social goods for the members of target minorities. With the minimal impairment step we move to the cost side. It has already been determined that the legislation strikes at (some or all of) the interests served by expressive freedom. The question now is whether the costs it imposes are greater than they need be in order to yield the legislation's expected benefits. If a similar or comparable enhancement of the equality rights of minorities could be achieved at less cost to expressive freedom, then the legislation will fail this part of the proportionality test.

In virtually all of the free expression cases which the Supreme Court has adjudicated the argument has focused primarily on these requirements of rational connection and minimal impairment. In every case the legislation in question has been deemed to pass the test of a pressing and substantial objective, and the question of its justification has come down to whether or not it satisfies these two elements of the proportionality test.[32] This has left the final proportionality requirement – proportional effects – with relatively little work to do. In its free expression cases the court has seldom paid more than perfunctory attention to this requirement; indeed, it has standardly functioned as a mere afterthought to the other components of the *Oakes* tests. In *Keegstra*, for example, Chief Justice Dickson's majority judgment allocates twenty pages of intense argumentation to rational connection and minimal impairment and one page to proportional effects. Dickson goes through the motions of insisting that this requirement is additional to and independent of all of the others: 'Even if the purpose of the limiting measure is substantial and the first two components of the proportionality test are satisfied, the deleterious effects of a limit may be too great to permit the infringement of the right or guarantee in issue.'[33] However, his subsequent discussion of proportional effects merely rehearses and summarizes his conclusions concerning the other tests. In her minority opinion Justice McLachlin gives it similarly short shrift but also provides a valuable clue as to its ambiguous status. She describes the requirement as follows: 'The third consideration in determining whether the infringement represented by the legislation is proportionate to the ends is the balance between the importance of the infringement of the right and the benefit conferred by the legislation. The analysis is essentially a cost-benefit analysis.'[34] Since the proportionality test as a whole constitutes a cost-benefit analysis,[35] it is easy to see why the final step in the test might be thought to be redundant.

The suspicion of redundancy makes even more sense when we take into account the evolution of the proportional effects requirement. In its earliest *Oakes* formulation, the condition stipulated that the deleterious effects of the infringement must not outweigh the objective of the legislation; this was the test applied by Dickson in *Keegstra.*[36] McLachlin, however, worked with a subtly but importantly different interpretation of the requirement as requiring a 'balance between the importance of the infringement of the right in question and the benefit conferred by the legislation'.[37] On this construal the costs of the legislation (its impairment of free expression) are to be weighed against its actual benefits (*not* its intended benefits), which is why she could refer to the condition as a cost-benefit analysis. This revision of the proportional effects requirement was formally endorsed by the court in *Dagenais* (1994), where Chief Justice Lamer wrote that it 'requires both that the underlying *objective* of a measure and the *salutary effects* that actually result from its implementation be proportional to the deleterious effects the measure has on fundamental rights and freedoms'.[38] From that point on, the court's standard interpretation of the requirement has been that the salutary effects (benefits) of the measure in question are to be weighed against its deleterious effects (costs).[39]

But these developments have merely reinforced the appearance of redundancy: if the proportional effects step involves conducting a cost-benefit analysis, and if all of the steps in the proportionality test collectively amount to just such an analysis, then isn't the part just replicating the whole? The most persistent advocate of the redundancy view has been Peter Hogg:

[Proportional effects] is really a restatement of the first step, the requirement that a limiting law pursue an objective that is sufficiently important to justify overriding a Charter right. If a law is sufficiently important to justify overriding a Charter right (first step), and if the law is rationally connected to the objective (second step), and if the law impairs the Charter right no more than is necessary to accomplish the objective (third step), how could its effects then be judged to be too severe? A judgment that the effects of

the law were too severe would surely mean that the objective was *not* sufficiently important to justify limiting a Charter right.[40]

While it is easy to see how Hogg could have come to this conclusion, it
is none the less mistaken. For one thing, the first *Oakes* test is limited to
determining the importance of the government's legislative objective; it
falls to the second (proportionality) test to assess the means the government is using to pursue this objective. It follows that none of the three
steps in the second test (including proportional effects) can be a mere
restatement of the first. Whether the objective of a legislative measure is
pressing and substantial is determined in the abstract by the kind of
benefits it is meant to deliver (or the kind of harms it is meant to prevent); only certain kinds will qualify as important enough to justify
infringing a constitutionally protected right.[41] The fact that some objective surpasses this threshold does not ensure that the expected benefits
of the measure will be proportional to its expected costs.

More importantly, the proportional effects requirement has a conclu-
sory function that is not performed by any of the other steps in the
Oakes tests. Once the government's objective has been deemed sufficiently weighty, the first two proportionality requirements focus respectively on the benefit and cost sides of the equation, in order to ensure
that the intended benefits can be rationally expected and that the costs
(to free expression) have been minimized. But only at the last step are
the cost and benefit sides brought together and compared in a calculation meant to determine whether the government's objective is worth
pursuing in this particular way, in the face of its predictable costs.[42] The
previous steps have the function of feeding necessary information into
the final cost-benefit balancing, but they do not conduct that balancing.
It is only at the final step that it can be determined whether a limit to
free expression is 'demonstrably justified', all things considered.

It might be thought, then, that Hogg has the redundancy issue backwards: it is not the proportional effects requirement which is redundant
(since it finally settles the question of justifiable infringement) but
rather rational connection and minimal impairment (since they are
merely accessory to it). However, this too would be an overly simple way
of conceptualizing the relationships among the three steps in the proportionality test. It is arguable that the kind of cost-benefit balancing
involved in the last step is already implicit in the other two.[43] Rational
connection requires a reasonable likelihood that the legislation will
realize its intended benefits. But when is a likelihood reasonable? Is a 30

per cent chance of success enough? 50 per cent? 70 per cent? It is difficult to see how any particular threshold of success could be established
independently of consideration of the legislation's costs to expressive
freedom: the greater those costs the more demanding we should be
about the probability of the benefits (as well as their importance). Unlike rational connection, minimal impairment is an explicitly comparative requirement, but the comparison cannot be limited to the cost side
alone. (The minimal impairment of free expression would always be no
restriction whatever.) Nor can it be limited to measures which promise
to deliver exactly the same benefits but at different levels of cost, since
the available policy options will rarely line up in this convenient Pareto
ordering. Presumably it will sometimes be rational to prefer a measure
with a slightly greater impairment of expressive freedom if it promises
to deliver substantially greater benefits. But in that case minimal impairment must take some account of the benefit side, just as rational
connection cannot ignore the cost side. The kind of cost-benefit comparison mandated by the proportional effects test therefore seems to
permeate the other two proportionality tests. This does not, of course,
make it redundant, since it remains true that only at the final stage are
all of the relevant costs and benefits in play.

It may seem perverse to insist that the least-used and most-ignored
component of the *Oakes* tests is actually the most crucial. But the confu-
sions concerning the status of the proportional effects requirement are
symptomatic of the questionable structure of the tests as a whole. Since
the *Oakes* procedure for determining the justifiability of a limitation to a
Charter right essentially mandates a cost-benefit balancing, and since
the final step in the procedure consists of just such a balancing, there is
an inevitable problem about the relationship of the part to the whole.
As we have seen, that problem has been highlighted by the evolution of
the final step into a comparison of actual effects (positive and negative).
It has also been highlighted by the court's increasing insistence that section 1 balancing be sensitive to context. We have already seen Justice
McLachlin's claim in *Keegstra* that 'the judge must situate the [cost-
benefit] analysis in the facts of the particular case, weighing the different values represented in that context'.[44] The intended contrast is with
an abstract approach in which the competing values at stake are identified generically – in *Keegstra* the underlying values of freedom of expression on the one hand and those of social equality on the other. The
contextual approach is intended to take into account both the particular form of expression being restricted (hate propaganda) and the par-

ticular harms (to target minorities) which the restriction is intended to prevent. The basic idea is that different forms of expression might differentially engage the free expression values, thus that some restrictions on expression might have higher costs than others, and that different objectives for the limiting legislation might not be equally important, thus that some restrictions might deliver greater benefits than others. As a result, according to McLachlin, 'it cannot be said that freedom of expression will always prevail over the objective of individual dignity and social harmony, or vice versa. The result in a particular case will depend on weighing the significance of the infringement on freedom of expression represented by the law in question, against the importance of the countervailing objectives, the likelihood the law will achieve those objectives, and the proportionality of the scope of the law to those objectives.'[45]

This demand that competing values or interests be balanced in context became a standard theme in the court's free expression cases during the 1990s. On the one hand it supported the developing consensus that different forms of expression might merit different levels of protection, depending on how closely they were situated to the 'core' values of free expression (a theme to which we will return in the next section). But it also underscored the importance, in section 1 balancing, of identifying the conflicting values or interests as concretely and realistically as possible, thus of weighing the expected benefits of legislation limiting expression against its actual costs. Since this function was allocated to the proportional effects requirement in the *Oakes* tests, the court's mantra of contextuality had the effect of accentuating the importance of this final calculus.

Their undoubted authority notwithstanding, the *Oakes* tests are formulated in a needlessly awkward and confusing manner. None the less, it has become clear that the tests collectively, and the proportional effects requirement individually, require a contextual, case-by-case balancing of the costs and benefits of any legislative measure found to infringe section 2(b) of the Charter. I have already noted the striking similarity between this procedure and a consequentialist justification of rights (and of their limitation). Equally striking, though perhaps now unsurprising, is the resemblance to the factors highlighted by J.S. Mill's harm-based approach to justifying restrictions on liberty.[46] According to Mill's Harm Principle the sole justification for interfering with individual freedom – including freedom of expression – is to prevent harm to others. It follows that any legislative measure imposing a content restriction on expression must pass a *harm test*: the government must be able to show that the particular kind of expression in question (hate propaganda, for instance) poses a significant risk of harm to third parties. The risk must be significant, as opposed to merely slight or trivial, in order to compete with the very substantial value of free expression. This threshold requirement corresponds to the first *Oakes* test, which stipulates that the content restriction must be in service of a pressing and substantial objective. Absent such an objective (which is to say, absent evidence of the harm to be prevented), the restriction cannot be justified.

In the more difficult cases (including hate propaganda) the restrictive legislation will pass the harm test. It does not follow, however, that it is therefore justified by Mill's argumentative framework. The Harm Principle makes harm to others a necessary condition for limiting liberty, but not a sufficient one. The further condition which the expression-limiting measure must satisfy is a consequentialist one: it must yield an acceptable balance of benefits over costs. This requirement, of course, has its counterpart in the second *Oakes* test of proportionality, with its components of rational connection, minimal impairment, and overall positive cost-benefit balance. As far as I am aware, Mill has never been acknowledged by the Supreme Court as the godfather of the *Oakes* tests. But he should have been, since the tests are a good approximation of the justificatory procedure, for any liberty-limiting measure, mandated by Mill's argumentative framework.

I have made much of the fact that the court's methodology for determining when an infringement of the right of free expression can be justified, and therefore its methodology for resolving conflicts between this right and competing rights (or social values), seems to be essentially consequentialist.[47] This result may seem surprising. After all, at least on the surface the Charter of Rights and Freedoms does not have the look of a consequentialist document. How then does it happen that in Charter adjudication judges come to behave as consequentialists (or quasi-consequentialists)? A full answer to this question would take us much too far afield, but it is easy to see in very rough outline how it might go. The political function of the Charter is to confer a special degree of legal protection on a set of selected social values by entrenching them as constitutionally guaranteed rights. Which values are to be protected in this way is itself a policy question, the best mix presumably being that which best safeguards the flourishing of a liberal democratic society. Whatever the favoured values may be, however, they will inevitably be capable of conflicting with one another. These conflicts will require interpretation of the abstract and perfunctory formulae enshrined in the Charter, interpretation which will perforce be carried out not by politicians but by judges. When judges are confronted by legislation which protects one constitutionally recognized value but trenches on another one, and when they have no unambiguous precedent to guide them, there seems no way for them to proceed except by seeking a reasonable balance between the conflicting values.

There is in this an important lesson about the nature and role of rights.[48] Legal rights are best regarded as instruments whose function is to safeguard important individual and social values. They are morally justified when they perform this function well – that is, when they strike an optimal, or at least an acceptable, balance among the values in question. It follows from this that rights cannot be the ultimate premises of moral/political argument; rather, they follow as conclusions from premises specifying the values which they are to protect, plus some understanding of how these values are to be weighed against one another. What may on the surface appear to be appeals to abstract right, therefore, are to be understood on a deeper level as consequentialist arguments concerning matters of public policy. In this respect constitutional adjudication conforms to the general pattern of moral/political argument, in which the good is prior to, and foundational for, the right.

What may be disquieting in all this is not that conflicting values need to be commensurated, nor that the optimal balance is the maximizing option, but that it is judges who are carrying out this entire exercise. Unlike politicians they are not answerable to the electorate, and unlike special committees or commissions they have little opportunity to collect empirical data. How can they be expected to reach informed judgments on large questions of social policy, such as the trade-off between freedom of expression and social equality, and how can they be held responsible for the judgments they do reach? The balancing mandated by section 1 of the Charter inevitably involves judges in the making, or remaking, of broad social policy. It therefore raises awkward and troubling questions about the relationship between the judiciary and the legislature in a functioning democracy. We turn to these questions in the next section, after a brief detour south of the border.

3.3 Land of the Free

In the United States any attempt to limit or regulate hate speech quickly runs up against the language of the First Amendment to the Bill of

Rights: 'Congress shall make no law ... abridging the freedom of speech.' In response to this seemingly absolutist injunction the U.S. Supreme Court has evolved a doctrine which distinguishes categories of speech receiving different degrees of First Amendment protection, some (such as political speech) enjoying the most stringent protection, others (such as commercial speech) only a lesser degree, and still others (such as defamation) none at all.[49] Where political speech is concerned, the court has permitted restrictions of 'time, manner, or circumstance' if they have some purpose (such as protecting the public against a nuisance) other than suppressing the circulation of the ideas being expressed, but no restrictions of content. Since the court counts hate speech as political speech, no prohibition of it similar to the Canadian hate propaganda law would withstand constitutional scrutiny in the United States.

In its 1992 *R.A.V.* decision, the court extended its prohibition of content discrimination to 'fighting words', defined as 'those which by their very utterance inflict injury or tend to incite an immediate breach of the peace'.[50] It was previously established doctrine that fighting words merited a lesser degree of First Amendment protection than political speech, because of their potential for provoking an immediate reaction in the target audience.[51] It appeared therefore that the state might enjoy somewhat more leeway to impose content restrictions on fighting words – for instance, to ban certain insults or epithets standardly directed at members of racial minorities. The *R.A.V.* case involved a group of white teenagers who burned a cross in the pre-dawn hours inside the fenced yard of a black family. One of the teenagers, Robert Viktora (who was a juvenile at the time of his arrest), was charged under the St Paul Bias-Motivated Crime Ordinance, which prohibited the display of any symbol 'which one knows or has reasonable grounds to know arouses anger, alarm or resentment in others on the basis of race, color, creed, religion or gender'.[52] Despite accepting the judgment of the Minnesota State Supreme Court that the ordinance applied only to fighting words, the Supreme Court none the less struck it down, primarily because it violated 'viewpoint neutrality' by prohibiting abusive speech directed against certain target groups (the ones enumerated in the ordinance) while permitting it if directed against other groups. By failing to observe viewpoint neutrality, the court concluded, the ordinance was a form of content restriction. In the wake of this decision, it now appears difficult for any content regulation of hate speech to survive scrutiny – even if narrowly drawn so as to target only fighting words

– unless it is drawn up in the most evenhanded manner.[53] Any attempt to offer special protection to minorities perceived to be particularly vulnerable because of past oppression or discrimination will be found inconsistent with the First Amendment.

As a result of the different constitutional climates in the two countries, Canada has a law targeting hate speech for which there could be no American counterpart. It therefore seems appropriate to conclude that, despite their many cultural and political similarities, the two countries have come to different resolutions of the conflict between liberal freedom and liberal equality: while Americans have tended to lean farther in the direction of the former, Canadians have been more zealous in the protection of the latter. How is this disparity to be explained? One possibility, which has been advanced by several commentators, is that the history of hate speech adjudication in the two countries reflects much broader differences in their political cultures.[54] Canadians, it is said, tend to be more communitarian in political outlook than Americans, and also more deeply committed to the values of equality and multiculturalism. The greater tolerance of hate speech in the United States must therefore be understood against this backdrop of American individualism and libertarianism, on the one hand, and Canadian collectivism and egalitarianism, on the other.

There is much evidence that can be mustered in favour of this contrast between the political climates in the two countries, including the historical role of social democratic parties in the Canadian political system, the fierce loyalty Canadians feel toward their publicly funded health care system, and the explicit recognition in the Charter of equality rights, group language rights, and multiculturalism.[55] These differences of political culture must be at least part of the explanation for the marked divergence between Canada and the United States where the legal regulation of hate propaganda is concerned. But it is worth exploring whether this is all that needs to be said, or whether a role has also been played by the different structures of free speech adjudication in the two countries.

Because the American Bill of Rights lacks a limitation clause similar to section 1 of the Canadian Charter, it makes no explicit room for the idea of a justifiable infringement of free speech rights. As we have seen, the Canadian courts enjoy the luxury of readily conceding the infringement and then raising separately the question of its justifiability. The quite different structure of American constitutional adjudication collapses these two stages of argument; if the law is found to infringe the

First Amendment there is then no way in which it might be saved. Everything therefore rests on interpreting the scope of the First Amendment protection of speech. It is in the service of this interpretative exercise that the American courts have developed the complex doctrine of categories of speech with varying degrees of First Amendment protection and (therefore) different burdens of justification on legislative restrictions. In this doctrine the decisive issue is the extent to which the form of expression in question falls under full First Amendment protection; if it does, then it is subjected to 'strict scrutiny', a burden of justification which is virtually impossible for the legislature to meet. Lesser degrees of protection, and more relaxed standards of scrutiny, are applicable to other forms of expression. Political speech (which includes hate speech) belongs to the first category, which is why virtually no content regulation is permissible for it. As we have seen, in principle at least, regulation of fighting words should be easier for a legislature to justify, but in the wake of the *R.A.V.* decision content neutrality is enforced even in this case. Why more stringent protection and stricter scrutiny for some forms of expression than for others? The reasoning of the U.S. Supreme Court seems to be that the more vital the form of speech to the operation of a functioning democracy the more vigorously it will be safeguarded; political speech therefore receives greater protection than, say, commercial speech. In assigning this priority to basic democratic rights the court seems to be embracing a different approach to justifying rights than the instrumentalism of its Canadian counterpart.

We have seen how rights can be justified as means to independently valuable ends. But they can also be thought to have a different kind of value, one which belongs to them as parts of a valuable whole. Let us call this kind of value constitutive, rather than instrumental. If we focus again on free speech rights, the larger whole of which they are an indispensable component is usually taken to be democracy itself.[56] On this view a well-ordered democracy is not a further end to which various rights, including freedom of expression, contribute as means. Rather, it is a political system which consists essentially in those rights: a system lacking them simply does not count as democratic. While freedom of expression is usually considered to lie at the core of the very concept of a democracy, it is not the only right implicated in that concept. Other rights matter too, possibly just as much; they include further freedoms (religion, association, peaceful assembly) as well as rights of participation in the political process. The justification of these rights is provided by their constituting a particularly valuable kind of political order. If we ask in turn what is so good about democracy then this further question may be answered by appeal to such values as justice (democratic procedures are uniquely fair means of arbitrating among competing views or interests) or the dignity or autonomy of citizens. But again the answer is constitutive rather than instrumental: democracy embodies basic principles of justice or respects dignity and autonomy. There is no further independent end to which it is a means.

So far we have found two points of difference between the Canadian and American judicial scene: Canadian courts limit expressive rights by excluding hate propaganda from their protection, American courts do not; Canadian courts take an instrumentalist view about rights and their limitation, American courts do not. It is tempting to connect these distinctions by using the latter to explain the former. Doing so yields our first hypothesis: instrumentalism supports the limitation of free expression, at least where hate speech is concerned. On this hypothesis Canadian courts permit the legal regulation of hate propaganda because the structure of the Charter compels them to be instrumentalists about rights.

There may be some truth worth preserving from this hypothesis, but it clearly will not work as it stands. For one thing, it ignores the fact that the hate propaganda law was upheld in *Keegstra* by the narrowest of majorities (4–3). More important, the dissenting minority in *Keegstra* was working with the same instrumentalist, quasi-consequentialist methodology as the majority. Both sides engaged in the same balancing exercise – they just emerged from it with different outcomes. Finally, the hypothesis also ignores the fact that in the *Zundel* case just two years later the court struck down a different section of the Criminal Code used to regulate hate speech, again by a 4-to-3 majority.[57] In *Zundel* the majority subjected the law in question to the same section 1 analysis employed in *Keegstra* but reached the conclusion that its objective was archaic and obscure and that it was not constructed so as to minimally impair the Charter right to free expression. Once again the minority disagreed, but this time the final verdict went the other way.[58] Instrumentalist reasoning about free speech rights, it seems, does not inevitably favour their limitation.

There also seems no compelling reason for thinking that constitutive reasoning about free speech rights must resist their limitation. We have seen how these rights can be defended as essential ingredients in a functioning democracy, rather than as means to an end. But equality rights easily lend themselves to the same defence. The traditional civil liberties (speech, association, assembly) certainly lie at the heart of the idea of liberal democracy, but so does the effective exercise of these liberties by citizens without discrimination on grounds such as race, ethnicity, religion, gender, and sexual orientation. Where the adjudication of hate speech is concerned, the constitutive approach requires the U.S. Supreme Court to determine whether free speech rights are more or less central to the best conception of democracy than equality rights. But how is this to be decided? If hate speech threatens the equal participation in the political process of its target groups, by silencing or intimidating them, then this exercise by hate groups of a democratic freedom can itself be seen as a threat to democratic freedom. Once democracy is recognized as a complex of values, the possibility of internal conflict among these values must be acknowledged. It is arguable that the best rationale for limiting the speech of hate groups is to protect and promote the speech of their target minorities.[59] If this line of argument is embraced then the constitutive approach might equally lead in precisely the opposite direction to that pursued by the court – that is, toward the justification of (selective) content restrictions and the consequent abandonment of the requirement of viewpoint neutrality.

The explanatory hypothesis under consideration therefore fails to connect both instrumentalism with the restriction of hate speech and constitutivism with its protection. However, its failure also points us toward a different hypothesis with a better chance for success. If constitutive arguments starting from the best conception of democracy are capable of supporting either the protection of hate speech or its restriction, it is unclear how this issue could be resolved one way or the other without looking behind the rights in question at the values which they protect – that is, without falling back on an instrumentalist (or even consequentialist) approach which aims to find the optimal balance between conflicting values. Indeed, it has been argued that even the U.S. Supreme Court, despite the absence from the Bill of Rights of an explicit limitation clause, has engaged in 'definitional balancing' in devising its various categories of speech with their different levels of constitutional protection.[60] The hypothesis is that the court has indeed weighed opposing interests in order to develop substantive principles (no content restrictions, viewpoint neutrality, etc.) which it can then apply in subsequent cases without reopening the balancing exercise. If this hypothesis is correct then it affords another way of understanding the difference between the Canadian and American approaches to the adjudication of rights. As we have seen, the *Oakes* tests engage the Canadian court in a balancing of conflicting interests whenever a legislative measure is found to infringe section 2(b) of the Charter. If a similar procedure is used by the American court to establish general principles, which are then applied in particular cases with no further balancing, we have a contrast between deliberative procedures reminiscent of the distinction between direct and indirect procedures for consequentialism.[61]

Any consequentialist theory provides a goal to be pursued, such as maximizing the balance of benefits over costs. It does not, however, stipulate any particular deliberative procedure for pursuing this goal. Abstractly, two options are available. A procedure is direct if it tells agents on each particular occasion to find the course of action which will best promote the theory's goal. It is indirect if it takes any other form, such as applying some antecedently determined rules or principles. Many consequentialists have argued that, for various contingent reasons, agents who seek to achieve their maximizing goal by indirect means are likely to be more successful over the long run than those who aim at it directly on a case-by-case basis. If so, then consequentialists have a good reason – the best sort of reason, given their own theory – for preferring an indirect procedure to a direct one.

Suppose, then, that both the Canadian and the American Supreme Courts approach the adjudication of free speech issues with the (implicit or explicit) goal of seeking an optimal balance among the competing (liberty and equality) interests at stake. In a particular case, the Canadian court must employ a two-stage deliberative procedure: first determine whether the law in question infringes the right of free expression and then determine whether the infringement is justifiable. It is at the second stage that the court, by engaging in balancing, must employ a direct consequentialist methodology; it must, that is, decide whether or not this particular restriction represents an optimal, or at least a satisfactory, balance of benefits over costs. There is no analogue to this direct balancing in the American case, where the first stage of the procedure is decisive. If a law is found to impose a content restriction on political speech then it is subject to a level of scrutiny which it is virtually impossible for it to survive – there is no further opportunity for balancing the law's expected benefits against the costs of its restrictions on speech. Whereas the Canadian court can readily concede an infringement of the constitutionally protected free speech right, because the infringement does not automatically condemn the law in question, the American court must be much more cautious at this stage. The elaborate network of principles which the U.S. Supreme Court evolved over the course of the twentieth century – the 'clear and present danger' test, the distinction between restrictions of content and restrictions of time, manner, or circumstance, the various categories of speech with their different levels of scrutiny, the requirement of viewpoint neutrality – have all been aimed at deciding the question of infringement. The development of these principles may indeed have embodied an implicit (or even explicit) balancing of (liberty and equality) interests. However, once the principles have been adopted, they are applied in subsequent cases without any further balancing. Thus in the opinion of the court majority in *R.A.V.* it is enough to show that the St Paul ordinance violated the principle of viewpoint neutrality; there is no occasion for pondering whether in this instance the additional protection the ordinance provided for vulnerable minorities might justify the violation. While the principle might have been justified in the first place in terms of a consequentialist goal, it is thereafter applied with no explicit reference to that goal.[62] Unlike the Canadian courts, which are permitted, indeed required, to invoke a consequentialist goal on each adjudicative occasion, the American pursuit of a similar goal is constrained by antecedently adopted principles.

So we now have a further distinction between the Canadian and American courts: when called upon to adjudicate conflicts between expressive rights and competing values, the former behave as direct consequentialists, the latter indirect. This enables us to formulate a second explanatory hypothesis: the direct procedure favours regulation of hate propaganda while the indirect procedure favours its protection. Does this hypothesis have a better chance of success than the first one? It is still, of course, embarrassed by the fact that in *Keegstra* and *Zundel* both the majority and the minority on the Canadian court used the same direct procedure to reach contrary conclusions. So direct optimization does not lead unambiguously to the limitation of free speech. However, it might still be the case that it has a pronounced tendency in that direction.

Both free speech interests and equality interests are varied and complex. The task of finding an optimal, or even a reasonable, balance among them requires the acquisition and processing of a great deal of empirical evidence concerning the harms both of hate speech itself and of its restriction. Courts are not ideally positioned to carry out this process. In applying the *Oakes* tests the Canadian court must determine the benefits which a restriction on hate speech will actually afford minorities in protecting them against the harms done by hate speech, the costs which it will impose on speakers, hearers, and bystanders, and, finally, whether the benefits outweigh the costs. In the face of this daunting task, the court has displayed a clear tendency to defer to the judgment of the legislature. This deference has manifested itself in three ways: a lenient attitude toward evidence, a relatively low standard of proof, and different levels of protection for different categories of expression.

When the government enacts legislation limiting the Charter right of free expression it assumes the responsibility of showing that the limitation is 'demonstrably justified in a free and democratic society'. Discharging this responsibility will require providing evidence relevant to the application of the *Oakes* tests, especially concerning the harm done by the form of expression to be restricted, the efficacy of the restriction in preventing or mitigating that harm, and the minimal damage done by it to the underlying interests protected by free expression. In *Keegstra* the evidence on which the court relied in order to establish the harms of hate speech was drawn primarily from the 1966 House of Commons committee report which led to the adoption of the hate propaganda law in the first place,[63] supplemented by reports by other governmental and quasi-governmental bodies.[64] The court imposed virtually no burden on the government to provide convincing empirical evidence concerning either the necessity of regulating hate speech or the minimal impact on free speech of doing so.[65] This relaxed attitude toward supporting evidence was even more apparent in the court's 1992 *Butler* decision, which upheld the obscenity statute despite conceding that the social science evidence concerning the causal relationship between pornography and risk of harm to society was 'subject to controversy' and 'inconclusive'.[66] These two cases can be contrasted with a third in which the court adopted a somewhat more demanding stance concerning evidence. In *RJR-MacDonald* (1995) the measure under section 1 scrutiny was the Tobacco Products Control Act, which broadly prohibited all advertising and promotion of tobacco products and the sale of such products without prescribed unattributed health warnings and a list of toxic ingredients. The majority of the court concluded that the act failed the minimal impairment requirement because the government had not shown that a partial ban on advertising and promotion would be less effective in achieving the objective of the legislation than a total ban. The problem with the government's case was not (merely) that the evidence on this issue was inconclusive, but that no evidence whatever had been adduced in support of the act's very broad scope. In Justice Iacobucci's words, 'When, as in the case at bar, the evidence is unclear whether a partial prohibition is as effective as a full prohibition, the *Charter* requires that the legislature enact the partial denial of the implicated *Charter* right. In the absence of the discharge of this evidentiary burden (which is to be wholly borne by the government), the least rights-impairing option is to be preferred.'[67]

With the noteworthy exception of *RJR-MacDonald*, the evidentiary burden which the court has imposed on the legislature has been pretty light. Besides the question of the kind and amount of evidence which the government should be expected to provide in defence of a right-infringing measure, there is also the closely related question of the standard of proof which it should be expected to meet. In *RJR-MacDonald* Justice McLachlin offered some tough talk on this issue as well: 'to meet its burden under s. 1 of the *Charter*, the state must show that the violative law is "demonstrably justified". The choice of the word "demonstrably" is critical. The process is not one of mere intuition, nor is it one of deference to Parliament's choice. It is a process of *demonstration*. This reinforces the notion inherent in the word "reasonable" of rational inference from evidence or established truths.'[68] We are therefore led to expect a high standard of proof to be imposed on the legislature.[69]

McLachlin considers three possible standards: scientific (demonstration satisfying the standards of social science), criminal (proof beyond reasonable doubt), and civil (proof on a balance of probabilities). In line with the court's earlier decisions,[70] she rejects the first two as imposing too heavy a burden of justification on the legislature and opts instead for the third.[71] The civil standard still looks pretty demanding and (one would think) impossible to meet without adducing good (though not necessarily conclusive) empirical evidence.[72] However, this appearance is deceptive. McLachlin first tells us that 'the balance of probabilities may be established by the application of common sense to what is known, even though what is known may be deficient from a scientific point of view'.[73] Then later, in her treatment of the rational connection requirement, she says that 'this Court has been prepared to find a causal connection between the infringement and the benefit sought on the basis of reason or logic, without insisting on direct proof'.[74]

McLachlin's citations of *Keegstra* and *Butler* in support of this last claim are revealing. In *Butler* Justice Sopinka, after conceding that the social-scientific evidence was 'subject to controversy', sidestepped the evidential issue by saying that 'while a direct link between obscenity and harm to society may be difficult, if not impossible, to establish, it is reasonable to presume that exposure to images bears a causal relationship

to changes in attitudes and beliefs'.[75] He also reached back to *Irwin Toy*
for the standard that 'in choosing its mode of intervention, it is sufficient that Parliament had a *reasonable basis*'.[76] Through the 1990s the
court coalesced around the consensus that the civil standard (balance
of probabilities) is the appropriate standard of proof to be imposed on
the legislature, that this is equivalent to demanding that the legislature
have a reasonable basis for its right-infringing measure, and that, in
determining whether its basis was reasonable, recourse may be had to
'common sense', 'experience', or 'logic', as well as to whatever social
science evidence may be available.[77] What this consensus amounts to is
that the legislature will be given the benefit of the doubt as long as it
can muster some evidence in favour of the measure, however inconclusive it might be, and as long as its case does not fly in the face of conclusive contrary evidence. In short, its basis for the measure is reasonable if
it is not either completely unsupported or contradicted by the evidence.

This relatively lenient standard of proof is further relaxed by the
court's concession that different kinds of expression merit different levels of constitutional protection. In *Keegstra* Chief Justice Dickson argued
that hate propaganda is 'of a special category [of expression], a category only tenuously connected with the values underlying the guarantee
of freedom of speech'.[78] He concluded that restrictions on it are 'easier
to justify than other infringements of s. 2(b)'.[79] Dickson's direction of
analysis here was undeniably influenced by the categories of expres-
sion/levels of scrutiny approach taken by the American courts in adjudicating First Amendment cases. Dickson took care to distance himself
from (what he saw as) 'an inflexible "levels of scrutiny" categorization of
expressive activity',[80] but it appears to have been the inflexibility of the
American doctrine which he found problematic, since it was inconsistent with the contextual, case-by-case approach which he favoured.[81]
None the less, he was comfortable speaking of the 'discounted value' of
hate propaganda and urging that 'it should not be accorded the greatest of weight in the s. 1 analysis'.[82]

Dickson therefore seemed to commit the court to different standards
of justification for different right-infringing measures, and different
levels of protection for different categories of expression, depending
on the extent to which the expression in question engages the values
underlying section 2(b). In subsequent cases the court has struggled
somewhat with this idea of a variable standard. In *Butler* Justice Sopinka
concluded that pornography also 'lies far from the core of the guarantee of freedom of expression',[83] but refrained from explicitly acknowl-

edging or endorsing the general levels-of-protection approach. However, a few years later Justice La Forest, writing for the court, could
claim confidently that 'this Court has consistently held that the level of
constitutional protection to which expression will be entitled varies with
the nature of the expression. More specifically, the protection afforded
freedom of expression is related to the relationship between the expression and the fundamental values this Court has identified as being the
"core" values underlying s. 2(b) ... This Court has subjected state action
that jeopardizes these "core" values to a "searching degree of scrutiny."
Where, on the other hand, the expression in question lies far from the
"centre core of the spirit" of s. 2(b), state action restricting such expression is less difficult to justify.'[84]

In this rendering of it, the levels-of-protection approach is virtually
indistinguishable from the doctrine of the American courts. Its effect has
been to impose an even lower standard of justification on the legislature
in cases concerning the restriction of 'peripheral' forms of expression,
including commercial advertising, hate propaganda, pornography, communication for the purpose of prostitution, defamation, and child pornography. However, it has not evolved without significant opposition. As
far back as *Keegstra*, Justice McLachlin objected to the idea of discounting the value of a form of expression in advance of conducting the section 1 analysis: 'The argument, moreover, is essentially circular. If one
starts from the premise that the speech covered by [the hate propaganda
statute] is dangerous and without value, then it is simple to conclude
that none of the commonly-offered justifications for protecting freedom
of expression are served by it.'[85] Her critique became a little more
focused five years later in *RJR-MacDonald*, where she argued (against Justice La Forest) that to discount the value of a form of expression (in this
case tobacco advertising) from the outset of the section 1 analysis was to
pre-empt the balancing involved in the third (proportional effects) stage
of the proportionality test.[86] She was joined on this point by Justice
Iacobucci, who expressed concern about the attenuated standard of justification which 'creates a risk that *Charter* violations will be too readily
justified and, as a result, *Charter* values too easily undercut'.[87]

McLachlin's critique achieved its mature form in her dissent three
years later in *Lucas*. There she complained once again about discounting the value of a form of expression in advance of applying the *Oakes*
tests: 'This risks reducing the s. 1 analysis to a function of what a particular judge thinks of the expression, thus shortcutting the cost-benefit
analysis proposed by *Oakes*. Instead of insisting that the limitation on the

right be justified by a pressing concern and that it be rationally connected to the objective and appropriately restrained, the judge may
instead reason that any defects on these points are resolved in favour of
the justification by the low value of the expression. The initial conclusion that the expression is of low value may thus dictate the conclusion
on the subsequent steps of the analysis in a circular fashion.'[88] McLachlin went on to argue that the value of the expression in question is irrelevant at every stage of the *Oakes* tests before the last: 'Legislative limits
on expression that falls far from the core values underlying s. 2(b) are
easier to justify, not because the standard of justification is lowered, but
rather because the beneficial effects of the limitation more easily outweigh any negative effects flowing from the limitation.'[89] In terms of her
own conception of the proportionality test as a cost-benefit analysis,
McLachlin's point could be stated as follows: the rational connection
requirement looks to the expected benefits of the legislation (the extent
to which it will achieve its objective), while minimal impairment ensures
that its costs to expressive freedom are as low as is compatible with real-
izing comparable benefits. Only at the proportional effects stage are the
costs of restricting the expression weighed explicitly against the expected benefits. If a particular form of expression is of low value – as
measured by the extent to which it engages the values of expressive freedom – then the costs of restricting it will necessarily be lower. But in that
case, the benefits of the restriction will more easily outweigh its costs.
The result will be that, *ceteris paribus*, restrictions on 'low value' expression will be easier to justify, but this will fall out as a result of the cost-
benefit analysis, instead of being imposed on it from the outset.

In terms of the logic of a cost-benefit analysis, McLachlin is surely correct: if the costs of a particular restriction are lower then the restriction
will be easier to justify. Furthermore, her analysis has the virtue of
underscoring the essential function of the proportional effects test, thus
rescuing it from the accusation of redundancy. She also puts the best
gloss on the court's mantra of contextuality. Whereas others have used it
to defend a flexible (i.e., variable) standard of justification,[90] her point
is that sensitivity to context, and to the differences between different
forms of expression, is required by the very nature of a cost-benefit analysis. The costs and benefits to be weighed and compared must be those
of *this particular* legislation restricting *this particular* form of expression.
If proper attention is paid to context, then no thumb is needed on the
scales of the cost-benefit balancing; the procedure itself will ensure that
all relevant variables are taken into account.

It appears, therefore, that the court's flirtation with the American categories of expression/levels of scrutiny approach has simply been a mistake born out of an insufficient appreciation of the advantages afforded by the opportunity of section 1 balancing. None the less, when combined with a minimal evidentiary requirement and an already low standard of proof, it has served to reinforce the court's tendency of deference to the legislature in its major freedom of expression cases. The results of this deferential posture are on the record. In ten cases since 1990 in which the court has ruled on challenges to legislation imposing limits on expressive freedom, it upheld the challenge in only three. In *Zundel* (1992) the 'spreading false news' section of the Criminal Code was found both to lack a pressing and substantial objective (or indeed any intelligible purpose) and to fail minimal impairment by virtue of overbreadth. In *RJR-MacDonald* (1995) the court ruled that the Tobacco Products Control Act also failed minimal impairment, since the government had adduced no evidence to show that a partial ban on tobacco advertising would be less effective than a total one. Finally, in *Thomson Newspapers* (1998) the court struck down the section of the Canada Elections Act prohibiting the publication of opinion polls within three days of a federal election, again on grounds of overbreadth. Meanwhile, in the remaining seven cases the court upheld the hate propaganda statute (*Keegstra* (1990)), the section of the Canadian Human Rights Act governing telephone hate messages (*Taylor* (1990)), the obscenity statute (*Butler* (1992)), the statute authorizing judges to exclude the public from the courtroom during legal proceedings (*New Brunswick* (1996)), the defamatory libel statute (*Lucas* (1998)), the section of the Customs Tariff governing the interception of obscene materials (*Little Sisters* (2000)), and the section of the child pornography statute governing simple possession (*Sharpe* (2001)). The targets which the court chose to invalidate were relatively small fish: an obscure and anachronistic section of the Criminal Code, a well-meaning but undermotivated restriction on commercial advertising, and a very specific but also pointless restriction on what newspapers could publish in advance of elections. In all of the 'big ticket' cases (hate propaganda, obscenity, defamatory libel, child pornography) the court allowed the legislature to have its way, in each instance further shrinking the territory protected by section 2(b) of the Charter. The contrast with the American judicial scene is, of course, starkest where hate speech is concerned. Though the regulation of pornography has evolved along different paths in the two countries, they have come to converge on a similar legal regime in which more or less the same materials can be freely produced, distributed, and consumed on both sides of the border. Not so with hate speech, where hate groups in the United States enjoy a degree of expressive freedom only dreamt of by their Canadian counterparts.

Deference to Parliament has been both practice and theory for the Supreme Court. Besides its actual record on the ground, the court has attempted to develop a doctrine concerning the appropriate relationship between the judiciary and the legislature. In *Irwin Toy* it drew a distinction between those cases in which the legislature is attempting to mediate between the interests of competing social groups and those in which the government is the 'singular antagonist' of the individual whose right has been infringed.[91] Free expression cases will normally fall into the former category, since they involve balancing the interests of the parties whose expression is limited (toy manufacturers, hate groups, pornographers, etc.) against the interests of the parties being protected against the risk of harm (children, minority groups, women, etc.). By the latter category the court had in mind cases concerning the criminal justice system in which the legal rights enshrined in sections 7 to 14 of the Charter were at stake. The distinction itself is not particularly well drawn, since many instances in which the court must decide important matters of criminal procedure involve balancing the interests of competing groups (defendants vs victims, to take an obvious example).[92] But what is important is the court's view of its own role in those cases which feature conflicts of interest: 'When striking a balance between the claims of competing groups, the choice of means, like the choice of ends, frequently will require an assessment of conflicting scientific evidence and differing justified demands on scarce resources. Democratic institutions are meant to let us all share in the responsibility for these difficult choices. Thus, as courts review the results of the legislature's deliberations, particularly with respect to the protection of vulnerable groups, they must be mindful of the legislature's representative function.'[93] The court therefore embraced the doctrine that the legislature is owed a greater degree of deference in these cases.[94]

This doctrine of degrees of deference obviously owed a great deal to a background political theory according to which representative institutions must be accorded considerable latitude to decide matters of broad social policy in a democracy. While such a theory is highly plausible, and no doubt widely supported, it is also true that the deference the courts owe to the legislature is constrained by their constitutional role. As was pointed out by Justice McLachlin, care must be taken not to extend the notion of deference too far. Deference must not be carried to the point of relieving the government of the burden which the *Charter* places upon it of demonstrating that the limits it has imposed on guaranteed rights are reasonable and justifiable. Parliament has its role: to choose the appropriate response to social problems within the limiting framework of the Constitution. But the courts also have a role: to determine, objectively and impartially, whether Parliament's choice falls within the limiting framework of the Constitution. The courts are no more permitted to abdicate their responsibility than is Parliament. To carry judicial deference to the point of accepting Parliament's view simply on the basis that the problem is serious and the solution difficult, would be to diminish the role of the courts in the constitutional process and to weaken the structure of rights upon which our constitution and our nation is founded.[95]

McLachlin's strictures notwithstanding, the court has generally given the legislature the very generous benefit of the doubt when it was perceived as attempting to strike a reasonable balance between competing interests. The stances we reviewed earlier – concerning evidence, standard of proof, and levels of protection – have operationalized the deference which the court has regarded as the legislature's due in free expression cases. The key to understanding this deferential attitude lies in the role assigned to the court by section 1 of the Charter. Let us assume that when the legislature enacts a measure which limits expression, it does so on the basis of a cost-benefit analysis (implicit or explicit) in which the negative effects on the group whose expression will be restricted are balanced against the positive effects on the group whose interests will be thereby protected. Because the measure imposes a content restriction on expression, it infringes section 2(b) of the Charter. When its constitutionality is challenged, the Supreme Court must determine whether the restriction is justified under the terms of section 1. In making this determination, the court employs the *Oakes* tests, which require it to conduct a cost-benefit analysis in which the negative effects of the measure are balanced against the positive. The court therefore finds itself in the position of replicating the process carried out in the first instance by the legislature. In this situation it is likely to second-guess the legislative outcome only if it can locate some discernible defect in it, such as absence of supporting evidence or neglect of some alternative means of achieving the same objective at less cost to expressive freedom. Absent any such defects, the court's conclusion is likely to be that the legislature had a reasonable basis for adopting the measure (i.e., it was not unreasonable of it to do so) and that, in that situation, the will of the representative body deserves to be respected. In this way, the balancing function imposed on the courts by section 1 structures and supports the posture of judicial deference.[96]

By contrast, the U.S. Supreme Court is freed of the burdens of revisiting the balancing exercise when considering each subsequent legislative restriction on speech. Instead, once it has evolved a body of doctrine (which may itself be the result of consequentialist balancing) then the principles which comprise this doctrine (categories of speech, content neutrality, viewpoint neutrality, etc.) take on a life of their own and can be applied to particular cases without any further cost-benefit calculation.[97] In such cases there will be no complex empirical question for the court to decide on which it might be tempted to defer to the judgment of the legislature. By comparison with its Canadian counterpart, the U.S. Supreme Court has not lacked the nerve to invalidate restrictions on hate speech, even when (as in *R.A.V.*) these restrictions specifically target 'fighting words' and do so in a manner intended to provide special protection for historically vulnerable minorities.

There may, therefore, be something to the second hypothesis, which connects the direct cost-benefit balancing practised by the Canadian courts to the limitation of free speech rights through the intermediate link of judicial deference. I have, of course, only sketched the case for this hypothesis, whose confirmation would require much more extensive evidence and argumentation. My aim has been the modest one of exploring the ways in which the different structures of constitutional adjudication in Canada and the United States might have led the courts in these countries to opposite conclusions about the regulation of hate speech. There still remains the possibility that the crucial background factor lies in the differences between the Canadian and American political cultures, the former more collectivist and egalitarian, the latter more individualist and libertarian. Without rejecting that explanation, I have focused on the possible roles played by two other lines of division: (a) between instrumentalist and constitutive justifications of rights, and (b) between direct and indirect procedures for pursuing instrumentalist ends. Because of the presence of section 1 in the Charter and the absence of any counterpart in the Bill of Rights, the Canadian courts have tended to be overt and direct instrumentalists while the American courts have tended to embrace either a constitutive justification for rights or a covert and indirect instrumentalism. Whatever the explanation, the American courts have stood firmer in the face of legislative restrictions on hate speech than have their Canadian counterparts. Whether or not this has been a good thing remains, of course, to be determined.

3.4 Conclusion

The phenomenon of hate propaganda confronts liberals with a conflict between rights to liberty and to equality, both of which they hold dear. Adjudicating the conflict requires some procedure for balancing the rights, which procedure is given to the Canadian courts by the doctrine of 'reasonable limits' in section 1 of the Charter of Rights and Freedoms and its articulation by the Supreme Court into the *Oakes* tests. Those tests in turn effectively operationalize the consequentialist criterion for justifying infringements of expressive freedom which is a central element in Mill's argumentative framework. In the *Keegstra* case both the majority and the minority on the Supreme Court engaged in essentially the same exercise of cost-benefit balancing, reaching diametrically opposed conclusions about the hate propaganda statute.

Canadian and American hate speech jurisprudence provide a contrast of both outcome (the extent to which hate speech can be legally regulated) and methodology (the extent to which limitations of rights are decided by an overt balancing of competing interests or values). It is at least tempting to correlate these two points of divergence, explaining the American tendency to protect hateful expression against legal interference by reference to the absence of an explicit limitation clause from the Bill of Rights. However, the deeper lesson may be not that American courts are less committed to consequentialist balancing than their Canadian counterparts but that they pursue their maximizing goal more indirectly, with a more robust commitment to intervening principles. The cost of the more direct procedure by the Canadian courts may be a higher degree of deference to legislative judgment.

Chapter 4

The Myth of Community Standards

Whoever would prohibit obscenity must first define it. In Canada the statutory definition of obscenity picks out publications 'a dominant characteristic of which is the undue exploitation of sex'.[1] Ever since the adoption of this definition by Parliament in 1959, the Canadian courts have struggled with the question of when a publication's 'exploitation' of sex should be considered 'undue'. The focus of this chapter is not on the conclusions they have reached on this question but on the way they reached them – in particular, on the role that has been played in Canadian obscenity adjudication by the community standards test. The rough idea behind this test is that a publication's exploitation of sex will be considered undue if it exceeds contemporary Canadian standards of tolerance. The test raises a number of important legal and philosophical questions whose exploration will be our main business. Before turning to them, however, we need a little historical background.

4.1 The Evolution of an Idea

Obscene materials have been subject to statutory (as opposed to common-law) regulation in Canada since the first enactment of the Criminal Code in 1892, section 179 of which made it an offence to offer for sale 'any obscene book, or other printed or written matter, or any picture, photograph, model or other object, tending to corrupt morals'. Aside from that reference to the corruption of morals, the 1892 statute refrained from offering a definition of obscenity, a lacuna in the law which endured until 1959. During that lengthy period the test of obscenity accepted in the Canadian courts was derived from the judgment of Chief Justice Cockburn in the 1868 *Hicklin* case in England.

That case concerned the distribution by one Henry Scott of a virulently anti-Catholic pamphlet entitled *The Confessional Unmasked: shewing the depravity of the Romish priesthood, the iniquity of the Confessional, and the questions put to females in confession.* The pamphlet consisted of extracts from the works of various Catholic theologians concerning the practice of confession, framed by notes and comments purporting to expose the immorality and blasphemousness of these authors.[2] While about half the pamphlet was considered by Lord Cockburn to relate to 'casuistical and controversial questions which are not obscene', the remainder was found to be 'obscene in fact as relating to impure and filthy acts, words, and ideas'.[3] In reaching this finding, the Chief Justice stated his 'test of obscenity' in the following terms: 'whether the tendency of the matter charged as obscenity is to deprave and corrupt those whose minds are open to such immoral influences, and into whose hands a publication of this sort may fall'.[4] The court found that the appellant had sold the pamphlet at cost to anyone who requested it, as part of his campaign to discredit the Roman Catholic church. As a result, Lord Cockburn observed, the pamphlet 'falls into the hands of persons of all classes, young and old, and the minds of those hitherto pure are exposed to the danger of contamination and pollution from the impurity it contains'.[5]

As long as the *Hicklin* test remained in force in Canada, the danger posed by obscenity was assumed by the courts to be the corruption of public morals, operating through the 'contamination and pollution' of the minds of those deemed particularly vulnerable to such influences – primarily women, minors, and members of the lower classes.[6] By the late 1950s, however, the test was beginning to unravel as it came to be subjected to increasingly intense criticism.[7] The movement which would eventually lead to its abandonment began in 1959 when the Criminal Code was amended so as to introduce the 'undue exploitation' definition, which remains unchanged today. It is clear from statements made in Parliament by the then Minister of Justice, E. Davie Fulton, that he intended the new definition to supplement, rather than replace, the *Hicklin* test in the adjudication of obscenity cases. Fulton's main target was the tide of cheap mass-produced pocket books and magazines which had begun to flood Canadian newsstands in the 1950s and which had not been prosecuted as vigorously as he thought appropriate. Rightly or wrongly, he suspected that the reluctance of the police and the courts to take action against these materials had much to do with the uncertainty and subjectivity inherent in the *Hicklin* test. Fulton therefore intended his statutory definition to be applied specifically to pulp fiction and magazines, while the courts would continue to use the common-law *Hicklin* test for 'serious' literature and art.[8] He clearly believed that the new definition was sufficiently clear and objective for the courts to apply it without difficulty, and that it would easily capture the kinds of materials he was aiming to bring under control without threatening more high-minded forms of literature. Subsequent history was to prove him overoptimistic on both counts.

In *Brodie* (1962), the first obscenity case to reach the Supreme Court of Canada, the nine justices divided on the issue of the status of the new statutory definition, four taking the view that it excluded the *Hicklin* test, two arguing that it did not, and three expressing no opinion on the question. In the long run, the opinion expressed by Justice Judson was to prevail. He argued that if the legislature intended a double standard for obscenity then both tests should have been expressly set out in the Criminal Code. Since the Code includes only the 'undue exploitation' definition, it must be meant to be exclusive: 'Otherwise, why define obscenity for the purposes of the Act, if it is still permissible for the Court to take a definition of the crime formulated 100 years ago and one that has proved to be vague, difficult and unsatisfactory to apply?'[9] So much for the explicit intentions of the Minister of Justice only three years earlier. The *Brodie* case must have been all the more poignant for Fulton, since it involved precisely the kind of serious literature (*Lady Chatterley's Lover*) for which he regarded *Hicklin* as still the applicable test.[10]

But Justice Judson was also influenced by his belief that the statutory definition would be less 'vague, difficult and unsatisfactory to apply' than the test it was replacing: 'In contrast, I think that the new statutory definition does give the Court an opportunity to apply tests which have some certainty of meaning and are capable of objective application and which do not so much depend as before upon the idiosyncrasies and sensitivities of the tribunal of fact, whether judge or jury.'[11] In this respect at least, he agreed with Fulton. In attempting to determine whether the treatment of sex in Lawrence's novel constituted 'undue exploitation', Judson formulated two tests, each of which was to have a long shelf life in Canadian obscenity adjudication. One was that the erotic passages in the novel must be read in the light of the work as a whole, the author's purpose, and the novel's literary merits. Lawrence's frank treatment of sex could not be considered undue if it was required by the 'internal necessities of the novel itself':

What I think is aimed at [by the phrase 'undue exploitation'] is excessive emphasis on the theme for a base purpose. But I do not think that there is undue exploitation if there is no more emphasis on the theme than is required in the serious treatment of the theme of the novel with honesty and uprightness. That the work under attack is a serious work of fiction is to me beyond question. It has none of the characteristics that are often described in judgments dealing with obscenity – dirt for dirt's sake, the leer of the sensualist, depravity in the mind of an author with an obsession for dirt, pornography, an appeal to a prurient interest, etc.[12]

The other test articulated by Judson was a reference to 'standards of acceptance prevailing in the community'.[13] Here he adapted to his own purposes some remarks by Justice Fullagar in a 1948 Australian case.[14] In his analysis of the *Hicklin* test, which was also in force at that time in Australia and New Zealand, Fullagar divided it into two parts: in order to qualify as an obscene libel, for legal purposes, a publication must be obscene in the more common meaning of the term – that is, indecent or disgusting or offensive – and must also tend to deprave and corrupt. As far as the first of these requirements is concerned, he argued that the mere fact that a publication dealt frankly with sexual matters was not enough to establish that it was indecent: 'in considering whether any given matter is indecent or offensive or disgusting, it must often be of vital importance to consider the character of the artistic or literary or scientific context in which that matter is found.'[15] Fullagar then continued as follows, in a passage which was to have a lasting impact on the Canadian courts:

There does exist in any community at all times – however the standard may vary from time to time – a general instinctive sense of what is decent and what is indecent, of what is clean and what is dirty, and when the distinction has to be drawn, I do not know ... that today there is any better tribunal than a jury to draw it. But the decency or indecency, the cleanness or dirtiness, cannot depend on the nature of the subject-matter treated ... [but instead] on the general purport of the thing in question and the purpose which the thing itself discloses ... I am very far from attempting to lay down a model direction, but a Judge might perhaps, in the case of a novel, say something like this: 'It would not be true to say that any publication dealing with sexual relations is obscene. The relations of the sexes are, of course, legitimate matters for discussion everywhere. They *must* be dealt with in scientific works, and they *may* be legitimately dealt with – even frankly and directly – in literary works. But they can be dealt with cleanly, and they can be dealt with dirtily. There are certain standards of decency which prevail in the community, and you are really called upon to try this case because you are regarded as representing, and capable of justly applying, those standards. What is obscene is something which offends against those standards. Do you think that the publication now before you is one in which these matters are dealt with artistically and, with whatever frankness, cleanly? Or do you think that there are passages in it which are just plain dirt and nothing else, introduced for the sake of dirtiness and from the sure knowledge that notoriety earned by dirtiness will command for the book a ready sale?'[16]

What Justice Judson thought he had found in this passage was a possible alternative to leaving the trier of fact to determine 'undueness' by reference to personal and subjective standards of taste: 'Either the judge instructs himself or the jury that undueness is to be measured by his or their personal opinion – and even that must be subject to some influence from contemporary standards – or the instruction must be that the tribunal of fact should consciously attempt to apply these standards. Of the two, I think that the second is the better choice.'[17]

Because the *Brodie* court was divided on the question of whether the 'undue exploitation' definition of obscenity superseded the *Hicklin* test, the status of the latter remained in some doubt until 1977, when the Supreme Court finally declared it to be obsolete.[18] No similar ambiguity impeded the growing judicial reliance on the community standards test. The court returned to the question briefly two years later in *Dominion News* (1964), when it accepted *in toto* the dissenting opinion by Justice Freedman of the Manitoba Court of Appeal, including his explication of the concept of community standards:

Those standards are not set by those of lowest taste or interest. Nor are they set exclusively by those of rigid, austere, conservative, or puritan taste and habit of mind. Something approaching a general average of community thinking and feeling has to be discovered. Obviously this is no easy task, for we are seeking a quantity that is elusive. Yet the effort must be made if we are to have a fair objective standard in relation to which a publication can be tested as to whether it is obscene or not. The alternative would mean a subjective approach, with the result dependent upon and varying with the personal tastes and predilections of the particular Judge who happens to be trying the case.[19]

The Supreme Court's endorsement of Freedman's analysis determined two of the enduring features of the community standards test. First, the standards in question will inevitably vary over time:

> Community standards must be contemporary. Times change, and ideas change with them. Compared to the Victorian era this is a liberal age in which we live. One manifestation of it is the relative freedom with which the whole question of sex is discussed. In books, magazines, movies, television, and sometimes even in parlour conversation, various aspects of sex are made the subject of comment, with a candour that in an earlier day would have been regarded as indecent and intolerable.[20]

Second, the community in question is the country as a whole: 'Community standards ... must be Canadian. In applying the definition in the *Criminal Code* we must determine what is obscene by Canadian standards, regardless of attitudes which may prevail elsewhere, be they more liberal or less so.'[21]

On the other hand, Freedman's analysis was indeterminate on a further crucial feature of the test. If appeal is being made to contemporary Canadian standards to settle the question of 'undueness', and thus of obscenity, then we need to know what these standards are supposed to be *about*. Under the *Hicklin* test the answer to this question was clear: they are standards of decency or purity. For courts applying that test, a publication exceeded contemporary standards if its treatment of sex would be found by the average member of the community, or the majority, to be distasteful or disgusting. The appeal was therefore to some shared standard of (depending on how one sees it) taste or morality. Since he was operating with the *Hicklin* test, this is clearly what Justice Fullagar had in mind in referring to 'certain standards of decency which prevail in the community' and 'a general instinctive sense of what is decent and what is indecent, of what is clean and what is dirty'.[22] In appropriating this notion of a community standard as the measure of 'undueness' in *Brodie*, Judson did not take issue with it as a standard of decency, but neither did he unequivocally endorse it as such; instead he referred ambiguously to 'standards of acceptance prevailing in the community'.[23] Freedman's language, adopted by the Supreme Court two years later, strongly suggested the decency interpretation when he spoke of discounting those of overly high or low taste and attempting to find 'a general average of community thinking and feeling'.[24]

Within a very few years, however, courts were routinely referring to standards not of taste but of tolerance. Again it was Justice Freedman who was one of the first to navigate this transition. In speaking of a number of paperback novels and magazines 'heavily imbued with sex' he wrote in 1970:

> It is not for the Court to determine whether publications of this kind hurt anyone or do any demonstrable harm. Parliament has already made that determination. It has spoken on the matter by defining obscenity in terms of undue exploitation of sex and proscribing the possession, sale, distribution, etc., of all publications falling within that definition. All that remains is for the Court to decide whether, according to contemporary Canadian standards, the present publications are within the definition or without it. In my view what is offered in these magazines goes beyond what the Canadian community is prepared to tolerate even in the relatively liberal atmosphere of 1970.[25]

Writing a separate opinion in the same case, Justice Dickson was even more explicit:

> The Court was urged to define 'community standards' as community standards of acceptance, *i.e.*, tolerance. I would accept this definition ... I have no doubt ... a distinction can be made between private taste and standard of tolerance. It can hardly be questioned that many people would find personally offensive, material which they would permit others to read. Parliament, through its legislation on obscenity, could hardly have wished to proscribe as criminal that which was acceptable or tolerable according to current standards of the Canadian community.[26]

Reference to community standards of tolerance as the determinant of 'undueness' quickly became standard in obscenity cases through the 1970s.[27] This interpretation of the test was eventually canonized by the Supreme Court in its 1985 *Towne Cinema* decision. Following a review of the precedent cases, Chief Justice Dickson (as he became) wrote: 'The cases all emphasize that it is a standard of *tolerance*, not taste, that is relevant. What matters is not what Canadians think is right for themselves to see. What matters is what Canadians would not abide other Canadians seeing because it would be beyond the contemporary Canadian standard of tolerance to allow them to see it.'[28]

Three features of the community standards test were therefore effectively settled by the late 1980s: the relevant standards are contemporary, national, and pertaining to tolerance rather than taste. A resolution had also been reached concerning the evidential issues unavoidably raised by this interpretation of the test: What was to count as evidence of a national standard of tolerance? To what extent was such evidence necessary, or at least desirable, in helping the trier of fact (whether judge or jury) reach a determination of 'undue exploitation'? To what extent was it the burden of the crown to introduce evidence on this point in order to prove a charge of obscenity?

The answers to these questions were to prove immensely important in distinguishing the 'undue exploitation' definition of obscenity from the *Hicklin* test. Under the old test, evidence concerning the literary merit of a publication or its probable effect on its readers was invariably ruled inadmissible.[29] As soon as judicial attention shifted to the community standards test, this barrier to the admission of evidence began to crumble. Already in *Dominion News* Justice Freedman was willing to consider a magazine's readership as a relevant factor in determining whether it exceeded community standards of tolerance.[30] A much stronger case for the admissibility, indeed the necessity, of expert evidence on community standards was made four years later in a remarkably bold opinion by Justice Laskin of the Ontario Court of Appeal. The case concerned the conviction of Dorothy Cameron for exhibiting erotic drawings in her Toronto art gallery. Arguing that the relevant standard is to be sought among those who appreciate the art form in question, Laskin continued:

> A Judge or a Magistrate may be as limited as any jury in the geographical range of his exposure, and this may mean a limitation of opportunity of appreciation and understanding of art in terms of composition or style or purpose. Expert evidence to assist the Judge or Magistrate or Judge and jury is accordingly indispensable. I think that such evidence would always be necessary to support the case for the Crown as well as to support the defence, especially where, as here, pictures by artists of repute are seized from a reputable gallery. Holding this view, I cannot but be surprised that the Crown in the case at bar produced no expert evidence and relied on the pictures themselves to convey obscenity to the Magistrate.[31]

None of his colleagues on the Court of Appeal joined Justice Laskin in this opinion, however, and a less demanding rule was destined to carry the day. Reviewing the case history on this question in 1970, Justice Dickson concluded: 'the Courts have not found it necessary to call upon expert testimony to describe the standards of the community. Such evidence is, of course, admissible but that is not the same thing as saying it is essential.'[32] In a different case decided in the same year, he allowed himself somewhat stronger language: 'Expert testimony describing the standards of a community is not only admissible but desirable.'[33] Desirable, but still not essential to proving the crown's case. This view of the matter became standard throughout the 1970s and into the 1980s,[34] and was ultimately confirmed by Dickson himself, writing as Chief Justice for the majority in *Towne Cinema*:

> Evidence of the community's standard of tolerance may well be useful and indeed desirable in many cases. Nonetheless, I do not consider that there must be evidence, expert or otherwise, which the trier of fact accepts before a particular publication can be determined to violate the community standard. It is the opinion of the trier of fact on the community standard of tolerance with which we are concerned. It ought not to be stated as a matter of law that the trier of fact must have evidence, expert or otherwise, to be able to form an opinion on the community standard of tolerance.[35]

The main contours of the community standards test were therefore well established by the mid-1980s. However, this was but one of three tests for 'undueness', and therefore obscenity, which had achieved judicial recognition. The second was the 'internal necessities' test, also dating back to Justice Judson's opinion in *Brodie*, according to which a publication's treatment of sexual matters would not count as undue if the publication had literary or artistic merit and if the treatment did not exceed what was necessary to the development of its sexual themes. This test had rather disappeared from view in subsequent adjudication, owing largely to shifts in the kind of material which tended to be targeted for prosecution. Arguments from literary or artistic merit were certainly appropriate when the items before the court were 'serious works of fiction' (such as *Lady Chatterley's Lover*,[36] *Last Exit to Brooklyn*,[37] or even *Fanny Hill*),[38] or drawings from a reputable art gallery,[39] or 'serious films' such as *Last Tango in Paris*.[40] But increasingly during the 1970s the attention of the police and courts shifted first to pulp fiction and magazines (Davie Fulton's intended targets in 1959), then to erotic films exhibited in cinemas, and finally to videos available for rental. For the vast majority of these materials no credible case of literary or artistic merit could be made, and in general defendants did not bother to try. Thus when Chief Justice Dickson reviewed the tests of 'undueness' in *Towne Cinema* he could give the internal necessities test mere passing mention since it was not relevant to the case at hand (a prosecution for exhibiting the film *Dracula Sucks*).[41] He also did not need to offer any opinion about the relationship between it and the community standards test.

However, in addition to the two established tests, the Chief Justice complicated matters by recognizing a third test of 'undueness': 'Sex related publications which portray persons in a degrading manner as objects of violence, cruelty or other forms of dehumanizing treatment, may be "undue" for the purpose of s. 159(8). No one should be subject to the degradation and humiliation inherent in publications which link sex with violence, cruelty, and other forms of dehumanizing treatment.'[42] The same theme was stressed by Justice Wilson:

> It seems to me that the undue exploitation of sex at which s. 159(8) is aimed is the treatment of sex which in some fundamental way dehumanizes the persons portrayed and, as a consequence, the viewers themselves. There is nothing wrong in the treatment of sex *per se* but there may be something wrong in the manner of its treatment. It may be presented brutally, salaciously and in a degrading manner, and would thus be dehumanizing and intolerable not only to the individuals or groups who are victimized by it but to society at large. On the other hand, it may be presented in a way which harms no one in that it depicts nothing more than non-violent sexual activity in a manner which neither degrades nor dehumanizes any particular individuals or groups. It is this line between the mere portrayal of human sexual acts and the dehumanization of people that must be reflected in the definition of 'undueness'.[43]

Both Dickson and Wilson appeared to be acknowledging a different test for 'undueness', one which targets the harm which might be done by 'degrading or dehumanizing' depictions of sexuality. If so, then the question must be raised of its relationship to the community standards test. Here the two justices parted company. For Wilson, if the harm test was to be appropriately objective and certain then it must be subsumed under the community standards test:

> As I see it, the essential difficulty with the definition of obscenity is that

'undueness' must presumably be assessed in relation to consequences. It is implicit in the definition that at some point the exploitation of sex becomes harmful to the public or at least the public believes that to be so. It is therefore necessary for the protection of the public to put limits on the degree of exploitation and, through the application of the community standard test, the public is made the arbiter of what is harmful to it and what is not.[44]

On the other hand, in Dickson's view not only were the two tests distinct, they could also yield conflicting results. While he thought that 'it is not likely that at a given moment in a society's history, such publications [those which degrade or dehumanize] will be tolerated', he did allow that it was possible:

> Ours is not a perfect society and it is unfortunate that the community may tolerate publications that cause harm to members of society and therefore to society as a whole. Even if, at certain times, there is a coincidence between what is not tolerated and what is harmful to society, there is no necessary connection between these two concepts. Thus, a legal definition of 'undue' must also encompass publications harmful to members of society and, therefore, to society as a whole ...
>
> ... there is no *necessary* coincidence between the undueness of publications which degrade people by linking violence, cruelty or other forms of dehumanizing treatment with sex, and the community standard of tolerance. Even if certain sex related materials were found to be within the standard of tolerance of the community, it would still be necessary to ensure that they were not 'undue' in some other sense, for example in the sense that they portray persons in a degrading manner as objects of violence, cruelty, or other forms of dehumanizing treatment.[45]

While the two opinions differ on the relationship between the community standards and harm tests, they both reflect two important developments in the early 1980s. One was the evolution of feminist thinking about pornography, which increasingly took the form of arguing that it threatened the security and equality of women by legitimizing sexual violence and portraying women in degrading or dehumanizing ways. This movement of thought irreversibly altered the landscape of public discourse about obscenity and censorship. At the same time, section 15 of the Charter, which came into effect in 1985, gave constitutionally protected status to the equality rights of women, thereby raising the question whether the distribution of pornography was protected under the section 2(b) right of freedom of expression. Henceforth, the question whether pornography harms women would be at least the ostensible focus of Canadian adjudication of obscenity.

The issue of obscenity next confronted the Supreme Court in the landmark *Butler* case (1992). In August of 1987 Donald Butler had opened the Avenue Video Boutique in Winnipeg, Manitoba, which stocked hard-core videotapes and magazines, dildos, vibrators, inflatable dolls, and other assorted sexual paraphernalia. Within days the shop was raided by the Winnipeg police and all of its inventory seized. Butler was charged with 173 counts of selling obscene material, possessing obscene material for the purpose of distribution, possessing obscene material for the purpose of sale, and exposing obscene material to public view. Notwithstanding these charges, he reopened the shop two months later and was quickly charged with a further 77 counts of the same offences. At his trial in 1989 he was convicted on 8 counts, relating to eight of the seized videotapes, and acquitted on all of the remaining charges. The crown appealed the 242 acquittals to the Manitoba Court of Appeal, and Butler cross-appealed the 8 convictions. In 1990, by a 3-to-2 majority, the Court of Appeal entered convictions with respect to all 250 counts. Butler then appealed these convictions to the Supreme Court.

The *Towne Cinema* decision had left three different tests of 'undueness' in play: the community standards test, the internal necessities test, and a harm test focusing on degrading or dehumanizing treatment. One of the tasks confronting the *Butler* court was to sort out the relationships among these three tests. Justice Sopinka, writing for the majority, resolved this issue in two steps. First, he sided with the opinion of Justice Wilson, and against that of Chief Justice Dickson, in taking community standards to be the measure of harm. Acknowledging that the harmfulness (or otherwise) of pornography is very much a matter of opinion, Sopinka appealed to community standards to resolve the issue: 'Because this is not a matter that is susceptible of proof in the traditional way and because we do not wish to leave it to the individual tastes of judges, we must have a norm that will serve as an arbiter in determining what amounts to an undue exploitation of sex. That arbiter is the community as a whole.'[46] He then continued:

> The courts must determine as best they can what the community would tolerate others being exposed to on the basis of the degree of harm that

may flow from such exposure. Harm in this context means that it predis-
poses persons to act in an anti-social manner as, for example, the physical
or mental mistreatment of women by men, or, what is perhaps debatable,
the reverse. Anti-social conduct for this purpose is conduct which society
formally recognizes as incompatible with its proper functioning. The stronger the inference of a risk of harm the lesser the likelihood of tolerance.
The inference may be drawn from the material itself or from the material
and other evidence.[47]

This paragraph is a veritable masterpiece of ambiguity, which can be
read in either of two very different ways:

1 The community's intolerance of (some particular form of) pornography is to be taken as an indicator, or perhaps a criterion, of the harmfulness of the material. Thus, from the fact that the material exceeds
  the community's limits of tolerance we may infer that it is harmful.
2 Independent evidence of the harmfulness of (some particular form
  of) pornography is to be taken as an indicator, or perhaps a criterion,
  of the community's intolerance of the material. Thus, from the fact
  that the material is harmful we may infer that it exceeds the community's limits of tolerance.

Both interpretations affirm a close link between the community standards and harm tests. But on the first interpretation, the community
standards test pre-empts an independent test of harm, while on the latter it does not. Since it seems clear from the context that Sopinka had
the first interpretation in mind, we may conclude that he meant the
community standards test to assimilate the harm test.[48] What then of the
internal necessities test? It comes into play only when a publication contains material which, taken by itself, would constitute undue exploitation (as determined by the community standards test). The question
then becomes whether that material is the sole or dominant theme of
the work, or whether it is essential to some 'wider artistic, literary, or
other similar purpose':

> Since the threshold determination must be made on the basis of commu-
> nity standards, that is, whether the sexually explicit aspect is undue, its
> impact when considered in context must be determined on the same basis.
> The court must determine whether the sexually explicit material when

viewed in the context of the whole work would be tolerated by the community as a whole.[49]

In *Butler*, therefore, the Supreme Court definitively established community standards as the measure of both harm and artistic merit for erotic materials, thus as the sole test of obscenity in Canadian criminal law. In so doing it also effectively consolidated the authority of the test for a number of related 'offences tending to corrupt morals' involving not obscenity but such cognates as indecency, immorality, or scurrilousness.[50] Because these highly charged and notoriously subjective notions are nowhere defined in the Criminal Code, not even in such vague and malleable terms as 'undue exploitation of sex', courts obliged to apply them have been quick to borrow from obscenity adjudication the only remedy they could find. Reference to community standards has therefore become as routine in cases involving indecency (and its various synonyms) as it has for obscenity.[51]

4.2 Which Community? Whose Standards?

Here is the way a democratic political system is supposed to work: laws are made by an elected legislature and interpreted and applied by the courts. Sometimes it actually works that way: a piece of legislation is fully and carefully crafted by the lawmakers and its application by judges becomes a relatively straightforward process. In those cases the judicial input to the actual shape of the law in practice is minimal. At other times, however, what the legislature comes up with is so indeterminate, so much in need of specification, that the courts cannot avoid inventing a more definite content for it. In theory at least, for any law in practice we should be able to distinguish how much it owes to its legislative origins and how much has subsequently been added by the courts. On this continuum, the obscenity statute clearly lies at the extreme end of judge-made law. On the crucial task of identifying the obscene, all Parliament contributed in 1959 was the unhelpful phrase 'undue exploitation of sex'. Since the courts have attached no meaning to 'exploitation' except that the publication in question deals, at least in part, with sexual themes, all of the weight of the definition has fallen on the modifier 'undue'.[52] But saying that a work will be deemed to be obscene when its treatment of sexual matters is 'undue' pretty well amounts to saying that it will be deemed to be obscene when it is thought to be obscene. Everything turns on the test(s) of undueness, to which the courts have been obliged to give some determinate shape and substance. It is in this process of judicial legislation that the reference to community standards has been the central theme.

As a result of the process, the integrity of Canadian law across a broad range of 'morals offences' depends almost entirely on the integrity of the community standards test. The idea that people might be subject to criminal sanctions just because they do something that exceeds the community's current level of tolerance raises a number of obvious and important legal, political, and philosophical issues. In the interest of sorting through these issues in some coherent fashion, we will begin by taking the idea of community standards at face value. Community standards are the standards of some community, and the courts have determined that the relevant community is a national one. The test therefore presupposes that Canada as a whole constitutes a community. So we may legitimately ask whether this is so. Since any answer to this question will depend on what we mean by a community, we need to give the notion some definition. The word 'community' derives from the same Latin root as 'common' or 'commonality', suggesting that a community is a group of persons who share some important feature or characteristic. In what is probably its most familiar sense we apply the term to a group united by such identifying features as language, culture, religion, history, ethnicity, or geography. The notion of a community seems especially apt when we can identify such a group by contrast with others among whom they live. It is this sense we have in mind when we speak of the Acadian community in the Atlantic provinces, the Jewish community in Montreal, or the gay community in Toronto. In each case we are relying on a degree of social cohesion within the group, induced both by a shared place and by common cultural markers with which members of the group strongly identify.

If we have this notion of a community in mind then we may doubt whether the country as a whole could count as a community. Because Canada is a multinational, multiethnic state, it is usual to think of it as composed of a large number of different cultural communities, each with its own identity. Canadians lack a common language, history, religion, ethnicity – and virtually every other characteristic which generally unites a group of people into a community. So it is tempting to answer the question in the negative: in no interesting or important sense is Canada a single community. However, this answer would be too hasty. Canadians are united by a common geography and perhaps also a certain common identity. This identity is usually expressed negatively by contrasting ourselves with our culturally more assertive neighbours to the south: we are the North Americans who have safe cities and universal health care, who don't own handguns and don't invade other people's countries. These commonalities are not strong enough to make us a cultural community, but they may be strong enough to make us a civic or political community. By virtue of our shared citizenship we are all subject to the jurisdiction of a common set of political and legal institutions. And it may be that there are certain values – a commitment to social and economic equality, for instance, to balance against the more American emphasis on individual liberty – with which we strongly identify and which therefore serve to mark us as Canadians.

If so, then one of those values surely is tolerance: the idea that we should respect different lifestyles and allow individuals to pursue their own conceptions of the good (as philosophers tend to put it). Tolerance is one of the pre-eminent virtues of the modern liberal state which embraces a plurality of distinct groups or cultural communities with divergent values, goals, and ambitions. So perhaps it is possible, after all, to say that Canada as a whole forms a single civic community united by, among other things, common allegiance to a standard of tolerance. If so, then the community standards test, as the courts have conceptualized it, would appear to have a meaningful reference point.

But the moment this idea is formulated, its problems become apparent. Suppose, for the purpose of argument, that all Canadians assign a positive value to tolerance – they all think it a good thing to be tolerant, consider themselves tolerant, esteem it in others, even take it to be a matter of national pride. It does not follow, nor is it true, that they agree on who or what should be tolerated or respected. White supremacists have no intention of tolerating Jews, or blacks, or Asians; many fundamentalist Christians refuse to extend tolerance to gays and lesbians; the self-appointed guardians of 'family values' may be intolerant of women who choose to work outside the home or employ professional child care; if they had the power, anti-choice groups would not tolerate women seeking abortions; and so on.

The absence of consensus on the appropriate objects of tolerance is nowhere more apparent than in the domain of sexuality in general and pornography in particular. Tolerance, like respect, is a virtue of self-restraint. Willingness to tolerate someone else's lifestyle presupposes disapproval of it, or at least enough qualms to rule out affirming its positive value. There is no need to tolerate that which we ourselves endorse;

instead, we can share in it, support it, applaud it, or promote it. Tolerance therefore requires difference – we tolerate others, not our own group – and it obliges us to make a crucial distinction between the moral and the political: though we may find some activity or practice morally repugnant or at least questionable, we will agree that the freedom of others to engage in it ought to be protected. This distinction has, of course, been enshrined in the community standards test for as long as it has been interpreted as a standard of tolerance rather than taste. Recall Justice Dickson's words in 1970: 'I have no doubt ... a distinction can be made between private taste and standard of tolerance. It can hardly be questioned that many people would find personally offensive, material which they would permit others to read.'[53]

There is obviously no consensus in Canada on the taste question concerning pornography. While it is a flourishing market, possibly still a growth industry, it is clearly not to everyone's taste. Some find it innocent or liberating while others condemn it as exploitative or demeaning. But there is also no consensus concerning tolerance. Groups advocating (civil or criminal) sanctions against pornography have been active in the public arena, including the *Butler* decision itself, as have civil liberties organizations on the other side of the question.[54] The tolerance issue continues to be a hotly contested one in Canadian political life, and one on which public opinion remains deeply divided. Many ordinary Canadians are not greatly bothered by the presence in their communities of 'adult' bookstores and video outlets or by the ready availability of pornography on the Internet. But others clearly are. One obvious line of division is geography: it would be naïve to expect community standards to be as permissive in rural Alberta as they are in Toronto or Montreal. Another is religious affiliation: fundamentalist Christians and ultraorthodox Jews are on the whole less tolerant of pornography than their more secular co-religionists. The censorship issue is divisive even within more ideologically homogeneous constituencies. Many feminists, though by no means all, find pornography at least unsavoury, if not downright repugnant. However, those who share this standard of taste part company on the issue of legal control; there are as many influential feminists opposing censorship as there are supporting it. In short, however we partition Canadians – by geography, religious affiliation, or political persuasion – there is simply no national consensus on the tolerance question to be found among them.

For the purpose of judicial procedure the community's standard of tolerance is deemed to be a matter of fact rather than law. Because prosecutions under the obscenity statute have almost invariably proceeded by summary conviction rather than indictment, the trier of fact in these cases has typically been a judge. For the most part judges charged with the responsibility of applying the community standards test have accepted that there is a fact of the matter which it is their job to discover and that they must not substitute their own individual views for the collective opinion of the community. However, alongside these expressions of judicial confidence in the existence of a national standard can be found occasional but persistent doubts. As early in the game as 1966 Justice Laskin was already musing about the possibility that 'a community standard is a will-o'-the-wisp, an unknown, and perhaps even an unknowable quantity'.[55] Nearly two decades later judges could still be found expressing scepticism about the possibility of a national standard of tolerance in a country as geographically and culturally diverse as Canada.[56]

This scepticism is clearly justified if the community standard which judges have been obliged to seek is interpreted as a consensus, requiring something approaching unanimity. The consensus interpretation is strongly suggested by the rhetoric of community, with its implication of bonds of attachment forged out of shared values. It is far from clear, however, that judges have generally assumed this interpretation. Indeed, it is far from clear what interpretation, if any, they have generally assumed, for there is remarkably little judicial discussion of this issue. We might wish to impute the consensus interpretation to those judges whose expressed scepticism about the possibility of locating a national community standard of tolerance is based on the pluralism or diversity of the Canadian populace. But they do not explicitly affirm it, and their doubts do not prevent them from applying (what they take to be) the standard of the community. The assumption of social consensus might also be thought to be implied by Justice Fullagar's reference to 'a general instinctive sense of what is decent and what is indecent',[57] which was cited with such approval by Justice Judson in *Brodie*. Perhaps Fullagar did really believe that a modern state could be homogeneous with respect to its sense of decency, but there is little evidence that Canadian judges have shared this assumption in more recent cases and clear instances in which they have rejected it.[58] The occasional passages in obscenity judgments which do suggest the consensus interpretation are very far from determinative.[59]

More frequent, but still far short of decisive, are references not to a consensus of community opinion but instead to an 'average'. This line of interpretation owes its origin to Justice Freedman's influential dissent in *Dominion News* (endorsed by the Supreme Court), in which he referred to 'a general average of community thinking and feeling',[60] and was subsequently affirmed in a number of cases.[61] However, the idea of an average level of community tolerance is conceptually problematic. Interpreted literally, an average is a statistical artifact computed from a set of quantified inputs. The average opinion of a community would therefore be a function of the several individual opinions of the community's members. The problem of computing such an average extends well beyond the fact that these opinions resist quantification. Suppose that the opinions of the members of some community are sought on the question of whether the sale or rental of hard-core sex videos ought to be permitted and that 55 per cent respond 'yes', 35 per cent respond 'no', and the remaining 10 per cent are undecided or have no opinion. What is the average opinion in this case? We can readily identify a level of tolerance supported by a majority in the community, but the notion of an average level seems to have no clear sense.

Those judges who have occasionally spoken of an average appear not to have meant it literally. Instead, they have conceived of the average of a community's thinking as a kind of midpoint between extremes. Again the idea goes back to Justice Freedman: '[The standards of the community] are not set by those of lowest taste or interest. Nor are they set exclusively by those of rigid, austere, conservative, or puritan taste and habit of mind. Something approaching a general average of community thinking and feeling has to be discovered.'[62] Freedman seems to have in mind here a middle ground of taste rather than tolerance, but the basic idea is readily adapted to the latter context. However, on this reading the interpretation of the community standard as an average of individual standards quickly mutates into a different one:

> I think it important to speak for a moment on tolerance. There are members of our community, a minority, who believe, sincerely, that all pornography, obscene or not, is evil and the work of the devil. One cannot deny them their beliefs. There are others, again a minority, who would say that anything goes, let me view whatever I please. The majority, as I perceive our current society, is sufficiently tolerant to allow viewing by others of video tapes of every kind and description, including the pornographic.[63]

Under this conception a community's standard of tolerance is a function of the distribution of opinion within it. Suppose that it could be ascertained that 20 per cent of the members of the community would permit the distribution of hard-core videos with no restrictions, 20 per cent would ban them outright, and the remaining 60 per cent would permit distribution but with some restrictions of content (no violence or degradation, let us say). In that case, the community's level of tolerance would be determined by discarding the minority views at either extreme and settling on the majority opinion in the middle.[64]

The identification of community standards with majority opinion is seldom explicitly affirmed in the Canadian cases.[65] However, it seems to be the most charitable interpretation of what judges have actually been doing when they seek the elusive national standard of tolerance. Whereas a national consensus does not exist and a national average makes no sense, there may well be a national majority on the tolerance question, one which, furthermore, could be ascertained by appropriate kinds of empirical evidence, such as opinion surveys.[66] By adopting this interpretation we at least credit judges with seeking something which it would be possible in principle for them to find.

The task of identifying the majority view has not been aided by the doctrine that evidence concerning community standards, while admissible, is not mandatory. Despite acknowledging that 'the state of mind or attitude of a community is as much a fact as the state of one's health',[67] courts have consistently held that no evidence concerning this state of mind – whether in the form of opinion surveys or expert testimony – need be adduced to assist the trier of fact.[68] Somehow or other judges were expected to identify the relevant standard, based on their experience, while at the same time avoiding the trap of substituting their own personal level of tolerance for that of the community. In *Rankine* (1983) Judge Borins noted the irony in this requirement that judges keep their finger on 'the pornographic pulse of the nation':

> The judge, who by the very institutional nature of his calling is required to distance himself or herself from society, for the purposes of the application of the test of obscenity is expected to be a person for all seasons familiar with and aware of the national level of tolerance. Thus the trial judge (or jury) is required to rely upon his or her own experience and decide as best he or she can what most people in Canada think about such material to arrive upon a measure of community tolerance of that material. Judges or jurors lacking experience in the field of pornography and the attitudes of others towards it face a substantial challenge in making the findings demanded by the law.[69]

By the end of the 1980s it was becoming evident that trial judges were experiencing real problems determining community standards in the absence of evidence. This is nowhere more apparent than in the decision by Judge Wright at Donald Butler's initial trial in 1989. Having acknowledged the difficulties involved in adducing reliable evidence on this question, Wright continued: 'Faced with the reality of these difficulties courts have followed an unusual judicial course by encouraging the decision on the issue of the contemporary Canadian standard of tolerance be made by the trier of fact alone without evidence beyond the impugned material. One might argue that this merely compounds the problem and does damage to judicial principles in the process.'[70] What kind of damage? Judge Wright's treatment of this question turned into a stimulating little essay on the place of evidence in the trial process which is worth reproducing at some length:

As noted, our case law emphasizes that the trier of fact may not identify the standard by his or her *personal* experience, for that experience has to mean the application of subjective opinions based on family, church and life influences. Rather the trier is expected to separate the assessment of the standard from these influences, while drawing on his experience in order to objectively identify the standard. It is difficult, however, to understand how this realistically can be accomplished in the absence of evidence, without relying on conclusions that are entirely personal. Indeed, whatever the approach, if there is no evidence (as to the standard) from which the trier can operate, any decision based only on his or her experience is bound to be subjective ...

The whole idea runs counter to the concept that a trier of fact makes decisions in respect of *contested* issues of fact (in the present case a significant disputed factual issue was the question of what is the community standard of tolerance) based on the evidence presented in the courtroom ...

If an important factual issue in dispute is not decided on the basis of evidence *on the record*, how is it possible to know on what basis the decision was made? How can an appellate court properly consider the finding of a trial court? Furthermore, how can the basis for the finding be tested during the trial? No cross-examination can occur. No rebuttal or response can be made because there is no evidence before the parties. It is all in the judge's mind ...

Judges are educated and trained, and juries are instructed, to submerge their own opinions and views in order to apply an objective and unbiased approach when called upon to assess conflicting positions in the adversarial presentation of evidence. On critical and controversial questions of fact it is not anticipated that the judge or jury will make findings based, *not on the evidence*, but rather on the then state of the judge's or jury member's own knowledge, education and experience ...

I have been a trial judge for many years and have endeavoured at all times to reach my judgements with impartiality on the basis of objective considerations. To render a factual decision on the basis of my experience is not in accord with the judicial role I have practised. I, of course, have certain opinions and perceptions as to what Canadian society would tolerate others to see or read, but they are nothing more than that. By the standards I utilize to arrive at a crucial finding of fact I would describe my own views in this area as entirely unreliable.[71]

Bound as he was by the Supreme Court majority in *Towne Cinema*, but perhaps emboldened by the two dissenting opinions on this issue, Judge Wright came as close as he could to stating that expert evidence on community standards was not only admissible and desirable but indispensable. At the subsequent appeal his concerns were echoed in the dissenting opinion of Justice Helper, who considered that the absence of evidence rendered the community standards test, and therefore the 'undue exploitation' definition of obscenity, objectionably vague and arbitrary.[72] That, however, is as far as this line of argument went, since the Supreme Court in *Butler* left undisturbed the *Towne Cinema* ruling that evidence of the community standard of tolerance was not mandatory, despite establishing this standard as the sole test of obscenity.

Notwithstanding the lack of subsequent judicial uptake, Judge Wright's diagnosis of the fundamental problem should be kept in clear view. Triers of fact in obscenity cases are put in the unenviable position of being obliged to determine what the majority of Canadians are willing to tolerate, often with no evidence whatever to guide them. Where such evidence has been introduced, it has been of doubtful assistance;[73] furthermore, judges have been free to disregard it, which they have frequently done, and rely instead on their own reading of 'the pornographic pulse of the nation'. The obvious danger is that judges working in an evidential vacuum will tend to project their own limits of tolerance, and their own reactions of distaste or disgust, onto the country at large; as Judge Wright so aptly put it, it is all in the judge's mind.[74] Any such tendency would of course completely subvert the original purpose of the community standards test, which was to provide a criterion of obscenity with 'some certainty of meaning and ... capable of objective application'.[75] Indeed, it would mean that the introduction of the statutory definition of obscenity, and the development of the community standards test as a way of operationalizing it, have amounted to little advance, if any, over the old *Hicklin* test.

The concern that, for all of its purported objectivity, the community standards test may ultimately be a subjective one has surfaced regularly in the adjudication of both obscenity and indecency.[76] It is reinforced by some egregious judicial lapses, one of the worst of which occurred only a few months after the Supreme Court decision in *Butler*. In 1989 officials of Canada Customs seized a shipment of books and magazines being imported by Glad Day Bookshop, a gay and lesbian bookstore in Toronto, on the ground that the materials were obscene. The owners of the bookstore appealed this seizure to the courts. The definition of obscenity, for the purposes of the Customs Act, was that laid down in section 163(8) of the Criminal Code; the issue of whether the materials were obscene would therefore be decided by applying the community standards test. At the subsequent trial, expert testimony concerning community standards was offered by three witnesses: the Chair of the Ontario Film Review Board, a Toronto city councillor with roots in the city's gay and lesbian community, and a sociology professor with expertise on sexual practices in the gay community. In his decision Judge Hayes first took note of the *Butler* decision, including the use made by the Supreme Court of community standards to determine both harmful and 'degrading or dehumanizing' portrayals of sexual activity. He then proceeded to reject all of the expert testimony as being of little or no assistance to the court in determining community standards and undertook his own review of the seized books and magazines, all of which contained stories, comic strips, or photographs depicting gay male sex. The rest of his judgment is a series of twelve brief assessments of these materials, of which the following are entirely typical:

> The description in the magazine of this sexual activity is degrading. I am of the opinion that this particular material does indicate a strong inference of a risk of harm that might flow from the community being exposed to this material. I am of the opinion that the community would not tolerate others being exposed to this item. The dominant characteristic is an undue exploitation of sex. It is obscene.

> The conduct depicted is such that society would formally recognize it as being incomparable [*sic*] with its proper functioning. There is a strong

inference of harm from the material. The community would not tolerate others being exposed to this material. The dominant characteristic is the undue exploitation of sex. It is clearly obscene.

There are stories of explicit sexual encounters of oral and anal sex and digital anal penetration. There is a description of a biker gang using one person for explicit anal intercourse and in violent and degrading circumstances with lewd descriptions of the activity and the alleged pleasures.

There is a strong inference of harm as referred to in R. v. Butler, supra. The community would not tolerate others being exposed to it and the dominant characteristic is the undue exploitation of sex. It is obscene.[77]

Reading through this remarkable sequence of unargued conclusions it is difficult to dispute the observation made by one legal commentator more than twenty years earlier that the community standards test 'is applied only by way of salutatory genuflexion, usually to the concealment of whatever real reason the tribunal may have had for its decision'.[78] All of the canonical post-*Butler* phrases are here: risk of harm, degrading, incompatibility with society's proper functioning, what the community will not tolerate, and so on. But no reasons are offered for the claims about harm or degradation except the obligatory invocation of the community's standards of tolerance, and no evidence is adduced concerning these standards at all. Judge Hayes's real reason for finding these materials to be obscene seems to be that they exceeded his own limits of tolerance, which were in turn determined by his responses of disgust and repugnance.[79] Any reference beyond his own subjective reactions to the standards of the community at large is purely notional.[80]

I do not mean to suggest that this particular decision is typical of the way in which judges have attempted to apply the community standards test. On the contrary, it stands out for being an especially blatant example of the dangers against which Judge Wright warned. (It is worrisome that it followed the Supreme Court's decision in *Butler*, though perhaps before its lessons could be properly digested.) Most judges have at least made a sincere attempt to apply community standards, as they understand them, and have generally come to more balanced conclusions. A good example of the norm may be found in Judge Borins's decision in *Rankine* (1983). This is the same decision in which Borins expressed scepticism about both the existence of a uniform national standard and the ability of a judge to keep his finger on 'the pornographic pulse of the nation'. None the less, recognizing that he was obliged to do so, he proceeded to apply the appropriate test to the materials in question (adult videotapes), concluding as follows:

> All of the films contain what the Crown described as 'standard, run of the mill scenes' of sexual intercourse. In my opinion, contemporary community standards would tolerate the distribution of films which consist substantially of scenes of people engaged in sexual intercourse. Contemporary community standards would also tolerate the distribution of films which consist of scenes of group sex, Lesbianism, *fellatio, cunnilingus*, and anal sex. However, films which consist substantially or partially of scenes which portray violence and cruelty in conjunction with sex, particularly where the performance of indignities degrade and dehumanize the people upon whom they are performed, exceed the level of community tolerance.[81]

The rubric here invoked by Judge Borins would prove to be enormously influential. His was the first decision to draw a distinction between the depiction of sex, on the one hand, and the depiction of sex with added elements of violence or degradation, on the other. These distinctions were destined to be taken up by the Supreme Court, first in *Towne Cinema* and subsequently in *Butler.* Judge Borins rested this distinction on his opinion about what the community would, and would not, tolerate. But on what was that opinion based in turn? Two 'expert' witnesses testified at the trial: Josephine Walker, a Toronto schoolteacher, and June Rowlands, a Toronto city councillor. The former viewed five of the twenty-five videotapes for whose distribution the defendant was on trial and expressed the opinion that the contemporary Canadian community would not tolerate any of them. Judge Borins elected to disregard Walker's testimony on the ground that she had no experience of community opinion outside Ontario and that she represented only a minority view within the province.[82] Rowlands viewed parts of three of the films and distinguished between the kinds of scenes she thought the contemporary Toronto community would tolerate (oral sex, masturbation, intercourse, group sex, etc.) and those she thought it would not (ejaculation on the face, insertion of objects into the vagina, anal sex, sex involving violence or cruelty, etc.). Judge Borins declared himself impressed by her testimony: 'There are well over a million women in Metropolitan Toronto. She has testified to what she believes to be the level of tolerance of a majority of them.'[83]

On what basis did Borins decide which 'expert' testimony to accept?

Both witnesses had lived in Toronto for many years, both were involved in public life, and both purported to speak for a large constituency of women. Neither offered any evidence, such as an opinion survey, to support her claim about what the women, or citizens in general, of Toronto would or would not tolerate, and neither was prepared to advance even an opinion about the rest of Canada (the relevant community standard is, remember, national and not local). Unlike both of the witnesses, Judge Borins viewed all twenty-five of the films in question. Before announcing his findings concerning them, he dutifully recited the standard judicial mantra: 'In determining whether it has been proved that a film is obscene I am mindful that my own personal tastes or prejudices must play no role. My decision must not reflect or project my own notion of what the contemporary Canadian community will tolerate. I must endeavour to apply what I, in the light of my experience, regard to be the contemporary standards of the Canadian community.'[84] His conclusion – that eleven of the films were obscene, the rest not – owed a great deal to Rowlands's testimony.[85] Yet there was no apparent reason to regard Rowlands as a more reliable informant about community standards than Walker, other than the fact that her views coincided more closely with Borins's own. Borins's reliance on his own level of tolerance is not nearly as blatant or offensive as that of Hayes, but it is difficult to resist the conclusion in his case as well that the reference to community standards, and the weighing of evidence concerning those standards, served only to conceal the real reasons for his conclusions.

The great defect of the *Hicklin* test was that it made the offence of obscenity depend on the judge's (or jury's) opinion on a moral issue – whether the material in question had a tendency to deprave and corrupt. Justice Judson's hope in 1962, and Davie Fulton's expectation in 1959, was that the statutory definition which (eventually) replaced the *Hicklin* test would be more objective, requiring judgment on a matter of fact – the community's standard of tolerance – rather than one of morals. More than forty years on, this hope now seems quaintly naïve. Judges routinely decide whether books, magazines, or (increasingly) films are obscene on the basis of their perception of what the community is prepared to tolerate, a perception which is usually based either on no evidence whatever or on very selective consideration of whatever evidence is available. The best explanation of their judgments is that they are conditioned not by a serious attempt to ascertain the tolerance level of the majority of Canadians but by the judges' own limits of tolerance, which are determined in turn by their sense of moral propriety. What the judge finds personally distasteful or disgusting is what he or she is likely to conclude exceeds the community's limits of tolerance.

There is an important issue of justice at stake here. It is an established principle of the rule of law that 'legislation which purports to regulate the conduct or actions of individuals must be sufficiently clear and precise to permit the individual to know, with a reasonable degree of certainty, that which is forbidden'.[86] Citizens must be given 'fair notice' that conduct they contemplate falls within the scope of a criminal offence as defined by the legislature. Laws which fail this condition due to vagueness engage section 7 of the Charter, which guarantees that individuals will not be deprived of the right to liberty and security of the person 'except in accordance with the principles of fundamental justice'. At the extreme such laws may even fail to qualify as 'reasonable limits prescribed by law' under the terms of section 1.[87]

If judgments about community standards, and therefore about obscenity, reflect little more than the subjective moral views of judges, then individuals in the business of producing, distributing, importing, selling, or renting erotic materials may be in no position to predict with a reasonable degree of certainty whether their activities will leave them vulnerable to prosecution and conviction. Whether a particular magazine or video will be found to be obscene may depend to a large extent on which judge hears the case in which part of the country. We can of course take the unsympathetic view that police raids, inventory seizures, criminal charges, and consequent legal expenses should simply be reckoned among the costs of conducting this rather unsavoury business. But even leaving aside the fact that everyone, including those in the sex trade, has a right to just treatment, we should bear in mind that the full weight of the law can descend not only on the major producers or distributors of pornography but also on very ordinary people, like Donald Butler, who manage or are employed in local video and magazine outlets. They are legally responsible for ensuring that none of the goods on their shelves run afoul of the law, a task that is a practical impossibility if that law is being applied in different ways in different courts in different jurisdictions (or even within the same one).

That the vagueness of the obscenity law and the subjectivity of the community standards test raise serious issues of justice has been noted by a number of commentators.[88] What is more interesting is that it has also been noted by some judges. The same Judge Borins who in 1983 wondered whether he and his fellows were qualified to keep their fingers on 'the pornographic pulse of the nation' raised the 'fair notice' issue in a different case (*Nicols*) a year later:

> the offence of dealing in obscene materials is unique among all of the offences created by the Criminal Code. With respect to all of the other offences created by the Code a person can be presumed to know that he or she is committing the offence when he engages in the prohibited conduct ... This is not so with obscenity crimes created by [sec. 163]. One does not know whether he or she is committing an offence under [sec. 163] until after a court has determined that the materials in issue exceed the standards of tolerance in the contemporary Canadian community ...
>
> ... No member of the public can say with certainty that material is obscene until the court, applying somewhat obscure standards, has pronounced it so ... Under the present regime, the criminal law has become a trap.
>
> ... For well over a century courts have had difficulty in defining obscenity with precision. To condemn people to the stigma of a criminal conviction for violating standards they cannot understand, construe and apply is a serious thing to do in a nation which, by its recent Charter of Rights, has affirmed its dedication to fair trials and due process.[89]

The 'fair notice' issue is, however, a complex one. Suppose it be conceded that both the statutory definition of obscenity and the community standards test are vague and that, at least in the absence of reliable evidence, the application of the latter by judges is unavoidably subjective. It does not immediately follow that it is also so uncertain as to fail the 'fair notice' requirement. It is noteworthy that while the constitutionality of the obscenity statute has been challenged on a number of occasions on grounds of vagueness or uncertainty, the challenge has never succeeded.[90] Courts have tended to take the view that some degree of vagueness is inevitable where a definition or test of obscenity is concerned, and that the judicial application of the community standards test has been sufficiently uniform to allow for reasonable certainty, at any given time, as to whether a particular type of erotic material will be found to be obscene. Because obscenity prosecutions have not been rare, at least prior to *Butler*, a certain density of adjudication tended to be built up over time which could serve as a reference point for subsequent decisions. At that point the best predictor of what a court will find to exceed community standards is what previous courts have found to exceed these standards; in effect, the missing evidence about the tolerance limits of the majority is provided by precedent cases.[91]

The predictive power of previous obscenity decisions is, however, strictly limited. Because the relevant community standard is supposed to be contemporary, cases quickly lose relevance with age; decisions more than a few years old provide no guidance whatever. The written decisions in obscenity trials show that judges tend to be acutely aware of what has happened recently in similar cases, either at the trial or appellate levels. However, the outcome of a trial in Toronto may be thought to have only slight probative weight for a prosecution in Winnipeg or Red Deer. Since even appellate decisions are only binding within their provincial jurisdiction, courts are not obliged to follow any outside authority except the Supreme Court. It is always open to judges, or prosecutors, to take the view that standards have changed – in one direction or another – since even very recent cases. A particularly striking instance of such a perceived shift could be seen in the *Nicols* case (discussed above). One of the three videos listed in the indictment for this case had been declared not to be obscene by the same Judge Borins a year earlier in *Rankine*. The *Nicols* charge was laid subsequent to the *Rankine* decision, despite the fact that the crown counsel conceded that he was unable to establish that Canadian community standards had changed during the intervening year. It was not withdrawn because just a few months before the *Nicols* case was heard a jury in another town in the same province found the video to be obscene. The unfortunate Mr Nicols gave evidence that he thought he could distribute this video with impunity because of the result in *Rankine*. Courts have long held that exoneration of erotic materials by other agencies – Customs officials, for example, or provincial film review boards – is no bar to a criminal prosecution for distributing the same materials.[92] But Nicols was relying on a court decision less than a year earlier in the same jurisdiction. The crown took the view that 'because community standards may change there may be situations in which the Crown might consider it appropriate to subsequently commence proceedings under [sec. 163] of the Code where materials have not been proved to be obscene in a prior prosecution'.[93] Even the seemingly most reliable precedents may therefore fail to provide entrepreneurs with 'fair notice'.

Though judges may attend to one another's obscenity decisions, this does not rule out significant disagreements among them. The 1980s were a particularly volatile period in Canadian obscenity adjudication, no doubt in part because of the flood of pornographic videos then coming on to the market. Reading through the decisions in this decade, one discerns two more or less parallel but utterly incompatible currents of thought. One began with Judge Borins's decision in *Rankine* and was carried on in a number of subsequent cases. On this view, contemporary community standards could tolerate explicit depictions of sexual activity as long as they contained no scenes portraying 'violence' and cruelty in conjunction with sex, particularly where the performance of indignities degrade and dehumanize the people upon whom they are performed'.[94] The parallel stream took the view that explicit sexual portrayals could exceed community standards even in the absence of these further elements of violence or degradation.[95] The vast majority of hard-core videos produced during this period for sale or rental contained little or no overt sexual violence; instead, they consisted of endless depictions of the kinds of sexual activity whose portrayal Judge Borins declared not to be obscene. What lesson was someone in the business of distributing, renting, or selling these videos supposed to draw from the obscenity decisions of the mid- to late 1980s? Were pornographic videos free of violence and 'degrading or dehumanizing' activities obscene or not? Was it safe to stock them or not? Not even the most attentive student of the judicial trends of the period would be able to predict with reasonable certainty whether his business practices would leave him vulnerable to a criminal charge.

By the end of the 1980s these inconsistencies at the trial level were becoming intolerable. Justice Sopinka attempted to resolve them in *Butler* by endorsing the threefold classification of pornographic materials ultimately derivable from *Rankine*: '(1) explicit sex with violence, (2) explicit sex without violence but which subjects people to treatment that is degrading or dehumanizing, and (3) explicit sex without violence that is neither degrading nor dehumanizing'.[96] Sopinka then concluded that items in category (1) will 'almost always' be obscene, those in category (3) will not be obscene unless they employ children in their production, and those in category (2) may be obscene 'if the risk of harm is substantial'.[97] These conclusions were based on Sopinka's reading of 'what the community would tolerate others being exposed to on the basis of the degree of harm that may flow from such exposure'.[98] In keeping with judicial tradition, Sopinka deemed evidence concerning community standards to be 'desirable but not essential'.[99]

The Supreme Court's opinion as to what contemporary community standards would or would not tolerate had no more evidentiary warrant than the opinions of judges in the lower courts. But because it was binding on lower courts across the country it should help to solve the 'fair notice' problem. In theory at least, after *Butler* importers, distributors, and retailers of erotic materials could be confident that they were immune from prosecution as long as their stock depicted neither violent nor 'degrading or dehumanizing' activities. But how were they to interpret these categories? What counted as sexual violence? Spanking? Bondage? Consensual domination and submission? More difficult still, which sexual activities qualified as degrading or dehumanizing? Ejaculation on a woman's body? Insertion of objects into her vagina or anus? Gay or lesbian sex?

In the post-*Butler* period these questions quickly became more than academic. I have already noted Judge Hayes's 1992 decision in *Glad Day Bookshop* which seized on the 'degrading or dehumanizing' category from *Butler* to find various gay male materials obscene, despite the fact that many of the sexual activities depicted therein were consensual and non-violent. Shortly thereafter an issue of a lesbian magazine, *Bad Attitude*, was found to be obscene on the basis of an article describing a sexual fantasy of a domination and submission (D & S) scenario between two women. Despite expert testimony at the trial concerning the place of consensual D & S within a subset of the lesbian community, Judge Paris concluded that 'This material flashes every light and blows every whistle of obscenity. Enjoyable sex after subordination by bondage and physical abuse at the hands of a total stranger. If I replaced the aggressor in this article with a man there would be very few people in the community who would not recognize the potential for harm. The fact that the aggressor is a female is irrelevant because the potential for harm remains.'[100] Once again, the material was declared obscene on the ground of being 'degrading or dehumanizing'. Meanwhile, seizures by Canada Customs of shipments of books and magazines imported by gay and lesbian bookstores continued unabated after *Butler*, despite the fact that Customs officers were mandated to apply the section 163(8) definition of obscenity.[101] There was no suggestion whatever in *Butler* that depictions of sexual activities could qualify as degrading or dehumanizing simply because they involve same-sex participants.[102] Furthermore, even if portrayals of gay sex were thought to fall into this inherently subjective category, they could not be found to be obscene on that account unless they also posed a substantial risk of harm. Like Judges Hayes and Paris, Customs officials seemed to think that this last requirement was automatically satisfied.

For at least a short while after *Butler*, trial courts continued to generate contradictory results concerning the same kinds of erotic materials. In 1993 the Ontario Court of Appeal considered five appeals of obscenity cases.[103] Three of those cases involved pornographic videos depicting consensual sexual activities entirely free of violence. In two of them the defendant was acquitted; in the third he was convicted. The trial courts differed over the interpretation of 'degrading or dehumanizing'; more specifically, they parted company over the question whether explicit depictions of sexual activities in contexts completely devoid of love or affection – that is, just repetitive, physical, mechanical sex – necessarily fell into this category. The conviction was based on the conclusion that they did, the acquittals on the opposite view. The appeal court ruled in favour of the latter interpretation.

That ruling seemed to induce a certain degree of stability, at least in the legal regulation of hard-core videos. My local video outlet in Toronto has a large room devoted to 'adult' materials portraying sexual activities ranging from the familiar to the bizarre, but nothing more violent than the occasional light spanking: no rape, no bondage and discipline, no domination and submission. All of the videos available for rent there have been approved by the Ontario Film Review Board, which applies its own interpretation of contemporary community standards in Ontario. Over the years it has developed checklists of activities which will be deemed to be degrading or dehumanizing. Some activities once checklisted (such as ejaculation on a woman's face) have since been delisted, presumably because (in the board's opinion) the contemporary Ontario community is now prepared to tolerate their portrayal. In effect, the board is providing distributors and retailers with the 'fair notice' they need, despite the fact that board approval of a film does not furnish immunity against prosecution. The Toronto police seem to have little interest in disrupting this cosy arrangement; their concern these days appears to be limited to child pornography.

By this roundabout route, therefore, the zone of vagueness or uncertainty in the obscenity law has been considerably reduced, at least for video outlets in Toronto. The same may or may not be true for Lethbridge or Corner Brook, and it is certainly not true for operators of gay and lesbian bookstores, who continue to be in the dark about the criteria applied by Canada Customs. However, to the extent that some entrepreneurs now have de facto 'fair notice', this has been achieved with little or no reliance on evidence of a national standard of tolerance. When Judge Borins declared in *Rankine* that hard-core porn was not *per se* 'undue exploitation of sex', in the absence of violence or degradation, he did so on the basis of nothing more than a reflex gesture in the direction of the level of tolerance of the majority of Canadians, and when Justice Sopinka endorsed this finding in *Butler* the complete absence of any evidence on this question was even more striking.[104] While neither judge could claim to be reporting what the majority *would* tolerate, they were effectively determining what the majority *must* tolerate. And what was that based on in turn except their own personal levels of tolerance?[105]

Nearly forty years of judicial infatuation with community standards has not brought us measurably closer to an objective test of obscenity. In fact, it has not even resulted in a great deal of advance over the subjectivity and inconsistency of the old *Hicklin* test. The reference to community standards of tolerance, introduced into obscenity adjudication in 1962, has not prevented judges from relying on their personal levels of tolerance (or standards of taste) in determining whether the materials before them are obscene. Instead of deciding, on the basis of no evidence beyond the work itself, whether some erotic material has a 'tendency to deprave and corrupt', judges are now required to determine when its depiction of sex is 'degrading or dehumanizing'. Their ritual genuflection toward community standards does little to disguise the essential arbitrariness of this exercise.

4.3 The Tyranny of the Community

Although the foregoing problems are serious, there are also deeper, more philosophical, objections to the use of the community standards test in obscenity adjudication. In order to highlight these objections, we need to make the following (unrealistic) assumptions: (1) at any given time there is a strong consensus, at least among the majority of Canadians, concerning the kinds of erotic materials whose distribution they are prepared to tolerate; (2) empirical evidence is available concerning this consensus which could be presented by the crown in the course of obscenity prosecutions; (3) the consensus is sufficiently determinate and stable as to constitute 'fair notice' whether particular materials exceed community standards of tolerance. Even under these ideal conditions for its practicability the community standards test would still be objectionable in principle.

To see why this is so, we need to return to J.S. Mill's Harm Principle, according to which the risk of harm to others is the only legitimate ground for legal restraint of an activity.[106] The Harm Principle excludes two competing justifications for restraints on liberty: paternalism (the protection of individuals against harm to which they willingly expose themselves) and moralism (the prohibition of activities with no potential for harm, to self or others, on the ground that they are immoral). The *Hicklin* test, with its reliance on the 'tendency to deprave and corrupt', was openly moralistic; as long as the test was in force, pornographic materials were condemned on the ground either that they were themselves indecent or that they encouraged indecent acts.[107] In the *Hicklin* case itself, Chief Justice Cockburn found the objectionable portions of the pamphlet at issue to consist of 'a series of paragraphs, one following upon another, each involving some impure practices, some of them of the most filthy and disgusting and unnatural description it is possible to imagine'.[108] This language of impurity and contamination permeates the case law during the *Hicklin* era, right through to the 1950s.[109] The demise of the test was occasioned in no small part by a growing disquiet with legal moralism as a justification for restraints on liberty,[110] accompanied by the conviction that a firmer basis needed to be found for the legal regulation of pornography. Following the introduction of the statutory definition of obscenity, the courts sought this basis in contemporary community standards. However, as long as these were interpreted as standards of decency, the rationale for regulating erotic materials remained moralistic.[111] Even under the *Hicklin* test courts recognized that public opinion about decency would be subject to change over time.[112] Since judges could not be expected to ascertain an eternal Platonic truth (if there is one) about the boundary between decency and indecency, reliance on contemporary community standards was inevitable. The community standards test therefore could not move obscenity adjudication out of the shadow of moralism until the standards in question were reinterpreted as providing a measure not of decency but of tolerance.

At least in principle, there is a clear difference between a standard of tolerance and a standard of taste or morality, since people may regard certain activities as indecent, and therefore prefer not to engage in them, while being prepared to tolerate their practice by others. Recall Chief Justice Dickson's definitive statement of the distinction: 'What matters is not what Canadians think is right for themselves to see. What matters is what Canadians would not abide other Canadians seeing ...'[113] This shift of focus from taste to tolerance is supposed to provide us with a more defensible justification for restricting liberties – to manufacture, distribute, and (by implication) consume erotic materials. The rationale can no longer be that these materials are indecent or scurrilous or otherwise immoral. Nor, since community intolerance is an unreliable indicator of genuine harm, can it be that they are harmful. So what is it? Stripped to its essentials, this is what the majority is saying to a minority with different tastes: 'You will not be permitted to exercise your taste, not because its exercise would be harmful to society, nor even because it would be immoral, but simply because we are not prepared to tolerate it. It *will* not be tolerated because we think it *should* not be tolerated.'

Reliance on the majority's limits of tolerance as a principle of restraint has been frequently, and justly, criticized either as objectionably conservative or as institutionalizing a (sexist or heterosexist) bias.[114] But these are mere symptoms of the fundamental problem. When Mill wrote the essay *On Liberty*, the danger against which he thought individual liberty principally needed protection was what he called the 'tyranny of the majority', which included 'the tyranny of the prevailing opinion and feeling ... [and] the tendency of society to impose ... its own ideas and practices as rules of conduct on those who dissent from them ... and compel all characters to fashion themselves upon the model of its own'.[115] The Harm Principle was Mill's proposed line of defence against this tyranny: unless it is possible to demonstrate a significant risk of social harm, there is no case for a restraint of liberty. The Harm Principle of course forbids moralism as a ground of restraint, whether in the form of the *Hicklin* test or a community standard of decency. But in protecting individuals against the tyranny of the majority it also forbids restraint on the basis of a community standard of tolerance.

The rationale behind the Harm Principle is obvious: since harm is (by definition) an evil, no one has an unqualified liberty-right to inflict it on others. The fact that some activity is socially harmful is therefore easily recognizable as a reason (in principle) for its legal regulation. There is no similar rationale for the community standards test: the fact that the majority is not prepared to tolerate some activity is, taken by itself, no reason at all for restricting it. Indeed, it appears to confuse the existence of intolerance with the justification for it; whereas harm can count as a reason for refusing to tolerate an activity, the mere fact that it is not tolerated cannot. The task of the courts is to determine what forms of expression must be tolerated, since they are protected by section 2(b) of the Charter. This important question cannot be settled by ascertaining what forms of expression are in fact tolerated. The idea that important individual rights can be circumscribed by the tolerance level of the majority is misconceived from the outset, since one of the principal functions of rights (and of their constitutional entrenchment in the Charter) is to safeguard minorities against the majoritarian decision making represented by the legislature.

Another way of putting this is to say that, if community intolerance is a poor epistemic indicator of genuine harm, reliance on community standards to identify the realm of the obscene effectively recognizes moral distress as a kind of harm.[116] In order to determine whether particular erotic materials will be legally tolerated, courts must try to determine whether most Canadians would morally tolerate them. But in that case the issue is decided by the level of moral distress experienced by some (the majority) at the very idea that others (the minority) are consuming these materials. This is not enough, by itself, to show that this result was reached through an application of the Harm Principle. But that step is easy to supply as well. According to the *Butler* court the rationale for regulating pornography in Canada has always been harm-based: it is the conception of the harm done by pornography which has shifted over time. Whereas this was once conceptualized as moral harm done to the male consumer, the locus of the harm has now been transferred to other groups considered to be vulnerable (especially women and children). What has all this to do with the appeal to community standards? It might be thought one thing to regulate pornography on a harm-based ground and quite another to do so by reference to the community's alleged standards of tolerance. The former fits unproblematically within the Harm Principle as traditionally conceived (that is, without expanding it by recognizing moral distress as a kind of harm) while the latter does not. But the court did not make this distinction; instead, it relied on community standards of tolerance as the measure of harm.[117] In doing so, the court maintained an official allegiance to the Harm Principle, but only at the cost of treating communal moral distress – grounded in a shared standard of tolerance – as a harm. Violent pornography counts as harmful, not because it can be causally linked to sexual violence (the court recognized that the evidence on this question is inconclusive), but because most people think it is so linked and are therefore not willing to tolerate its consumption by anyone (else).

Just as the inadequacies of moralism gradually became apparent to an earlier generation of judges and scholars, so questions are now being raised about tolerance as a basis for restraint. These questions achieved some degree of judicial recognition in the Supreme Court's decision in *Towne Cinema*, where for the first time social harm was acknowledged as a relevant factor. Recall the disagreement in that decision between Chief Justice Dickson and Justice Wilson over whether harm was to be determined independently of the community standards test. Ultimately, in *Butler*, the court favoured Wilson's opinion (that community standards are the appropriate measure of social harm) over Dickson's (that the two factors could diverge, so that independent evidence of harm would be appropriate). Some commentators on the *Butler* decision have hailed it as the final step in the evolution from moralism to a harm test for obscenity.[118] It is certainly true that the *Butler* court devoted considerable attention to the harm question, at least so far as it concerned depictions of sex which are 'degrading or dehumanizing'.[119] However, it also subsumed that question under the community standards test.[120] The result is an unstable union of two quite different grounds for the legal regulation of pornography: harm and tolerance. While the former is the only legitimate ground, the *Butler* decision suggests that the harm test is to be applied by means of the community standards test, on the assumption that community standards of tolerance are based, at least in part, on the perception of harm. It is difficult to think of any other legal context in which the fact that some activity is harmful is taken to be established by people's belief that it is.[121] If, for instance, the state wishes to justify restrictions on smoking in public places, then it must provide evidence that exposure to secondhand smoke is a health hazard, not just that people think it is.[122] Only in the case of pornography is mere opinion considered to be sufficient to establish the fact of the matter.

Whether pornography has the potential for social harm (and, if so, what kind of harm) is a complex empirical question for whose resolution it is appropriate to consult the best available social-scientific evidence. It is not a question to be answered by a public opinion survey. If the evolution of judicial and academic thinking about obscenity has brought us now to the point of accepting the harm test as dispositive, then we should apply that test directly by requiring evidence of the harm caused by pornography. Doing so will render the community standards test redundant and obsolete. The test was devised in the first place to fill the legislative vacuum left by the vague and unhelpful 'undue exploitation' definition of obscenity. Over the course of some forty years, it has gradually evolved from its roots in moralism to an unreliable surrogate for a harm test. It cannot now carry judicial thinking about obscenity any farther along the road to an open endorsement of the Harm Principle; indeed, it is an obstacle to further progress in that direction. The *Butler* court inherited the community standards test which had already been shown (in *Towne Cinema*) to have at best an uneasy relationship with the harm test. The court had the opportunity to steer the course of obscenity adjudication in a new direction by repudiating community standards altogether, and it did not have the courage to do so. Now it is time to decide, as a matter of political morality, what can justify restraints on the freedom to circulate erotic materials. If it is the majority's level of tolerance, then the community standards test still has a role to play. But if it is the risk of harm, then the test has outlived its usefulness.

4.4 Conclusion

The definition of obscenity in Canada is a judicial construct filling a legislative vacuum. Having been given nothing more specific to work with than the unhelpfully vague phrase 'the undue exploitation of sex', the courts have attempted to operationalize it by adopting the community standards test as a reference point. Doing so has raised a number of legal problems: In a country as diverse as Canada, how can we speak of a national community? If there is such a community, how do we determine what its level of tolerance is for (some particular kind of) erotic materials? In the absence of a national consensus, is the community standard decided by the majority? If so, how are triers of fact to determine what the majority view is when they are given no empirical evidence on the question? How do we avoid having judges substitute their own personal tolerance level for that of the community? If this is what judges are doing, does the obscenity law not fail to provide potential offenders with 'fair notice' of the legal status of their actions?

Although these practical difficulties attending the application of the obscenity law are serious enough, there is also a deeper and more philosophical issue raised by the community standards test. Criminalizing conduct solely on the ground that the majority are not prepared to tolerate it is inconsistent with Mill's Harm Principle and with the rejection in liberal societies of legal moralism. In its *Butler* decision and thereafter, the Supreme Court has insisted that restrictions on expressive freedom must be harm-based rather than morality-based. Since there is no good reason to think that the community's level of tolerance accurately tracks harmfulness, there remains a contradiction at the heart of Canadian obscenity adjudication.

Chapter 5

In Harm's Way?

In two landmark decisions in the early 1990s the Supreme Court of Canada gave the legal landscape concerning hate speech and pornography a structure which remains intact today.[1] Unsurprisingly, given their subject matter, both decisions were highly controversial. In *Keegstra* (1990) the court was divided against itself by the narrowest of margins, with lengthy and thorough arguments on both sides of the question. In *Butler* (1992), by contrast, the justices achieved unanimity, but the absence of internal dissent was amply compensated by vigorous external criticism.[2] In the decade or so that has elapsed since these decisions no social consensus on either of these limits to expression has emerged in the country at large. While a substantial majority of Canadians favour anti-hate laws, this support still falls well short of unanimity; meanwhile, public opinion is divided pretty well down the middle on the censorship of pornography.[3]

The court's substantive conclusions may have been divisive, but its decisions did achieve a different sort of consensus, one not of outcome but of methodology. As we noted in chapter three, the application of the *Oakes* tests has meant that limits to expressive freedom are subjected to a cost-benefit analysis, the benefit side consisting primarily in the prevention of whatever kinds of harm are thought to flow from the expression in question. It is therefore a clear implication of the court's developed approach to section 1 of the Charter that in order to justify an infringement of the section 2(b) right of free expression, it must be possible to demonstrate a link with some recognizable type of harm.[4] In *Keegstra* the majority and minority alike pointed to the different kinds of harm to target groups which can result from the dissemination of hate propaganda.[5] In *Butler* the court continued the same theme by insisting that the case for legal regulation of pornography must be made out not as the enforcement of morals but as the prevention of harm (though, of course, it chose to filter harm through the lens of community standards).[6] Through the 1990s the court continued to employ this harm-based approach when considering limits to other forms of expression.[7] In doing so it displayed its allegiance, at least where expression is concerned, to J.S. Mill's Harm Principle, which tells us that the sole justification for restricting freedom is the prevention of harm to others.[8]

This convergence on the centrality of the harm issue has, however, left a number of important questions unanswered. What kinds of effects on others count as harms to them? What kinds of harm might be caused by, or otherwise associated with, hate propaganda or pornography? Who are the victims? What kinds of evidence do we have of these harms (and how reliable is it)? Thus far we have reached only a negative result with respect to these questions, by excluding moral harm and moral distress as legitimate harms on either normative or descriptive grounds.[9] The time has now come to consider the real harm issues.

5.1 Pornography and Sexual Violence

One category of harm clearly has impeccable credentials, both normative and descriptive: being the victim of sexual violence. For clarity, sexual violence will here be understood to include any sexual treatment by a man of an adult woman which is characterized by the use of force, threat, or deception.[10] The clearest case, though not the only one, is rape. The link with sexual violence has always been at the heart of the feminist critique of pornography. To the extent that pornography can be associated with violence of this sort – to the extent that such violence can be shown to be one of its effects – then it will have been demonstrated not to be harmless.

Pornography is both a product – a form of expression consisting of words or pictures on the page or screen – and a system of production. When we ask whether pornography is a cause of sexual violence against women we can be thinking either of the product or of the process. If it is the product we have in mind then our attention will be focused on the mediation of the male consumer: it is because *he* buys, reads, rents, views, is aroused by the book, magazine, video, website that *she* – who is not a consenting party to the transaction – subsequently gets hurt. I shall call these effects *third-party harms*. On the other hand, if we are thinking about the means by which (heterosexual, male-oriented) pornography is made, then a different class of potential victims comes into view: the women involved as models and performers (as well as writers, producers, directors, etc.) in the pornography industry. To differentiate these effects, I shall call them *participant harms*. Feminist critics of pornography have based their opposition to it largely on the claim that it causes both third-party and participant harms to women. In fact, the two kinds of claim are often mutually supportive: pornography causes harm to third parties by virtue of the sexual violence it depicts, and it depicts this violence by inflicting it on its participants.[11] Although it is doubtless artificial to separate these two different sites of harm, that is none the less exactly what I propose to do. I will first consider the issue of violence inflicted on the women involved in the making of the pornographic product and then turn attention to the wider issue of harms to women in general flowing from the consumption of that product.

Catharine MacKinnon's recitation of the harms done to women in the pornography industry is characteristically trenchant: 'Women in pornography are bound, battered, tortured, harassed, raped, and sometimes killed; or, in the glossy men's entertainment magazines, "merely" humiliated, molested, objectified, and used.'[12] Just to be absolutely clear: MacKinnon is not saying that women are merely *represented* in pornography as being bound, battered, tortured, and so on; she is saying that these things are really done to them and then photographed for men's pleasure. The issue is not the representation, which might be objectionable on other grounds, but the reality. That it is reality follows for MacKinnon from the very nature of explicit, hard-core pornography, in which the performers do not simulate the activities captured on film but really engage in them.[13]

Before we proceed any farther we need to recognize the fundamental fallacy in this assumption. What makes a representation of sexual activity explicit is that it is shown in full detail with nothing hidden. Hard-core pornography is, by definition, explicit in this way: the performers who are represented as engaged in fellatio, cunnilingus, intercourse, and so on, really are doing it. The lack of simulation is what distinguishes hard-core from soft-core pornography, or pornography from depictions of sexual activity in mainstream films. However, from the fact that the sex depicted in a hard-core video actually happened it does not follow that *everything* depicted in the video actually happened. A female character (or a male one, for that matter) can be depicted as being beaten, tortured, or killed without really being beaten, tortured, or killed. To say this is merely to point out the obvious: even hard-core pornography involves some *acting*, some simulation. When women are depicted in a hard-core video as being brutalized in some way, we should not – must not – conclude from that fact alone that women really were brutalized in the making of the video.

This is not merely a philosophical point about the gap between representation and reality. Rather, it is a reminder that allegations of brutalization require confirming evidence. The need for such evidence is illustrated particularly well by the strongest, and most shocking, of MacKinnon's claims: that women are sometimes killed in the making of pornographic films in order to depict their murders for the sexual gratification of the (male) audience. MacKinnon is here referring to so-called snuff films.[14] However, no snuff film has ever been shown to exist. There is no credible first-person report of one, though many people claim to know people who know other people who have seen one. Snuff films, in short, appear to be an urban legend. There was, of course, once a film called *Snuff*, released in 1976 and advertised as 'the film that could only be made in South America ... where life is cheap!', whose final scene purported to show the actual torture, murder, and mutilation of a young woman. However, *Snuff* fails to satisfy MacKinnon's conditions for a snuff film in two important respects. First, it is not a piece of pornography; instead, it belongs to the genre of 'slasher' film, with little sex depicted, none of it explicitly. Second, and more important, it was a hoax whose brilliant marketing campaign capitalized on rumours circulating of snuff films being smuggled into the United States from South America. Furthermore, it has been known to be a hoax since shortly after its premiere in New York, when the understandably alarmed district attorney interviewed the actress who was purportedly murdered in the film's notorious final scene.[15] It would of course be foolhardy to claim that there has never been a case of a woman's actual murder being recorded for a pornographic film. However, we still await reliable evidence of one.

What, then, of MacKinnon's allegation that women in pornography are bound, battered, tortured, harassed, or raped? Visual pornography comes in many forms and is produced in many countries, including third-world locations where violence or coercion against female models and performers may be subject to less stringent control than in western Europe or North America. Thus again it would be foolhardy – and almost certainly false – to claim that no woman has ever been subjected to this kind of treatment in the production of pornographic photographs, films, or videos. However, if we confine ourselves to MacKinnon's own jurisdiction – the pornography industry in the United States – there is reason to treat her claim with considerable scepticism.

That reason stems from the evolution of the industry over the past three decades or so. The three principal media for visual pornography are the glossy men's magazines (*Playboy, Penthouse, Hustler,* and innumerable others), videos (and now DVDs), and Internet websites. The magazines standardly depict nudity and sexual activity, but little violence.[16] While the market for magazines has remained relatively constant during this period, the market for videos expanded dramatically during the 1980s with the increasing availability of VCRs and has remained robust ever since. In 1997 sales and rentals of adult videos in the United States generated some $4.2 billion, which is larger than the annual revenue of Major League Baseball, the National Football League, or the National Basketball Association.[17] Some 11,000 new adult titles were released in 2000, as opposed to 400 new releases by Hollywood.[18] In every respect pornography has become big business, including its involvement with major corporations such as hotel chains (in-room X-rated movies), telephone companies (phone sex), and cable and satellite companies (adult channels and pay-per-view movies).[19] As it has expanded, the industry has also become more respectable and mainstream. Whatever connections might once have existed to organized crime seem now to have largely disappeared.[20] Adult videos are now stocked by most general-purpose video outlets, while shops devoted exclusively to the product (and other sexual paraphernalia) stand alongside convenience stores and fast-food outlets on urban streets and strip malls across the country. The videos are rented by a wide variety of consumers, white collar and blue collar, old and young, gay and straight, male and female.[21] As one of the people in the industry put it: 'We realized that when there are 700 million porn rentals a year, it can't just be a million perverts renting 700 videos each.'[22]

With respectability has come an informal system of industry self-regulation. The major American producers of video pornography are located in the San Fernando Valley ('silicone valley') in southern California. They range from large enterprises churning out hundreds of titles every year to small mom-and-pop operations. They all abide by an industry code which prohibits, *inter alia,* the use of models or performers under the age of eighteen and the depiction of forced or coerced sex. As a result, the two forms of sexually explicit materials of most concern to law enforcement agencies and government commissions – child pornography and violent pornography – are not produced by the main-

stream American industry.[23] This is not to say that they are not produced anywhere. The (equally mainstream) industry in Europe, largely
concentrated in Scandinavia, Germany, and the Netherlands, is somewhat more adventurous in its inclusion of some themes of violence,
especially BDSM (bondage and discipline, sadomasochism). Even in
these materials, however, it is important to distinguish between consensual and non-consensual scenarios. In most BDSM depictions, the sex,
although violent (involving beatings, torture, etc.), is also mutually consensual, with the 'victim' having control over the direction of the
action.[24] It is therefore arguably different in kind from the depiction of
genuinely non-consensual rape or torture, at least as far as harms to the
participants are concerned.

If mainstream American (and Canadian) pornography does not standardly depict women being bound, battered, tortured, harassed, or
raped then there is little reason to think that it inflicts this treatment on
its models or actors. Furthermore, we have testimony by women who
have pursued careers in the adult video business that it does not.[25]
MacKinnon's own claim to the contrary is based largely on the experience of Linda Marchiano, aka Linda Lovelace of the 1972 Gerard Dami-
ano film *Deep Throat*. Marchiano has published an autobiographical
account in which she claims that her participation in that film was the
result of coercion by her then husband Chuck Traynor.[26] If we accept
that account at face value, then every sex scene in the film is a depiction
of her rape. However, there is no reason to think that Marchiano's experience is typical of the pornography industry even in its early days, let
alone the mainstream industry into which it has since developed. More
recent testimony by women in the industry provides no evidence that
their performances in X-rated videos are forced or coerced.[27]

Even if women are not subjected to violence in the making of pornography, there may still be a causal link between the pornographic product and violence against women in general. Let us turn, then, from
participant to third-party harms. The question whether pornography
causes sexual violence seems to be one for the social sciences to answer.
Unfortunately, as we shall see, such evidence as is available concerning
the effects of pornography tends to be inconclusive; worse, there seems
no likelihood of finding conclusive evidence. But in addition to this evidential problem, there is a prior epistemological one: When we are
seeking evidence of a causal relationship between a form of expression
and violent acts, what exactly are we looking for? What would establish
the existence of such a relationship?

It would be easy to detour here into an extended philosophical discussion of the nature of causation. Fortunately, for our purposes, most of the essential work has been done by others. As a member of the 1986 United States Attorney General's Commission on Pornography, Frederick Schauer was largely responsible for drafting the chapter of the commission's *Final Report* dealing with 'The Question of Harm'.[28] In that chapter the commission, under Schauer's leadership, stated its understanding of what it means to show that pornography is a cause of a particular kind of consequence, such as sexual violence: 'It means that the evidence supports the conclusion that if there were none of the material being tested, then the incidence of the consequences would be less. We live in a world of multiple causation, and to identify a factor as a *cause* in such a world means only that if this factor were eliminated while everything else stayed the same then the problem would at least be lessened.'[29] Schauer subsequently elaborated his analysis of the causal issue in an article published after the release of the commission's *Final Report*.[30] He there offered reasons for rejecting deterministic and attributive conceptions of causation, at least in this context, in favour of a probabilistic conception under which 'a factor (C) is a cause of an effect (E) if, and only if, the presence of C raises the incidence of E for a large population and raises the probability of E for an individual case when all factors other than the presence or absence of C are held constant'.[31] It is important to note (as Schauer does) that under this probabilistic conception a factor will qualify as a cause of an effect as long as it raises the probability of the effect, other factors equal, even though (1) the effect is still unlikely, given the existence of the cause, and (2) other factors are greater causes, by virtue of raising the probability of the effect by a greater margin.

Given this understanding of the question, what is the evidence of a causal relationship between pornography and sexual violence? No brief summary can possibly do justice to the enormous amount of material that has been generated on this issue over the past twenty years or so. However, it will help us to find our way through it if we distinguish four different kinds of evidence which have been advanced in support of such a relationship: (a) *Aggregate studies*, examining possible correlations between the availability of pornography in a society and its incidence of sexual violence; (b) *Retrospective studies*, aiming to determine whether sexual offenders have had more, or different, exposure to pornography than non-offenders; (c) *Laboratory studies*, attempting to determine whether exposure to pornography leads to an increase in aggressive behaviour, or hostile attitudes, toward women; and (d) *Narrative testimony*, consisting of first-person accounts by women of ways in which pornography has been implicated in their victimization.

We will work through each of these categories of evidence in turn, beginning with the aggregate, or macrosocial, evidence. If pornography causes sexual violence then, where all other relevant factors are equal, we should expect a higher rate of consumption of sexually explicit materials to be accompanied by a higher rate of such violence. Whether these factors are correlated in this way could be tested either by a cross-sectional analysis comparing different societies at the same time or by a longitudinal analysis comparing the same society at different times. Whichever approach is favoured, a number of methodological problems must be confronted. Since consumption rates for pornography cannot be measured directly, some appropriate surrogate (such as circulation rates for male-oriented sexually explicit magazines) must be utilized, in which case there must be good reason for thinking that this is an equally reliable indicator of consumption in different places and at different times.[32] As for rates of sexual violence, the usual practice is to focus exclusively on rape. Most of the available statistics, however, concern *reported* rapes, and rape may not be reported at the same rate in different places or at different times. These complications, however, are relatively slight compared to the problem of satisfying the 'all other factors equal' condition, since different societies, and the same society at different times, tend not to match neatly for all relevant variables save one (availability of pornography), so that the influence of other factors can be screened out. For this reason, the most that any aggregate study could generate would be a correlation between the two phenomena in question. It could not, in principle, demonstrate that one is a cause of the other.

Notwithstanding these methodological limitations, some studies of both kinds (cross-sectional and longitudinal) have been undertaken. The most influential cross-sectional studies were done during the 1980s by Larry Baron and Murray Straus, who compared the fifty U.S. states in terms of their rate of rape and the circulation rate within them of eight of the most popular sexually explicit magazines.[33] Baron and Straus reported a fairly strong correlation between the two rates, even when a number of other possible confounding factors were taken into account. However, one specific problem with their methodology is that states constitute relatively diverse (urban, suburban, rural) populations, with the result that state-level aggregate data can conceal important internal variations. When a similar study was undertaken by Cynthia Gentry using more compact and homogeneous units (Standard Metropolitan Statistical Areas) no such correlation could be detected.[34] The presence or absence of a correlation between these variables may therefore be an artifact of the selected unit of analysis.

Rather more data are available from longitudinal studies within single jurisdictions. Since the distribution of sexually explicit materials has increased dramatically in many countries over the past thirty years or so, it would be interesting to compare trends in the rate of sexual offences in the same countries during the same period. Most of this work has been done by Berl Kutchinsky, one of whose studies compared rape rates from 1964 to 1984 in Denmark, Sweden, West Germany, and the United States to rates for non-sexual violent offences.[35] What he found was that in none of the countries did rape increase more than these other violent offences and in three of them (Denmark, Sweden, West Germany) it increased less (in fact, in West Germany it did not increase at all). In the United States, rape and non-sexual assault followed exactly the same pattern. Kutchinsky drew from these results the conclusion that 'the aggregate data on rape and other violent or sexual offences from those countries where pornography has become widely and easily available during the period we have dealt with would seem to exclude, beyond any reasonable doubt, that this availability has had any detrimental effects in the form of increased sexual violence'.[36] Another study found that as the availability of pornography dramatically increased in Japan from 1972 to 1995 the incidence of rape and other forms of sexual assault substantially decreased.[37]

Not all studies have reported similar results. John Court's examination of rates of reported rapes from 1964 to 1974 in a number of jurisdictions led him to advance the hypotheses that these rates increased in places which liberalized their obscenity laws during this period, that this rate of increase exceeded that for non-sexual violent offences, and that similar increases did not occur in jurisdictions which either did not liberalize their laws or actually tightened them.[38] However, the data on which Court relied do not unequivocally support these hypotheses. As Court himself admits, for example, 'there are many instances where no differences [between rape and non-sexual violent offences] can be detected, or where little association exists at all'.[39] If this is the case – that is, if the increase in the rate of rape over a specified period simply paralleled the increase in violent crime in general – then the argument is significantly weakened that it is due to an increase in the availability of pornography.[40] Furthermore, though he wishes to attribute the increase in the rape rate over this period specifically to wider distribution of violent pornography, he presents no data which disaggregate this form of pornography from others (both hard- and soft-core).[41] For these reasons, among others, his analyses and interpretations have been the subject of considerable criticism.[42]

The aggregate evidence of a correlation between the availability of pornography and the incidence of rape is therefore at best inconclusive. (At worst, if we accept Kutchinsky's results, the data tend to disconfirm any such correlation.)[43] But there is another way to come at the question of a causal relationship between pornography and sexual violence. If pornography is a cause of such violence then we should expect sex offenders to have a history of more than normal consumption of sexually explicit materials (especially those featuring themes of sexual violence). We are led, therefore, to the second category of evidence: retrospective studies of men with a history of sex offences.[44] Some people who have worked with such offenders have claimed that pornography plays a crucial causal role in their pattern of aggressive behaviour toward women,[45] and some offenders themselves have implicated pornography in their history of sex crimes.[46] This latter testimony clearly must be interpreted with some caution, since offenders might be tempted to minimize their own responsibility for their violent behaviour by claiming that 'pornography made me do it'. In any case, it needs to be supplemented by more scientific studies of patterns of pornography use among populations of offenders. These studies also must be interpreted with care, since they may use different categories of sex offenders (rapists, child molesters, incarcerated, non-incarcerated, etc.) and compare them with different control groups (non-offenders, non-sexual offenders, etc.). None the less, some generalizations appear to be possible. The early studies relied on by the 1970 Commission on Obscenity and Pornography tended to show that sex offenders had a history of no greater exposure to sexually explicit materials than non-offenders and that they did not differ from other adults in their responses to such materials.[47] The additional research available to the 1986 Attorney General's Commission showed somewhat more mixed results, but still no clear patterns of abnormal or distinctive consumption of pornography by sex offenders.[48] Most subsequent studies have confirmed this result.[49] The available evidence seems therefore to suggest that, at least where consumption of pornography is concerned, sex offenders are not significantly different from average adult males.[50]

Besides their inconclusive, or even negative, results, these first two categories of evidence share a further common limitation: since the studies
test only for a correlation between pornography consumption and sexual violence, they are incapable of establishing a causal relationship.
Even if such a correlation were discovered, it would on its own be consistent with any of three causal hypotheses: (1) the pornography consumption causes the violence, (2) the violence causes the pornography
consumption, or (3) both are caused by some third factor. Much of the
motivation for undertaking the third kind of scientific study – laboratory experiments – has derived from the desire to impose controlled
experimental conditions capable of yielding genuine causal results. By
far the greatest quantity of social-scientific evidence concerning links
between pornography and sexual violence falls into this experimental
category. Work in this area began to develop momentum in the late
1970s, reached its peak in the 1980s, and has tailed off since then. It
generated the scientific (as opposed to narrative) evidence relied on
most heavily by feminist critics of pornography (and advocates of its
legal regulation).[51]

Both the sheer volume of published laboratory studies and the controversies over their interpretation render any summary of their results
particularly hazardous. Although the studies vary in their design,
they usually incorporate the following elements. Subjects are randomly
assigned to one of two groups: experimental and control. Members of
both groups are initially 'angered' by a confederate of the researcher
and their levels of aggression measured. The experimental group is
then exposed to some sexually explicit materials, which may or may not
include scenes of sexual violence, while the control group instead views
a 'neutral' source (such as a wildlife film). Both groups are subsequently
given the opportunity for aggression against the confederate (e.g., by
administering phony electric shocks). The level of aggressive behaviour
by members of the experimental group is then compared both with
their initial levels of aggression and with the behaviour of the control
group. Alternatively, the results of an initial test administered to both
groups to determine levels of aggressive or antisocial attitudes toward
women may be compared with results for both groups after exposure
to the differential stimuli. Whatever the particular methodology
employed, the aim is to determine whether exposure to pornography
increases the subjects' level of either aggressive behaviour or aggressive
attitudes.

In summarizing the results of these studies it is important to distinguish two different varieties of sexually explicit materials: violent and non-violent. While the former contains scenes of sexual violence or coercion against women (most commonly rape), the latter is a mixed bag, consisting basically of 'anything else', ranging from mutually consenting 'vanilla' sex to scenes involving subordination or degradation, as long as no actual force was employed or threatened. The distinction is important because the experimental results have tended to be different for the two categories of materials. There is a fairly strong consensus among the researchers that exposure to violent pornography increases subjects' aggressive behaviour and/or attitudes.[52] No such consensus exists for non-violent pornography. Some researchers have found no negative effects for these materials,[53] while others have claimed that long-term exposure may induce antisocial attitudes toward women.[54] The differences in these results may be due in part to the use of different types of 'non-violent' pornography (e.g., the presence or absence of scenes of subordination or degradation).[55]

The evidence for a causal linkage with aggression, at least under laboratory conditions, is obviously strongest for sexually explicit materials featuring scenes of violence against women. It is this evidence, for instance, that was accepted by the 1986 Attorney General's Commission in support of its conclusion that 'there is a causal relationship between exposure to sexually violent materials and an increase in aggressive behavior directed towards women'.[56] However, there is a problem with the interpretation of these results.[57] The materials in question have three distinct features: (1) they depict violence, (2) the violence they depict is distinctively sexual in nature (usually involving rape), and (3) the depiction is explicit. It is therefore possible that one or more of these features is causally inert – that is, that similar results will be found in its absence. This appears to be the case for the explicitness factor. A depiction is explicit if it does not shrink from showing or describing the full details of the scene in question, such as penetration. Studies appear to show that depictions of sexual violence which are similar in all other respects, save for being non-explicit, have comparable effects on aggressive behaviour and/or attitudes.[58] Likewise, the fact that it is violence that is depicted (whether explicitly or not) is also causally irrelevant (or, more accurately, insufficiently specific). Depictions of non-sexual violence (prize fights, gang wars, alien invasions, etc.) also appear to have no discernible effect on male attitudes or behaviour toward women.[59] What appears to be essential to the effect is the sexual nature of the violence, combined with the implicit endorsement that comes with its presentation as a source of erotic entertainment.[60] The strongest laboratory effects have been found for sexualized (or eroticized) depictions of sexual violence (again, whether explicit or not). These effects have been associated with violent pornography, which tends to present the rape victim's plight as a source of arousal, but also with mainstream non-pornographic movies.[61]

A more general question about all of the laboratory studies concerns the significance of their results. After all, what we want to know is whether pornography (of any variety) causes sexual violence in the real world, not under the artificial conditions of the laboratory. Commentators have identified a number of problems involved in extrapolating the laboratory results to real-world settings.[62] One obvious limitation is that, for ethical reasons, researchers cannot actually test directly for the dependent variable – namely, sexual violence against women. They can employ a measure of aggressiveness, such as willingness to administer electric shocks to a female confederate, but the 'violence' then is not specifically sexual.[63] Alternatively, they can test for surrogates of sexual aggressiveness, such as acceptance of 'rape myths', but these are attitudes as opposed to actions based on them.[64] There is also a further issue concerning the durability of the observed effects. Most of the laboratory studies measure only short-term increases in levels of aggression, leaving open the question whether repeated exposure to violent pornography has more lasting consequences.[65]

The various limitations of these studies, which are integral to the laboratory setting, are not enough to invalidate their findings or to deprive them of all relevance or interest. It is easy – too easy – to trap the social scientist in a dilemma: either a study is carried out in a real setting (as in the first two kinds of evidence), in which case it cannot confirm a causal relationship, or it is done in an artificial one, in which case it can tell us nothing about attitudes and behaviour under realistic conditions. This is far too quick a way with the only scientific evidence we have on the possible causal linkages between pornography and sexual violence. However, it does go some way toward explaining the reluctance of some official bodies to rely on the evidence as the basis for social policy. As noted earlier (in chapter 3), the Supreme Court in the *Butler* case found the social science evidence as a whole to be 'inconclusive'.[66] In this it was echoing similar reservations expressed in the 1985 Canadian report by the Special Committee on Pornography and Prostitution.[67] The 1986 U.S. Attorney General's Commission is rather the exception to the rule in this respect, since it was willing to extrapolate from the laboratory studies, especially those concerning violent pornography, to the causes of sexual violence in the real world:

> Since the clinical and experimental evidence supports the conclusion that there is a causal relationship between exposure to sexually violent materials and an increase in aggressive behavior directed towards women, and since we believe that an increase in aggressive behavior towards women will in a population increase the incidence of sexual violence in that population, we have reached the conclusion, unanimously and confidently, that the available evidence strongly supports the hypothesis that substantial exposure to sexually violent materials as described here bears a causal relationship to antisocial acts of sexual violence and, for some subgroups, possibly to unlawful acts of sexual violence.[68]

The commission made it clear that this conclusion was based not only on the experimental evidence but also on supporting assumptions, especially the assumption that exposure to favourable depictions of sexual violence – depictions which are capable of stimulating aggressive attitudes and behaviour toward women in the laboratory – will tend to increase the incidence of such violence. Here we are clearly in the domain of what the Supreme Court has called 'common sense' or 'logic', as opposed to scientific proof.[69] However, to disparage the commission's conclusion on that ground would effectively rule out the use of social-scientific evidence to determine the harmful effects of pornography. Furthermore, as Frederick Schauer has rightly emphasized, the conclusion, properly understood, is actually quite modest.[70] Given its own conception of causality, all that the commission is entitled to claim is that, when all other factors are held constant, we should expect a somewhat greater incidence of sexual violence against women when violent pornography is available than when it is not. This claim is quite compatible with thinking that (1) exposure to this material will seldom lead to sexually violent behaviour, and (2) violent pornography is a relatively minor factor in the incidence of sexual violence, since other social conditions will have a much greater effect on it.[71]

The mixed results emerging from the social-scientific studies, and the controversies concerning their significance, have led even some anti-pornography feminists to advocate a shift away from reliance on scientific evidence toward 'listening to women' when they relate their experiences with male consumers of pornography.[72] This narrative evidence has long served as one of the main foundations of the activities of anti-pornography activists such as Andrea Dworkin and Catharine MacKinnon. Both because of research studies focusing on this issue and, especially, because of opportunities presented by various public hearings, we now have a considerable amount of testimony by women (and some by men as well) concerning the impact of pornography on their lives.[73] While the testimony is impossible to summarize briefly, certain themes run persistently through it: women who were forced by their husbands or lovers to view pornography against their will; women who were forced to perform sex acts which their husbands or lovers had seen in pornographic materials; women who were raped or otherwise sexually abused by men aroused by pornography; and, most disturbingly of all, women who were victims of sexual assaults which appear to have been choreographed to imitate specific pornographic scenarios. By contrast with the various forms of scientific evidence, it is easy to impugn this first-person testimony as 'merely anecdotal'. It is true that the narrative evidence, because of its individual nature, cannot demonstrate a causal relationship between the availability of pornography and the overall incidence of sexual violence. But it can point to the role pornography appears to have played in particular instances of such violence.

However, we do need to exercise caution in drawing causal conclusions from the testimony. In all of these cases pornography is implicated, in one way or another, in violence inflicted on women by men. However, according to the conception of causation with which we are working, the pornography can qualify as a cause of that violence only if its consumption by the men in question increased the probability that the violence would occur. It might seem obvious in these cases that this condition is satisfied. If, to use but one example, a man forces his lover to perform fellatio on him because he has been turned on by watching this being done in a pornographic video, then surely the probability of the coercion was raised by his viewing of the video. In fact, we would naturally go farther than this and say that, but for his viewing of the video, she would not have been coerced in this way at all. However, the qualifier 'in this way' is important. Suppose it is true that had he not seen the oral sex in the video, he would not have forced his lover to do it to him. Then the specific injury 'being forced to perform fellatio on him' is indeed a result of his viewing the video. But suppose it is also true that had he not seen that video, or indeed any piece of pornography, he would still have forced her to perform sex acts to which she objected. In that case, the more general injury 'being forced to perform sex acts on/ with him' is not a result of his viewing the video: it would have occurred anyway with just as high a probability. The general point is this: from the fact that a woman suffers a particular injury in which pornography is implicated we cannot conclude that she would not have been injured in the absence of pornography; she might just have been injured in a different way. In order to qualify as a cause of sexual violence in a particular case, pornography must increase the likelihood of such violence. It does not do this whenever (some form of) violence would have occurred anyway. Nor is this possibility merely a fanciful and far-fetched thought experiment. The kind of men likely to sexually abuse women after having consumed pornography may be just the kind of men likely to abuse women (in one way or another) even without this stimulus. In that case, it makes more sense to identify the abusive male, rather than the pornography, as the cause of the violence.[74]

There are doubtless some cases, perhaps many, in which women would have been less likely to suffer injury, or injury of comparable seriousness, in the absence of the pornographic stimulus. In those cases, we do indeed have evidence that pornography can cause sexual violence. However, this conclusion needs to be put into perspective. It is difficult to imagine any genre of literature or film for which similar evidence could not be collected, were one to set out to solicit it at public hearings. How many copycat murders have been inspired by scenarios in mainstream films or mystery novels (or by media reports of real killings, for that matter)?[75] How many people have been involuntarily subjected to readings from the Bible or suffered violence inspired by its messages?[76] Pornography is not benign and can be used by nasty people for nasty ends. But so can most words or images.

5.2 Pornography and Inequality

In the previous section we found little evidence to suggest that women in the pornography industry are subjected to violence. However, the claim that their participation is coerced often takes a different form, citing not physical force or threats but such circumstances as economic hardship, drug use, or an abusive background as the factors explaining women's decisions to perform in hard-core videos. The general form of this critique is that the pornography industry exploits its female performers by taking advantage of their inequality. Catharine MacKinnon again: 'Empirically, all pornography is made under conditions of inequality based on sex, overwhelmingly by poor, desperate, homeless, pimped women who were sexually abused as children. The industry's profits exploit, and are an incentive to maintain, these conditions. These conditions constrain choice rather than offering freedom. They are *what it takes* to make women do what is in even the pornography that shows no overt violence.'[77]

Before working through MacKinnon's various claims, it is important to note that no broad social-scientific study has ever been undertaken of the backgrounds and working conditions of models or performers (male or female) in the pornography industry. The evidence MacKinnon adduces in support of her claims is therefore inevitably particular and narrative, as is the evidence against them. This is, once again, not to disparage it, but merely to point out how limited it is when we are talking about literally thousands of men and women. In the absence of a more systematic study, we simply do not have very reliable information about the participants in the industry and their treatment by it.

With this evidential limitation in mind, we can begin to work backwards through MacKinnon's list of 'conditions of inequality based on sex'. There is certainly evidence that some women in the pornography industry have come from family backgrounds featuring physical and/or sexual abuse. But there is equally evidence that many, probably most, have not. Many performers in hard-core videos seem to have emerged from remarkably normal childhoods and family circumstances.[78] We must keep in mind here that any industry producing more than 10,000 new titles every year will need to recruit new performers continuously (especially since the demand for youth will limit the average length of a career in the business). Recruitment, however, does not seem to be a problem. Once they reach the minimum legal age of eighteen, a surprisingly large number of young women appear to be eager to get into this line of work, whether motivated by the financial rewards, the degree of freedom involved, a taste for sexual variety, a streak of exhibitionism, or the desire for fame. Given the very large numbers of women making X-rated videos, we should expect considerable diversity in their backgrounds, circumstances, and motives. And diversity is what we appear to get. Indeed, the closer one looks at women in pornography – or, more generally, at women in sex work – the more they come to resemble women in general.[79] Certainly the suggestion, also advanced by MacKinnon, that they are being pimped (presumably by someone, male or female, with undue power over them) does not seem accurate. Whatever one may think of the decisions by women to get into the industry, they are the ones making them.[80]

Are they then poor, desperate, or homeless? Typically neither desperate nor homeless, but the money is definitely one of the principal incentives. Women making hard-core videos typically earn about $800 (U.S.) per day of filming.[81] Assuming that steady work is available (which is very likely, given the volume of product being generated), the financial rewards compare very favourably with other forms of unskilled labour available to the average, not highly educated, eighteen-year-old (by comparison, workers in the fast-food business seldom earn more than the minimum wage). Working conditions seem to be pretty much what you would expect in an unregulated industry hiring workers on a casual basis.[82] The daily rate includes no royalties or residuals for the videos produced and no benefits. Furthermore, while performers do reliably get paid for their work, written contracts are rarely involved. Probably the closest analogue to this kind of sex work is found in casual domestic labour: the hiring of (mostly female) babysitters, nannies, or cleaners. There is, however, one important disanalogy. Female performers in X-rated videos typically earn twice as much as men, are treated with more respect, and enjoy a greater veto power over the partners with whom they will work.[83] This differential is unsurprising, given that the women are, after all, the main attraction for the heterosexual male audience. However, the men who make it in the business tend to enjoy longer careers than the women, since their primary function is to serve – as one of the top (female) executives in the business aptly put it – as 'props'.

The current structure of the pornography industry certainly lends itself to economic exploitation of its workers, though most of the women involved seem to be reasonably satisfied with their treatment by producers (the vast majority of whom are men). However, the allegation of economic exploitation, which has been raised against the industry by MacKinnon and others,[84] cuts deeper than the issue of working conditions. Indeed, paradoxically, it is because those conditions, especially the financial rewards, are as tempting as they are that the industry is alleged to exploit the unequal condition of women. In a more egalitarian society, the argument goes, where women had more and better employment opportunities, no one would choose to do this kind of work. The industry therefore takes advantage of the absence of these other opportunities; this is the way it exploits women in a patriarchal, capitalist society. This critique is open to (at least partial) refutation by finding examples of women who elected a career in pornography over other equally remunerative and fulfilling options.[85] It is also arguable, indeed highly plausible, that even under conditions of sex equality there would still be demand for the pornographic product; it takes a particularly romantic view of sex to suppose otherwise. (Indeed, there might be even more demand than now, if equality led women to feel freer to shop for erotic stimuli.) Where there is demand, then, in a market economy there will be supply, which will require offering women (and men) employment opportunities in the pornography industry competitive with whatever other options are open to them. This is likely to improve working conditions in pornography, which would certainly be a good thing; but any such improvement would also have the perverse effect (from the standpoint of some feminists) of making careers in the industry all the more attractive. If the egalitarian tide rises it seems likely to carry the pornography boat along with it.

There is also something a little odd about the economic exploitation argument. It seems to run as follows: it is a regrettable fact that women do not have available to them the full range of employment opportunities they deserve; therefore we should deprive them of this one, however remunerative it might be. If things are already bad for women, why would eliminating this option make them better rather than worse off? What is particularly objectionable about offering women the opportunity to make pornography? Bernard Williams has suggested that 'a particular kind of moralism is involved in pressing the charge of exploitation with respect to participation particularly in pornography, when that participation is by ordinary criteria voluntary. It may be that much employment which by those standards is voluntary can justly be seen as exploitation, but there is no particular reason to pick out employment in the production of pornography.'[86] Anti-pornography feminists such as MacKinnon must think, on the contrary, that there is such a reason – one which explains why this kind of work is different from other employment sectors which might also be thought to exploit the disadvantaged circumstances of the women who work in them. Williams is, I think, right to suspect that the reason is moralistic: posing for nude pictorials or performing for X-rated videos is thought by MacKinnon to be degrading. Since no one would voluntarily choose to be degraded, the women who do this kind of work *must* be coerced or exploited. Understood in this way, it is possible to see how the exploitation argument might continue to be maintained even in the absence of confirming empirical evidence of bad treatment of models and actors. The argument has ceased to be vulnerable to empirical disconfirmation, since it has ceased to be an empirical thesis about the way in which women are treated in the industry. However voluntary their participation might be, however attractive they may find the work, however ideal working conditions might become – the fact remains that they are being degraded, or are degrading themselves, by doing this kind of work. But if the argument takes this form then it is appealing to a kind of moral harm which we have already found reason to reject.[87]

Feminist concerns about inequality do not focus solely on the working conditions of women in the pornography industry. We have already observed that mainstream, non-violent, male-oriented pornography portrays women as subordinate to men's sexual needs and desires and that this is part of its appeal to its male consumers.[88] In that case, feminists have argued, by eroticizing women's inequality – by making it a source of sexual arousal for men – pornography contributes to reinforcing and perpetuating women's subordinate social status. In MacKinnon's words, pornography 'eroticizes hierarchy, it sexualizes inequality. It makes dominance and submission into sex ... It institutionalizes the sexuality of male supremacy, fusing the erotization of dominance and submission with the social construction of male and female.'[89]

At least in its simplest form, this is once again a causal hypothesis: pornography tends to maintain and reinforce inequality. However, it is even less susceptible to scientific confirmation (or disconfirmation) than the analogous hypothesis about sexual violence explored in the previous section. We cannot here identify a select body of offenders to test for abnormal consumption of pornography, and it is difficult to imagine a controlled laboratory experiment designed to determine whether exposure to pornography increases the discriminatory treatment of women. If gender inequality can be measured on some reliable scale then we could, in principle, carry out aggregate studies comparing its level in different countries (or in the same country at different times) with rates of distribution for sexually explicit materials. However, the prospects that such studies will support the causal claim seem slim. Intuitively and unscientifically, it appears that (1) women enjoy a greater degree of equality in liberal societies in which pornography is also widely available,[90] and (2) women enjoy a greater degree of equality in those societies now than they did before obscenity laws were liberalized. It is therefore far from clear that the availability of pornography makes women less equal than they would otherwise have been, holding all other factors constant, or that its impact on women's social status is greater than that of many mainstream media, including advertising and mass-circulation women's magazines.

5.3 Defaming, Degrading, Subordinating, Silencing

All of the possible harms we have canvassed to this point share the important feature of being instrumental. Something is instrumentally harmful when it satisfies two conditions: (1) it is a cause of some state or condition which (2) is intrinsically harmful. Our problem so far has been to find a kind of harm associated with pornography which meets both conditions. Moral harm and moral distress may satisfy the first condition but they fail the second, since neither qualifies as an intrinsic harm within the meaning of the Harm Principle. Sexual violence and inequality satisfy the second condition, but it is difficult to find convincing evidence of the causal link with pornography (except perhaps for some types of pornography with violent content). But not all the harms attributed to pornography have this instrumental character. For anti-pornography feminists, it has been tempting to bypass the troublesome evidential problems by finding some respect in which pornography – or at least some pornography – is intrinsically harmful to women. We will examine some such lines of analysis in this section: claims that pornography defames, degrades, subordinates, or silences women.

The defamation point has been made forcefully by Helen Longino:

> What is wrong with pornography, then, is its degrading and dehumanizing portrayal of women (and *not* its sexual content). Pornography, by its very nature, requires that women be subordinate to men and mere instruments for the fulfillment of male fantasies. To accomplish this, pornography must lie. Pornography lies when it says that our sexual life is or ought to be subordinate to the service of men, that our pleasure consists in pleasing men and not ourselves, that we are depraved, that we are fit subjects for rape, bondage, torture, and murder. Pornography lies explicitly about women's sexuality, and through such lies fosters more lies about our humanity, our dignity, and our personhood ... Each work of pornography is on its own libelous and defamatory, yet gains power through being reinforced by every other pornographic work.[91]

Longino's analysis locates the harm of pornography not in what it does (or causes) but in what it says. The same line of thought – that pornography's content defames women – can be found in Catharine MacKinnon: 'Construed as defamation in the conventional sense, pornography says that women are a lower form of human life defined by their availability for sexual use.'[92] However, MacKinnon ultimately rejects the defamation approach to identifying pornography's harm, and her reasons for doing so are instructive. The theory of group defamation, she argues, is not a good fit for the kind of harm pornography does to women. For one thing, its exclusive focus on content or representation – on what pornography says – invokes constitutional protections of free expression and invites courts to strike down restrictions on pornography as failing the test of content-neutrality. Construing pornography as defamatory also invites the defence of truth: it cannot defame women if it does not lie about them.

Any attempt to determine whether pornography presents a distorted picture of women's sexuality quickly runs up against a problem which we have thus far sidestepped: the sheer variety of the pornographic product. Pornography, both verbal and visual, comes in a bewildering variety of forms and genres. Some, such as gay male porn, have little to say (at least on the surface) about women at all. Others, such as erotic stories and some lesbian pictorials and videos, are both created by and marketed to women. There is a small but robust sector of the industry, largely run by women, which produces 'woman-friendly' visual materials aimed at a couples market. And then there is the mainstream product: magazines, videos, websites, and so on, which are largely produced by men and target a heterosexual male audience. When feminists accuse pornography of lying about women's sexuality, it is usually this last (and largest) category which they have in mind. So we will henceforth focus on it.

Standard, male-oriented pornography typically represents women as being sexually available for men and frequently also as sexually subordinate to them. (As we have noted earlier, it does not typically portray women as 'fit subjects for rape, bondage, torture, and murder'.) If this is taken to be a representation of the totality of women's sexuality then it is fair to call it a lie. But pornography also typically depicts women as initiating, welcoming, and enjoying casual, recreational sex outside the constraints of either marriage or procreation. Since mainstream pornography exists primarily for the purpose of fulfilling (heterosexual) male fantasies, it is scarcely surprising that it fails to present an ideally fully rounded picture of women's sexual nature (whatever that would be). But other media, including fashion magazines, romance novels, and detergent commercials, offer portrayals of women which could also be accused of lying by virtue of their one-sidedness. If pornography's depiction of women qualifies as a lie, then it is in very respectable company.

The defamation approach to pornography thus faces the difficult task of showing that pornography's portrayal of women's sexuality is sufficiently distorted to preclude the truth defence. There are, however, deeper and more serious problems with it. In Canada defamation is both a tort and a crime. Both are aimed primarily at protecting the reputation of individuals who can be harmed by the publication of false allegations about them. There are therefore two obstacles in the way of construing mainstream male-oriented pornography as defamatory. The first is that it typically does not target particular individuals whose reputation could thereby be injured. A piece of pornography could, of course, target a particular person in this way – if, for instance, it took the form of an explicit satirical cartoon portraying a known figure engaged in various creative and unusual sexual practices. But in that case, while it might be actionable, its pornographic character would be secondary to the offence; it could be equally defamatory without the explicitness. Bringing most pornography within the ambit of the law of defamation would require acknowledgment of group defamation either as a tort or as a crime. In Canada, at least, this expansion of the offence has not yet occurred.

The more serious obstacle, however, concerns the necessity of proving injury as a result of the defamation. The crime of defamatory libel is defined in the Criminal Code as the publication of material 'likely to injure the reputation of any person by exposing him to hatred, contempt, or ridicule',[93] and the corresponding tort also requires injury to reputation.[94] Making the case that mainstream pornography defames women as a group would therefore require showing at least the likelihood of reputational injury to them. This would take the form of establishing that the publication of pornographic materials has rendered women more susceptible to attitudes of hatred or contempt (presumably on the part of men). Any such showing, however, would merely take us back to the ground we have previously covered: does exposure to pornography change men's attitudes toward women for the worse? We have already seen how unsettled and unhelpful the evidence is on this causal question (with the possible exception of pornography with overtly violent content). Taking the defamatory route as a means of restricting or controlling pornography therefore does not avoid these difficult issues; instead it reopens them.

Longino accuses pornography not only of lying about women but also of depicting them in a degrading manner. Earlier we considered the claim that the process of producing pornography degrades the women who participate in it as models or actors.[95] That claim was vulnerable to the response that if these women do not experience their work, or their working conditions, as degrading then at worst they can be said to be suffering a moral harm. (Of course, if sex work of this sort is not actually degrading then they are suffering no harm whatever.) But now we are considering a different issue – namely, whether the pornographic product portrays women in a degrading way. It is quite possible for it to do so, even if no women have been degraded in the making of it. Whether standard, male-oriented pornography degrades women in this way is not an easy question to answer (especially for a man). We can note once again that neither the Canadian courts nor ancillary agencies such as film review boards think that it necessarily does (though they do regard certain scenarios as degrading). The distinction they thereby draw between degrading and non-degrading pornography obviously lends no support to the thesis that pornography *as such* defames women by portraying them in a degrading or dehumanizing manner. Of course, these institutions may just have got it wrong: perhaps *all* mainstream porn, by its very nature, degrades women. The feminist case for this thesis (which Longino appears to be defending) is, however, seriously weakened by the testimony of many other feminists who claim not to find all of this material degrading.[96]

If we reject the idea that all mainstream pornography portrays women in a degrading fashion, then we need a criterion of degradation – one which will enable us to distinguish degrading from non-degrading portrayals. This is the point at which the courts cease to be helpful, since their reliance on community standards essentially tells us that a piece of pornography is degrading when people generally – or the majority of them – think it is.[97] What we are seeking instead is a normative criterion, one which will tell us when a portrayal is *really* degrading. One way of working toward such a criterion would be to take seriously the literal meaning of 'degrading' as reducing to a lower grade or status. This interpretation would suggest that a pornographic representation of a woman is degrading when it depicts her as something less than a full person or subject – as an object, say, or an instrument.[98] In that case, it would mesh nicely with another frequently voiced critique of pornography – namely, that it objectifies women. The notion of objectification is not much less contestable than that of degradation, but in this case some of the needed interpretive work has been done by Martha Nussbaum.[99] Nussbaum performs a valuable service by distinguishing a number of different ways in which a person can be treated as an object, three of which are *instrumentality* (the person is treated as a tool of another's purposes), *denial of autonomy* (the person is treated as lacking self-deter-mination), and *denial of subjectivity* (the person is treated as someone whose own experiences and feelings need not be taken into account). If we apply these categories to mainstream, male-oriented pornography then it is difficult to support the view that it objectifies women by its very nature. Even the fact that its portrayal of sexuality is male-centred, and in that sense sexist, does not imply that it portrays women as objects.[100] However, it is not difficult to support the view that *some* pornography of this genre objectifies women, for some of it portrays women as under the direction or control of men and as being used in a passive manner to satisfy male sexual desires. Alternatively (or additionally), some of it affixes to women such objectifying labels as 'slut', 'bitch', 'cunt', and so on, and openly suggests that they are to be used or exploited by men for men's purposes. In these respects some pornography crosses the bound-ary between the merely sexist and the openly misogynistic.[101]

Suppose we accept the foregoing analysis, at least to the extent of agreeing that on any reasonable normative criterion of degradation, some (but not all) mainstream pornography will qualify as depicting women in a degrading fashion. None of this yet yields any conclusion about *harm*. If harm is something that happens to persons – something they suffer – then it cannot be right to say that women in general are harmed simply by virtue of the fact that degrading representations of them are being marketed to men. And we have already ruled out the conclusion that the women who participated in the making of these rep-resentations were thereby harmed, unless we can show that they experi-enced the process as degrading or exploitative. So we still appear to lack evidence of either third-party or participant harms, *even if some pornogra-phy is genuinely degrading*. Furthermore, the evidence we would need in order to demonstrate such harms is once again causal. If it could be shown that men's exposure to degrading depictions of women increases the likelihood that they will treat women (real women: their wives or girlfriends) in a degrading or disrespectful fashion then we would have good reason to think that these depictions harm women. But in that case the harm would be of the familiar instrumental kind. Like the defa-mation approach, the degradation analysis does not seem to provide a way of bypassing the bothersome causal issues in order to show that por-nography is somehow intrinsically harmful.

MacKinnon prefers to conceptualize pornography not as defamation of women but as discrimination against them and therefore a violation of their civil rights. This approach is reflected in the various municipal civil rights ordinances which she and Andrea Dworkin sponsored during the 1980s, all of which defined pornography (in part) as 'the graphic sexually explicit subordination of women' combined with various objectionable representations of women.[102] Note that pornography is not here characterized as the *depiction* of the subordination of women but as their actual subordination. As MacKinnon comments, the definition 'includes the harm of what pornography says – its function as defamation or hate speech – but defines it and it alone in terms of what it does – its role as subordination, as sex discrimination, including what it does through what it says.'[103] Pornography is itself a practice of sex discrimination and calls for restriction on that ground, rather than its defamatory content. But what exactly does it mean to allege that pornography is a discriminatory practice? This is partially clarified in the text of the ordinances themselves, of which the following is typical:

> Pornography is a discriminatory practice based on sex which denies women equal opportunities in society. Pornography is central in creating and maintaining sex as a basis for discrimination. Pornography is a systemic practice of exploitation and subordination based on sex which differentially harms women. The bigotry and contempt it promotes, with the acts of aggression it fosters, harm women's opportunities for equality of rights in employment, education, access to and use of public accommodations, and acquisition of real property; promote rape, battery, child abuse, kidnaping and prostitution and inhibit just enforcement of laws against such acts; and contribute significantly to restricting women in particular from full exercise of citizenship and participation in public life, including in neighborhoods.[104]

On one reading of this passage what makes pornography a practice of discrimination is the fact that it treats the women involved in its production in a discriminatory way and that it reinforces and perpetuates violence or discrimination against women in general. These are, of course, the instrumental harms (to participants and third parties) which we have already canvassed. On this reading, then, pornography can be shown to be a discriminatory practice if and only if there is credible evidence of those harms (which explains why MacKinnon has devoted so much time to collecting and presenting that evidence). To the extent that the evidence is inconclusive, the case for pornography as a civil rights violation is weakened. However that may be, it is clear that this line of argument opens up no new ground.

However, MacKinnon's point is also open to a different interpretation which may provide a way of circumventing the awkward evidential issues. This approach to the harm question, which borrows heavily from the speech act analysis of J.L. Austin,[105] is no more than sketched or suggested by MacKinnon herself,[106] but it has been developed to a much higher degree of philosophical sophistication by others sympathetic to her project.[107] Austin's analysis distinguished various sorts of acts which speech can be used to perform. For our purposes, the important distinction is between two categories of such acts: illocutionary and perlocutionary. Suppose that Ann says to Bill, 'You should apply for that job,' as a result of which Bill does apply. Then we may say that Ann *persuaded* Bill to apply, where the act in question (persuading) requires a further causal consequence (Bill's applying) in order to be performed. Persuading is a perlocutionary act: it is a further end accomplished through or by means of saying something. But we may also say that Ann *advised* Bill to apply, where this description holds whatever Bill subsequently decides to do. Advising is an illocutionary act: it is constituted, in context, by the speaking itself, without reference to any of its further effects. In general, the performance of illocutionary acts requires certain (linguistic or other) conventions to be in place, but does not require causal efficacy. Perlocutionary acts, by contrast, are identified by their causal consequences.

Now consider the claim that pornography subordinates women. Thus far we have understood this as a perlocutionary act: pornographic expression brings about or reinforces or perpetuates the subordination of women. Evidence that it has this perlocutionary force will, of course, be causal in nature; perlocutionary harms are instrumental. But could pornography's subordination of women be instead an illocutionary act, in which case no evidence of its causal consequences would be necessary? Suppose we understand subordinating someone to consist, roughly, in placing her in an inferior rank or status.[108] If so, then it seems that subordinating can be an illocutionary act. When the Taliban, for instance, decreed 'Henceforth Afghan women are not to be educated,' then that decree had the (perlocutionary) effect of subordinating Afghan women (by bringing it about that they were denied education). But the very issuing of the decree also had the illocutionary effect of subordinating Afghan women – it would have been true that they had been subordinated even if the decree had been widely disregarded or subverted, so that many or most women were not denied education. However, as this example shows, merely saying something can constitute the act of subordinating only in the appropriate conventional setting. In particular, the illocutionary act requires that the locution be uttered by someone who possesses the necessary authority for it to have legal effect – it must be a decree. If a private Afghan citizen had said the same thing, it would not have constituted the act of subordination. How, then, might it be the case that pornography could have the illocutionary force of subordinating women? In the first place, presumably this could be said only of pornography which depicts women as subordinate to the sexual demands of men (i.e., roughly speaking, the kind of pornography which we earlier identified as portraying women in a degrading way). So let us continue to assume that some (but not all) pornography does depict women in this way. In order for that pornography to subordinate women (in the sense currently under discussion), it must somehow have the authority to do so. But it is difficult to see how this condition could be satisfied. Unlike the Taliban (in their day), pornographers do not have the legal, or normative, authority to determine the rank or status of women; they have, as we might say, no jurisdiction over this matter.[109] Their portrayal of women in a degrading or subordinating fashion might, of course, contribute to or reinforce women's actual, social subordination, but that would be a perlocutionary effect which could be established only by providing evidence of subordination as a causal consequence.

Thus far, then, the speech act approach does not look promising. However, a further possibility remains to be explored: not that pornography subordinates women, but that it silences them. Silencing must here be understood once again as an illocutionary act, that is, as something pornography accomplishes without reference to its causal efficacy. To see how this line of argument might go, we need to introduce a further feature of illocutionary acts. Consider again the example of Ann and Bill. Suppose that in saying 'You should apply for that job' Ann intends to advise Bill. Bill, however, thinks that Ann is rehearsing a line for the play in which she is currently performing and therefore does not take her to be advising him. In this case, Ann's attempt to advise has been unsuccessful because it did not secure the necessary uptake on Bill's part; in Austin's terms it has *misfired*. In general, Austin claims, the successful performance of an illocutionary act requires that the act be recognized as such by its audience.[110] So consider now the illocutionary act of *refusing*. Suppose that a woman intends to refuse a man's sexual advances by saying 'No, stop.' In order for her act to have its intended illocutionary force the man must understand that by saying this she is refusing his advances. If he does not interpret what she says in this way, but instead takes it to be coyness or playfulness or even encouragement to his advances, then her attempt to refuse will have misfired. There is therefore an important difference between his recognizing her refusal for what it is and continuing anyway (in which case he is knowingly forcing or overpowering her) and his failing to so recognize it (in which case he believes that she is consenting). In the latter case, we may say that in an important sense she has been silenced: she has been rendered unable to refuse.

Speech may have the effect of disabling other speech, by undercutting the possibility of its performance. This is again clearest in the case of authoritative speech. By refusing to acknowledge contracts for sexual labour, for instance, the legislature or the courts make it impossible for sex workers and their clients to perform the illocutionary act of contracting; they have been deprived of the power to do so. Could pornography similarly silence women by disabling them from refusing sex with men? As with subordinating, this power could presumably only be attributed to pornography with a certain content: depictions, say, of women who feign refusal of male sexual advances but who clearly mean to encourage them, or of women who come to enjoy rape after initial resistance. (It is worth reminding ourselves at this juncture that very little commercially available pornography actually features scenarios of this sort.) Men who had been exposed to these depictions might come to suppose that a woman's 'no' does not really mean 'no', thus failing to recognize 'no' as refusal. In that case, pornography might have the effect of disabling women's refusal of sex, but the effect would be causal and the disabling would be (in Austin's schema) a perlocutionary act.[111] In order for it to constitute an illocutionary act, pornography would again have to possess the normative authority to deprive women of the power of refusal. But there seems no reason to attribute this authority to it.

If pornography could be shown to have the illocutionary force of silencing women then it could also be shown to have the force of subordinating them, since it would be lowering them to an inferior status by depriving them of the ability to perform the illocutionary act of refusing. But it seems too much of a stretch to attribute either speech act to pornography. In general, illocutionary act analysis is most at home in the context of a well-defined conventional rule system, whether normative (as in a legal system) or linguistic. The rules of such a system can both create the power to do certain things with words (e.g., marrying) and deprive specified groups of this power (e.g., minors, same-sex couples). These background conditions are conspicuously lacking in the case of pornography. No one – including men in general – has conferred on pornography the power to determine the social status of women or to deprive women of the ability to do their own things with words, including refusing sex with men. The attempt to show that pornography subordinates or silences women through its illocutionary force therefore seems doomed to failure. These outcomes could still, of course, be among its causal consequences, but showing that they are will require empirical evidence. The need to provide such evidence therefore seems inescapable.

5.4 Pornography and Children

To this point we have explored a number of possible linkages between pornography and harm to women. It remains to consider the other group commonly advanced as victims of pornography, namely children. The harm in question in this case is usually taken to be sexual abuse – the analogue of sexual violence against women. However, whereas the latter concept is relatively clear, the former must be treated with some care. What is to count as sexual abuse of a child? Who, for that matter, is to count as a child? The age of consent for sexual activity varies across jurisdictions, and often for different purposes within a single jurisdiction. The commonly accepted minimum legal age for modelling or performing in pornography is eighteen, while the minimum age for consenting to sex may be as low as twelve or fourteen.[112] We do not want to define sexual abuse so broadly that it captures all sexual activity involving participants younger than eighteen, unless we are comfortable with the implication that a sexual relationship between a pair of seventeen-year-olds is necessarily abusive. We do not even want to define it so as to capture all sex between adolescents (under eighteen) and adults, if for no other reason than because the partners may be legally married. What we need is some characterization of what would make sex involving a minor abusive: when is the child being abused? In order to be able to focus on the clearest cases, I will confine attention in this section to sexual activity between an adult and a minor under the minimum age of consent to sex (for convenience, fourteen) *where the activity is unwanted by the child*. The category of unwanted sexual activity initiated by an adult will include any sexual exposure or touching under conditions of force, threat, or deception.[113] This characterization preserves the analogy with sexual violence against women, while leaving open the question whether adult-child sexual contact is also abusive where these particular conditions are not in play.

There is ample evidence of the harms that sexual abuse can do to its victims.[114] The short-term harms may be physical (laceration, bruising, infection, pregnancy, etc.) or, more commonly, psychological (distress, sleep disorders, behavioural problems, etc.). The long-term negative effects may take the form of depression, anxiety, antisocial behaviour, substance abuse, eating disorders, post-traumatic stress disorders, problems of sexual adjustment, and (in the extreme cases) suicidal or self-damaging behaviour. Unsurprisingly, these symptoms are very similar to those found in adult women who have been subjected to sexual violence. When we considered this case earlier, in section 5.1, the issue was not whether being a victim of sexual violence constitutes a genuine harm but whether there was reliable evidence that pornography is one of its causes. The main difficulty we found in providing this evidence was the lack of a reliable, direct link between cause and effect. Pornography might be one factor, among many, which increases the risk of sexual violence, but if so its causal contribution is very difficult to isolate and to measure. We would have some reason to suspect a cause-effect link if there were evidence that perpetrators of sexual offences against women had a history of greater consumption of pornography, or consumption of a different kind of pornography, as compared with non-offending males.[115] That evidence, however, is lacking. Our question now is whether we have better evidence of a causal link between pornography and the sexual abuse of children.

If we do, that link would be provided by the activities of pedophiles. While some sexual abuse of children is carried out by parents or other members of the child's immediate family, many perpetrators are either acquaintances (neighbours, teachers, coaches, etc.) or strangers.[116] Many, perhaps most, perpetrators can be aptly characterized as pedophiles, where pedophilia is understood as a primary sexual orientation on the part of an adult toward children.[117] Law enforcement authorities specializing in child pornography and/or child sexual abuse claim that nearly all active pedophiles are collectors (and very often also distributors and producers) of child pornography, while approximately 35 to 40 per cent of known collectors have themselves been directly implicated in abuse.[118] Unlike mainstream adult pornography, child pornography has not been produced and distributed for a commercial market since legislation specifically targeting it was passed in most countries in the late 1970s or early 1980s.[119] Since that time the Internet has become virtually the sole medium for the circulation of visual images and stories, through such means as websites, chat rooms, newsgroups, and peer-to-peer filesharing protocols.[120] While some pedophiles are members of organized networks, many operate on their own, trading materials with other like-minded individuals.[121] In this way child pornography is the currency of choice for child sexual abusers. It also plays an important role in the abuse.

In tracking the harms done to children by child pornography, it will once again be convenient to distinguish between participants and third parties. Children are participants in the making of child pornography when they are photographed, filmed, or videotaped in sexual activities or in sexually inviting or suggestive poses. In those cases the pornographic product is itself the visual record of the sexual abuse of the children who are being exploited or manipulated for the sexual purposes of adults.[122] The key difference between children and adult women as models or performers in pornography is the incapacity of the former to give meaningful consent to their involvement. To the extent that this involvement results in any of the sequelae commonly associated with sexual abuse, the children have thereby been harmed. The harm to third parties stems from the use of child pornography by pedophiles to groom further victims by 'normalizing' sexual activity for children, thereby overcoming prior inhibitions against involvement.[123] In this way the abuse of earlier victims can contribute to the later abuse of new recruits.

There is one final issue concerning pornography and children remaining to be considered. Children are routinely protected against exposure to sexually explicit materials by devices such as age limits, the v-chip, and Internet filters. The standard justification for these restrictions is that exposure to these materials may be harmful to minors. There is, however, remarkably little empirical evidence in support of this proposition. An entire social science industry has developed to investigate the cognate question of the impact on children of exposure to media violence, and its results to date remain equivocal and inconclusive.[124] While many researchers remain convinced that children's viewing of violent images will tend to increase aggressive behaviour, others are sceptical about this causal relationship.[125] By contrast, there has been little or no research concerning the psychological impact on children (either short-term or long-term) of exposure to explicit sexual images.[126] In the absence of any reliable social-scientific evidence of harm, the basis for the ubiquitous restrictions on children's access to erotic materials appears to lie entirely in a sexual morality which regards childhood or adolescent interest in sex as inappropriate, pathological, or downright sinful. But in that case, the harm against which children are being protected is not physical or psychological but moral.[127]

5.5 Hate Speech and Hate Crimes

In this section we turn from the possible harms of pornography (of all kinds) to those of hate propaganda. Our treatment of this issue can be much briefer, since we can adapt to the present purpose some of the results of our earlier discussions. For one thing, we can exclude from consideration the entire category of participant harms. Unlike pornography, hate literature in either print or visual form does not involve members of its target group in its production. There are therefore no harms to participants to be taken into account. Furthermore, two kinds of putative harm to third parties can be safely ignored. Hate messages vilifying groups on the basis of such markers as race, religion, ethnicity, disability, and sexual orientation are rightly found to be offensive, indeed outrageous and disgusting, by anyone with liberal sensibilities. However, this response, however justified, falls squarely within the category of moral distress, since it depends on the conviction that the messages transgress appropriate standards of tolerance or respect. If conservative moral distress stemming from pornography cannot qualify as harm for the purposes of the Harm Principle, then neither can liberal distress occasioned by hate propaganda. We have also seen how claims that pornography does various kinds of non-instrumental harm – by defaming, degrading, subordinating, or silencing – cannot provide a way of evading the evidentiary burden of showing a causal relationship between pornography and harm to women. Exactly analogous arguments can be, and have been, made for hate speech,[128] and they are subject to exactly the same limitations.

We are left, therefore, with the familiar questions concerning evidence of the effects of hate literature on the minority groups which it disparages. By contrast with the social science industry which emerged in the 1980s to examine possible links between pornography and harms to women, there has been relatively little empirical work done on this question. Thus we have here no aggregative studies looking for correlations between the availability of hate literature and the incidence of hate crimes, no retrospective studies attempting to determine whether perpetrators of hate violence have a history of differential consumption of such literature, no laboratory studies designed to determine whether exposure to hateful materials increases the likelihood of negative attitudes toward, or aggression against, members of the target groups, and no formal hearings with witnesses testifying about injuries which were incited or motivated by hate messages. It is interesting to speculate on the reasons for the comparative lack of attention to the harm issue where hate speech is concerned. Is it thought to be just obvious that material alleging the inferiority of a particular social group must in some way be injurious to members of that group? Or is it that hate literature is regarded as a fringe product largely circulating out of the public eye, by contrast with the mass distribution of pornography? Or that hate is a less glamorous – and, yes, less sexy – subject for investigation than sex?

Whatever the reason, we will have to get by here with a relative (but not absolute) vacuum of evidence on the harms of hate speech. In order to sort through what is available, it will be convenient to distinguish two different (though not mutually exclusive) causal pathways by means of which hate messages targeting a particular minority might harm the members of that minority.[129] We will say that the harm is direct if it results from exposure to the messages by members of the target group. This may occur when individuals are subjected to verbal abuse in the form of racist or homophobic epithets or insults, but also when hate messages intrude upon the lives of their targets in the form of anonymous telephone calls or notes, graffiti spraypainted in public spaces, crosses burned in front yards, pamphlets delivered through the mail, the desecration of sacred places, or other means. Mari Matsuda has enumerated these direct harms as follows:

> Victims of vicious hate propaganda experience physiological symptoms and emotional distress ranging from fear in the gut to rapid pulse rate and difficulty in breathing, nightmares, post-traumatic stress disorder, hypertension, psychosis, and suicide ...
>
> Victims are restricted in their personal freedom. To avoid receiving hate messages, victims have to quit jobs, forgo education, leave their homes, avoid certain public places, curtail their own exercise of speech rights, and otherwise modify their behavior and demeanor. The recipient of hate messages struggles with inner turmoil ...
>
> As much as one may try to resist a piece of hate propaganda, the effect on one's self-esteem and sense of personal security is devastating. To be hated, despised, and alone is the ultimate fear of all human beings. How-

ever irrational racist speech may be, it hits right at the emotional place where we feel the most pain.[130]

Even if there were no empirical evidence to support Matsuda's claims, they have a pretty secure footing in common sense. After all, hate messages which are imposed on members of their target group are not meant to engage the audience in a rational debate or persuade them of some important truths. Rather, they are meant to hurt – by insulting, humiliating, or intimidating – and it would scarcely be surprising if they were often to succeed in this aim. Many of the immediate responses Matsuda describes are the ones all of us evince when subjected to abuse or insult, whether motivated by prejudice or not. Fortunately, however, we do not need to rely solely on common experience here: there is also scientific support for the attribution to victims of hate speech of these kinds of emotional, attitudinal, and behavioural effects.[131] It is also worth noting that they bear more than a passing resemblance to some of the short-term effects on children of sexual abuse, and on women of sexual violence. There is no clean line here between abusive speech and abusive conduct – or, rather, the former is just one type of the latter.

The harm of hate speech, however, does not end with its direct impact on its victims. Its indirect effects are more systemic and pervasive, requiring the mediation of attitudes and conduct on the part of a wider audience. The two broader social conditions to which hate propaganda is most frequently said to contribute are analogues of the ones we explored earlier in the case of pornography and women: the social inequality of target minorities and an increase in the incidence of violence against members of these minorities. These outcomes are not, of course, really distinct, since the experience of living in fear of racist or homophobic violence is itself one form of social inequality. However, for analytic purposes I will deal with them separately, first with inequality and then, finally, with violence.

Whatever their precise content, hate messages preach the inferiority of the groups they choose to single out and advocate one or another form of discrimination against the members of those groups. Actual discriminatory practices against minorities would therefore count as success for the producers and distributors of these messages. But hatemongers themselves have little power to impose such practices beyond the confines of their own narrow circles. Success therefore will necessarily require enlisting a much wider public in the cause. That, in turn, will require an impact on the attitudes of non-members of the target minorities – members, that is, of the dominant social groups. It is this mechanism of subtle and pervasive attitudinal change that Matsuda also attributes to hate speech:

> Research in the psychology of racism suggests a related effect of racist hate propaganda: At some level, no matter how much both victims and well-meaning dominant-group members resist it, racial inferiority is planted in our minds as an idea that may hold some truth. The idea is improbable and abhorrent, but because it is presented repeatedly, it is there before us. 'Those people' are lazy, dirty, sexualized, money grubbing, dishonest, inscrutable, we are told. We reject the idea, but the next time we sit next to one of 'those people,' the dirt message, the sex message, is triggered. We stifle it, reject it as wrong, but it is there, interfering with our perception and interaction with the person next to us.[132]

Clay Calvert has pointed to the same effect: 'It is a long-term, cumulative harm that accrues with repeated use of racist epithets directed at targeted minorities. The harm is the subordination of racial minorities, including the perpetuation and reinforcement of discriminatory attitudes and behaviors. In brief, use of racist expressions creates and maintains a social reality of racism that promotes disparate treatment of minorities.'[133]

We are obviously dealing here with an alleged causal relationship between the availability of hate literature within a society and the discriminatory treatment of that society's minorities, one which parallels the alleged relationship we examined earlier between the availability of pornography and the social inequality of women. In that case we found the evidence for the relationship disappointingly thin; indeed, there was some reason to suppose that women have taken greater steps toward equality in those societies in which pornography is plentiful. The connection in the present case has a stronger basis in common sense since, unlike at least most forms of pornography, hate propaganda openly advocates an unequal social status for minorities. However, advocacy is one thing and successful advocacy quite another. Just as it was plausible to suppose that at least some (violent, misogynistic) pornography makes some contribution toward the unequal social status of women, so it is plausible to suppose that hate propaganda makes some contribution toward the unequal social status of blacks, Asians, Jews, aboriginals, and gays. But no serious scientific attempt has been made in either case to factor out and measure the extent of this contribution, nor is it easy to see how this could be done. It seems that in the territory of equality no advances are possible beyond what common sense can teach us.

Things are rather different when we turn to the issue of violence. Hate violence takes the form of assault on a person or damage to property motivated by hostility toward the group with which the person or property is associated. Most legal jurisdictions now classify certain cases of murder, assault, vandalism, and so on, as hate crimes on the basis of evidence of such motivation. Whereas the literature on the effects of hate speech may be limited, there is ample evidence of the harms (both immediate and long-term) that hate crimes do both to their immediate victims and to other members of the target communities.[134] None of this, of course, is surprising: we know that being the victim of racist or homophobic violence is a harm, just as we know the same for sexual violence. The question in this case, as in the earlier, is whether there is a causal connection back to a particular form of expression. In brief: does hate speech cause hate crimes?

Many hate messages either imply or openly advocate the legitimacy of violence against Jews, blacks, or gays. By so doing, it is arguable – indeed highly plausible – that they contribute to a climate which fosters hate crimes and which members of vulnerable minorities experience as threatening or intimidating.[135] The extent of this contribution is, of course, difficult to measure with any degree of certainty, but we can point to one quite tangible link in the causal chain from speech to crime. While some hate propaganda is produced and disseminated by isolated individuals, most of it is generated by organized neo-Nazi, white supremacist, or homophobic groups. For these groups the primary purpose of the materials they circulate, largely now through websites, is not to contribute to a broad public debate concerning Jews or blacks or gays. Rather, the materials are used to reinforce the shared ideology that binds the group together and to recruit new group members.[136] For a hate group, hate propaganda is its creed or ideology, and its call to action.[137] That action frequently involves acts of violence against members of target groups or their property. It is impossible to determine with any accuracy what proportion of the overall incidence of hate crimes can be attributed to individuals affiliated with hate groups.[138] Some studies have suggested that most such crimes are committed for thrills or in defence of 'turf' against 'outsiders', and only a small proportion by individuals for whom racism or homophobia is a long-term mission.[139] On the other hand, we have good evidence that many hate groups have a history of involvement in racist violence.[140] Furthermore, there have been a number of prominent instances of hate violence in recent years where the perpetrator has had a personal history of involvement with a hate group.[141] When the group has advocated violence against members of a particular minority and one of its adherents comes to practise just such violence, it is difficult to resist a cause-and-effect conclusion. If that conclusion is at least sometimes justified then hate messages can do more than merely legitimize or endorse violence against target minorities – they can also encourage or even instigate it.[142]

5.6 Conclusion

The case for legal restraints on either pornography or hate propaganda depends crucially on the harms done by these forms of expression. In the case of pornography a good deal of attention has been devoted to this question, but the resulting evidence is inconclusive at best. The pornography industry employs thousands of women in its production process, but there is no good reason to think that they are standardly abused, brutalized, or exploited, though their working conditions could undoubtedly stand considerable improvement. Social scientists have focused primarily on the pornographic product as a possible factor in the incidence of sexual violence against women, but most studies have resulted in little evidence of a cause-and-effect relationship. The evidence is strongest in the case of materials which eroticize sexual violence by portraying it for male arousal, but most commercial pornography is free of such themes. Pornography is also cited by feminists as a contributing factor in women's social inequality, but there seems to be no way to verify this claim and considerable reason to doubt it.

The difficulties in the way of showing a causal relationship between pornography and harms to women have led some feminists to reconceptualize its impact in non-instrumental terms. Thus the harm of pornography has been claimed to lie in the fact that it defames women or degrades them or subordinates them or silences them. But all of these claims suffer from one or another of two shortcomings: either they require supporting causal evidence of harmful consequences (defamation and degradation) or they rest on questionable presuppositions about the authority of pornography to determine the social status or linguistic powers of women (subordination and silencing). If pornography is to be shown to harm women, there seems no way around the evidential burden of establishing its empirical effects.

While the case for the harmfulness of standard commercial pornography is problematic, a much stronger case can be made for child pornography, which harms children both in its production (which itself constitutes sexual abuse) and in its use by pedophiles to groom new recruits for abuse. Pedophiles provide a causal link between the production of child pornography and child sexual abuse. However, there is little reason to think that children are standardly harmed simply by exposure to sexually explicit materials.

There is reason to think that target groups are harmed by exposure to hate propaganda, which they will often experience as humiliating or intimidating. Common sense would also suggest a role for hate speech in supporting or reinforcing social practices of discrimination against minorities, but there is little or no social-scientific evidence to confirm this suggestion. Hate propaganda is, however, implicated in hate violence against minorities, primarily through its role in recruiting members to hate groups and reinforcing their attitudes of hostility and contempt toward the groups' favoured targets. Hate groups appear to serve as a link between hateful expression and hate violence which parallels the role of pedophiles in the case of child pornography and the sexual abuse of children.

The aim of this chapter has been to understand the kinds of harm which we have good reason to think are caused by pornography and hate speech. Its aim has not been to decide when, if ever, these harms are either serious or probable enough to justify criminal restrictions on these forms of expression. From Mill we learned earlier that the fact that some form of conduct is harmful to others opens up the possibility of justified interference with it, but it does not itself justify that interference. If pornography (in at least some of its forms) or hate propaganda causes significant harm to some target group then its restraint by legal means is not prohibited by the Harm Principle. However, it may still be ill-advised as a matter of public policy, because contrary to the general good. From the approach taken by the Supreme Court to free expression cases we have learned that in deciding when a restriction on freedom of expression is justified, the harms done by a particular form of expression must be balanced against the harms that would be done by the restriction itself. In advance of this balancing, no conclusion can be drawn about the justification of limits to free expression. One crucial piece of our business is therefore still unfinished.

Chapter 6

From Principle to Policy

This book began with the avowed aim of developing a principled framework – a theory of free expression – capable both of grounding expressive rights and of determining the limits to those rights. The preceding chapters have put in place all of the main ingredients of such a theory. Rights, I have argued, are valuable for the interests they protect and promote. Expressive rights are valuable because freedom of expression is intimately connected to two kinds of interests: some of our most basic interests as individuals and as citizens – recognition, self-respect, political participation, empowerment, and the like – and equally important social interests, including the search for truth, diversity of forms of life, artistic experimentation, and the effective functioning of democratic government. This much J.S. Mill recognized a century and a half ago. He also recognized that all rights, including expressive rights, have their limits, and he provided us with the framework for determining where those limits are to be drawn. Mill's framework focuses our attention on the harm that expression can do, and on the need to balance that harm (where it exists) against the harm of its regulation. For the particular cases of pornography and hate speech, therefore, the route to a principled regulatory policy begins with an objective assessment of the evidence concerning the kinds of harm these expressive materials might do – to whom, how serious, how probable, and so on. This assessment was the business of the preceding chapter.

While we now have all the pieces, we have not fitted them together into a coherent whole. What remains is to move from our principled framework via the empirical evidence concerning harm to a defensible policy concerning the regulation of pornography and hate speech. That is the business of this chapter. Before we turn to it, however, there is one further area to explore. The preceding chapters have focused exclusively on two state-imposed limits to free expression: the Criminal Code statutes governing hate propaganda and obscenity. Before beginning to draw conclusions about the justifiability of these limits, it would be well to recognize that the state also has other means at its disposal for regulating expression. The hate propaganda and obscenity laws have attracted most of the attention in the public and academic debates in the past decade or so, not only because of the inherent seriousness of bringing criminal penalties to bear on the distribution of prohibited materials, but also because of the high profile of the landmark Supreme Court decisions in *Keegstra* and *Butler*. However, other legal provisions in place in Canada – both criminal and non-criminal – have been at least as effective, if not more so, in limiting expression and have also had their day in court. It is time to give them the attention they deserve, if only because they may offer us interesting alternatives to the traditional criminal restraints.

6.1 Restraint by Other Means

1. The child pornography law. For reasons explored in the preceding chapter, child pornography has seemed to many the most dangerous of all sexually explicit materials and the most in need of regulation (or outright prohibition). Whether or not they already had more general obscenity statutes on the books, during the 1970s and 1980s most Western jurisdictions responded to this perceived danger by enacting legislation specifically targeting child pornography.[1] Canada was a relative latecomer in this trend toward specialized regulation. The application of the more general obscenity statute (sec. 163 of the Criminal Code) to sexually explicit materials depicting children was confirmed in Justice Sopinka's majority opinion in *Butler* (1992), which declared that the depiction of 'explicit sex that is not violent and neither degrading nor dehumanizing' will not count as obscene 'unless it employs children in its production'.[2] None the less, one of the last acts of the Conservative government in 1993 was to pass legislation (sec. 163.1 of the Criminal Code) specifically governing child pornography.[3] At the time of its enactment the new legislation encountered considerable criticism, on the ground that it was either unnecessary (to the extent that it overlapped with the existing obscenity law) or objectionable (in those respects in which it departed from it).[4] Since then it has survived a constitutional challenge and has come to serve as the means by which child pornography is policed in Canada.

The child pornography statute departed from the pre-existing obscenity law in two principal ways. First, instead of relying on community standards, the definition of child pornography was content-based. That definition came in two parts, the first of which targeted any visual representation 'that shows a person who is or is depicted as being under the age of eighteen years and is engaged in or is depicted as engaged in explicit sexual activity, or the dominant characteristic of which is the depiction, for a sexual purpose, of a sexual organ or the anal region of a person under the age of eighteen years'.[5] The second part of the definition covered 'any written material or visual representation that advocates or counsels sexual activity with a person under the age of eighteen' that would itself be an offence under the Criminal Code.[6] The second respect in which the child pornography statute differed from its predecessor was in the offences which it enumerated. Besides the production or distribution of child pornography (both of which would be offences under the obscenity law), it also prohibited simple possession (which would not).[7]

Both the definition of child pornography and the possession offence were at issue in the constitutional challenge raised in *Sharpe* (2001), and they were linked together in the Supreme Court's majority judgment.[8] As far as simple possession of child pornography was concerned, it was conceded on all sides that its prohibition was an infringement of section 2(b) of the Charter. The question, consequently, was whether or not it could be saved as a 'reasonable limit' within the terms of section 1. When the *Oakes* tests were invoked in order to settle this question, the principal point at issue was whether the legislation failed the minimal impairment test by reason of overbreadth. That point in turn implicated the definition of child pornography which determined the kinds of materials whose possession the legislation prohibited. The court therefore subjected that definition to lengthy scrutiny.

That scrutiny addressed a number of possible concerns about overbreadth. What, for instance, is to count as a depiction of 'explicit sexual activity'?[9] Is this meant to include activities such as stroking, hugging, or kissing, in addition to obvious instances such as fellatio or intercourse? On this question the court concluded that the phrase 'refers to acts which viewed objectively fall at the extreme end of the spectrum of sexual activity – acts involving nudity or intimate sexual activity represented in a graphic and unambiguous fashion'.[10] It therefore does not catch photos of teenagers kissing at summer camp. Likewise, in interpreting the phrase 'for a sexual purpose' the court held that this qualifier applied only when a depiction could be 'reasonably perceived as intended to cause sexual stimulation to some viewers'.[11] This interpretation was clearly intended to ensure that the depiction fell within the customary definition of pornography as material whose primary purpose or function is sexual arousal.[12] Innocent family photos of naked youngsters in the bath would therefore not qualify as child pornography.

The court also addressed the question of what is meant, under the second part of the definition, by advocating or counselling criminal sexual activity with a minor, concluding that 'in order to meet the requirement of "advocates" or "counsels", the material, viewed objectively, must be seen as "actively inducing" or encouraging the described offences with children ... The mere description of the criminal act is not caught. Rather, the prohibition is against material that, viewed objectively, sends the message that sex with children can and should be pursued.'[13] What the court appeared to have in mind here are materials which portray children as welcoming, enjoying, or even initiating sexual activities with adults, or which describe such activities for the purpose of sexually arousing the viewer or reader.[14]

To this point the court had confined itself to clarification of the definition of child pornography, in order to provide guidance both to courts and law enforcement agencies charged with the responsibility of applying the law and to private individuals who might have legitimate doubts whether materials in their possession constituted child pornography. However, the court majority also took the view that, without further specification of the definition, the inclusion within the statute of the offence of simple possession would fail the *Oakes* test of minimal impairment by reason of overbreadth.[15] The object of their concern was the fact that the unamended definition would criminalize the possession of two sorts of materials: (1) 'works of the imagination', such as self-created and privately held journals, diaries, writings, or drawings, and (2) visual representations, such as photographs or videos, created by the person or persons depicted in them and intended only for private use. The court majority had no difficulty with the idea that the distribution of these materials could legitimately be prohibited. However, a prohibition of private possession (and, of course, production) was another matter. On the one hand, in the court's opinion, by intruding on the realm of private expression any such prohibition would implicate such section 2(b) values as self-fulfilment and self-actualization. On the other hand, the risk of harm to children is minimal since no children are involved in the production of the first category of materials and those involved in producing materials of the second sort are also the subjects of them. The court recognized four different ways in which child pornography might involve the risk of harm to children: (a) by normalizing the sexual abuse of children, it may reduce the inhibitions of pedophiles against committing such abuse; (b) by fuelling their sexual fantasies it may incite pedophiles to offend; (c) it may be used by pedophiles to groom or seduce further victims; and (d) children may be abused in the production of the materials. Where 'works of the imagination' or personal photographs or videos are held privately by their creators and not circulated to others, the court held that some of these potential risks did not apply at all, while the probability of others was substantially reduced. Its conclusion was that the risk of harm in these cases was 'small, incidental and more tenuous' than that posed by most child pornography. In order to prevent the child pornography law from failing the test of minimal impairment, the court elected to read exceptions for the two categories of materials into the possession offence in section 163.1, thereby effectively narrowing the definition of child pornography for the purpose of the production and possession offences in the statute.[16]

The practical impact of this narrowing for law enforcement agencies targeting child pornography has been minimal.[17] The creators of pedophilic 'works of the imagination' (stories, drawings, cartoons, computer simulations, etc.) seldom keep them solely for their own personal use; indeed they are typically eager to circulate them to others. Furthermore, those who have such self-created materials in their collections invariably have many other materials as well (photographs, videos, etc.) which involve children in their production. Consequently, virtually anyone in possession of the kinds of materials excluded by the court will be subject to prosecution either for distribution of those materials or for possession of non-excluded materials.

In its decision the court took another step which has been of greater concern to law enforcement agencies. The child pornography statute provided a defence on grounds of the 'artistic merit' of the impugned materials.[18] As we saw earlier,[19] the analogous defence in the case of obscenity was incorporated into the community standards test. Since community standards play no role in the definition of child pornography, the question the court needed to settle was whether they were to have a role in determining artistic merit. In the end the court rejected this importation of the community standards test and considered two possible alternative interpretations of 'artistic merit': (1) having artistic character, and (2) having artistic value. On the first interpretation, the defence would apply to any materials (visual or written) which counted as works of art at all, while on the second it would apply only to those judged to be good or meritorious by some appropriate aesthetic standard. The court chose the first option, concluding that '"artistic merit" should be interpreted as including any expression that may reasonably be viewed as art. Any objectively established artistic value, however small, suffices to support the defence.'[20] The court's conclusion on this issue has opened up the possibility of having expert witnesses testify at trial that stories, photos, or videos that clearly constitute child pornography have some redeeming literary or visual merit. Law enforcement agencies have been understandably fearful that the defence, so interpreted, may impede successful prosecution for materials which otherwise lie at the heart of the definition of child pornography.[21]

2. *Human rights legislation.* While the child pornography law differs in important respects from the obscenity law, it is still a piece of criminal legislation. The regulation of expressive materials in Canada is not, however, confined to criminal procedure. Where hate speech is concerned, an important alternative is embodied in the policy and procedure of human rights legislation. In Canada this legislation falls within both provincial and federal jurisdiction. The original model was provided by the province of Ontario, whose Human Rights Code was first adopted in 1962, but over the next quarter-century similar legislation was passed by the other nine provinces, the Yukon and Northwest Territories, and the federal government. The principal aim of these human rights acts is to prohibit discriminatory practices in a wide variety of contexts, including employment, housing, and the provision of goods or services. Among the prohibited practices is hate speech. For example, section 13(1) of the Canadian Human Rights Act (adopted in 1977) defines as one discriminatory practice the telephone communication of 'any matter that is likely to expose a person or persons to hatred or contempt by reason of the fact that that person or those persons are identifiable on the basis of a prohibited ground of discrimination'.[22] The prohibited grounds of discrimination enumerated in section 3(1) of the act include (but are not restricted to) race, national or ethnic origin, colour, religion, sex, and sexual orientation.

This provision in the Human Rights Act obviously overlaps with the hate propaganda statute in the Criminal Code. However, the two measures for regulating hate speech are not an exact fit. For one thing, the range of protected groups in the act is much wider than the list of 'identifiable groups' for the purpose of section 319(2) of the Code, which is limited to 'any section of the public distinguished by colour, race, religion or ethnic origin'. Just to pick two obvious examples, hate speech targeting women or gays is prohibited by human rights law, but not by criminal law.[23] Secondly, the criminal statute requires specific intent, by stipulating that the promotion of hatred must be 'wilful', whereas the human rights legislation focuses on the likely effect of the communication (exposing members of a protected group to 'hatred or contempt'). It is therefore possible for someone to be found to be in contravention of section 13(1) in the absence of any evidence of intent to promote hatred against the group in question. Third, the Human Rights Act, but not the criminal statute, would apply to private communications (by telephone) between consenting parties. Finally, the act also omits the defences (including truth) which are made available to defendants in the hate propaganda law. The scope of the human rights legislation is therefore considerably broader than that of the criminal law, and the threshold for a successful proceeding against an offender is also measurably lower.

In 1990 the constitutionality of section 13(1) of the Canadian Human Rights Act was upheld by the same 4-to-3 majority on the Supreme Court that decided *Keegstra*.[24] The dissenting minority would have struck the section down, principally on grounds of overbreadth. While the majority took due note of the various respects in which the act was broader than the corresponding criminal legislation, they none the less concluded that it imposed a reasonable limit upon freedom of expression, partly on grounds of the procedural differences between the administration of human rights and criminal law. In a criminal procedure there is a trade-off between the seriousness of the penalties attached to offences (in the case of hate promotion, a maximum of two years' imprisonment) and the protection of the accused provided by such safeguards as the burden on the prosecution of proving its case beyond a reasonable doubt. In the case of the Human Rights Act a hearing conducted by a tribunal is a quasi-judicial proceeding in which the presumption of innocence is still in place for the respondent but the standard of proof required is that of the civil law (proof on a balance of probabilities).[25] Should it conclude that a contravention of section 13(1) has occurred, the tribunal is empowered to impose remedies, including a cease and desist order, compensation to a specific victim of the communication (to a maximum of $20,000), and a fine (of up to $10,000). These remedies do not include incarceration, nor do they carry the additional stigma of a criminal conviction. More serious sanctions, including a stiffer fine or a prison sentence, can be applied only by a court after the respondent is found to have been in contempt for non-compliance.[26] The Supreme Court majority took the view that the greater breadth of the offence defined in section 13(1) and the greater ease of establishing that it has been committed were both tolerable in the absence of criminal sanctions.[27]

The very considerable overlap between this section of the Canadian Human Rights Act and the hate propaganda section in the Criminal Code means that a person suspected of communicating hate messages could in principle be open to either criminal or administrative proceedings (or both). Ernst Zundel makes an interesting case in point. For years Zundel distributed a pamphlet from his home in Toronto denying that six million Jews were killed by the Nazis and claiming that the Holocaust is a myth spread by a worldwide Jewish conspiracy. During all this time no prosecution was ever initiated under the hate propaganda statute, probably because the Attorney General of Ontario took the view that there would be only a slim chance of obtaining a conviction. Instead, Zundel was prosecuted, and convicted, under the then section 181 of the Criminal Code, which prohibited 'spreading false news'. This statute, however, was then struck down by the Supreme Court on section 1 grounds.[28] Finally, in 1996 a complaint was filed with the Canadian Human Rights Commission concerning materials posted on Zundel's website questioning the existence of the Holocaust. Because of a series of procedural delays, the Canadian Human Rights Tribunal took more than four years to render the judgment that Zundel was in contravention of section 13(1) of the Human Rights Act and order him to cease posting discriminatory materials on his website.[29] By that time he had moved to the United States, beyond the tribunal's jurisdiction.[30]

3. *Customs regulation.* Broadly speaking, the state has two means available of restraining a particular kind of activity: it can impose a penalty on the offender once the activity has occurred or it can act to prevent its occurrence in the first place. Both criminal and human rights legislation are examples of subsequent restraint: criminal prosecution or a proceeding before a human rights tribunal requires the defendant (or respondent) to have already done what is alleged to be unlawful. Customs regulation, on the other hand, is an example of prior restraint: expressive materials considered to fall into a prohibited category are intercepted at the border in order to prevent their distribution within Canada.

Ernst Zundel notwithstanding, Canadian citizens or residents are not world-class producers of hate propaganda – or of pornography. In one way or another, most materials in these two categories which are distributed in Canada enter the country from the outside. Nowadays much of that inflow is digital, via the Internet; indeed, where hate propaganda and child pornography are concerned, virtually all materials originating from abroad reach Canadian endusers via e-mail, the World Wide Web, chat rooms, or other forms of electronic transmission. The proliferation in recent years of commercial sexually explicit websites means that the same holds for much adult pornography as well. But not for all. Canadians still import erotic materials in physical form – books, magazines, videos, and so on – for domestic distribution and consumption. When these materials cross the border they fall within the jurisdiction of Canada Customs.

Under the terms of the Customs Act inspectors at the border have the authority to determine the tariff classification of any imported goods. Schedule VII of the Customs Tariff includes tariff code 9956, which, among other things, covers 'Books, printed paper, drawings, paintings, prints, photographs or respresentations of any kind that (a) are deemed to be obscene under subsection 163(8) of the *Criminal Code*'.[31] To assist them in the task of applying code 9956(a), Customs inspectors are provided with guidelines in Memorandum D9-1-1, including an interpretation of the statutory definition of obscenity as determined by the Supreme Court in its *Butler* decision. Inspectors are therefore alerted to look for depictions or descriptions of sexual activities which are violent and/or degrading or dehumanizing, such as sexual assault, bondage, sadomasochism, incest, bestiality, and necrophilia. They are also supplied with an illustrated manual of prohibited materials for comparison purposes. Once a particular publication has been determined to be obscene the importer is notified that it will be detained at the border. The decision of the inspector is then reviewed by a Commodity Specialist, a Customs official who deals only with materials suspected of falling under the provisions of tariff code 9956. If the initial decision is confirmed the importer then has the option of requesting a redetermination by a Tariff and Values Administrator and, if necessary, a further redetermination by the Prohibited Importations Directorate in Ottawa. Once these review procedures within the Customs bureaucracy have been exhausted the decision can be further appealed to the courts.

Over the years a wide variety of erotic materials have been denied entry into Canada by these processes.[32] For many distributors or private consumers the detention of materials they are attempting to import has doubtless amounted to little more than an irritant. In other cases, however, it has become a serious economic problem, particularly for the proprietors of gay and lesbian bookstores. Most of the erotica (books, magazines, newspapers, manuals, etc.) stocked in these bookstores are imported. As far back as the 1980s, a pattern began to emerge of selective seizures by Customs of gay and lesbian materials. It became apparent that shipments ordered by bookstores specializing in these materials were being targeted for special scrutiny by Customs inspectors, since very often the same items were imported without difficulty by general-purpose bookstores. Confiscations and delays resulted in serious disruptions in the normal business of these establishments, since items such as periodicals went out of date quickly and in any case were often readily available elsewhere. The internal review mechanisms within Customs were lengthy and unwieldy, and very often resulted in confirmation of the original decision, while recourse to the courts was expensive and even more time-consuming. In the 1980s and early 1990s Glad Day Bookshop in Toronto mounted a series of court challenges to Customs procedures[33] which did little to change the system except to establish that the Customs Tariff must incorporate the statutory definition of obscenity (with its dependence on community standards). A more serious challenge was initiated in 1994 by Little Sister's Book and Art Emporium in Vancouver, which alleged that the selective targeting of gay and lesbian materials constituted a violation of sections 2(b) and 15(1) of the Charter.[34] The trial judge agreed that the Charter rights of the complainants had indeed been violated, but attributed this to faults in the administration of the Customs Tariff rather than in the legislation itself. Customs officials therefore retained the authority to intercept materials on grounds of obscenity, but were admonished to exercise this authority in a manner which did not discriminate against gay and lesbian erotica. The trial court's judgment was upheld by the British Columbia Court of Appeal, though on a split decision.[35]

When the case reached the Supreme Court, it too was split.[36] The majority and minority agreed on two important matters: that Customs officials had been applying code 9956(a) of the Customs Tariff in a manner which unjustifiably discriminated against gay and lesbian erotica, and that the statutory definition of obscenity (as interpreted in *Butler*) applied equally to straight and gay pornography. In the light of some problematic court decisions immediately following *Butler*,[37] it was particularly useful to have the court declare that erotic materials with gay or lesbian content are not obscene as such; rather, the same standards (of violent or degrading or dehumanizing content) are to be applied to them as to straight pornography. The court was emphatic that the mere fact that the sexual activities depicted involve same-sex partners does not render them degrading or dehumanizing.

Where the majority and minority differed was in their analysis of the source of the discriminatory treatment by Customs officials, and therefore also in their favoured remedy. The minority argued that the Customs legislation itself, and not merely its faulty administration, was responsible for the constitutional violations. They would therefore have struck down code 9956(a) of the Customs Tariff on the ground that it lacked the procedural safeguards necessary to ensure its equitable administration. The majority chose a less adventurous route, defending the legislation as a reasonable limit on freedom of expression and attributing the problems to its misapplication.[38] It therefore upheld the Customs legislation, with the exception of the provision which imposed a 'reverse onus' on the importer, at the redetermination and appeal stages, to establish that the material in question is not obscene. Otherwise the court majority limited itself to requiring that the administrative procedures be both equitable and timely. It also invited Little Sisters to go back to court were they to experience further problems of the kind that led them to initiate the legal challenge in the first place. As of this writing they had elected to do so, following Customs seizure of two erotic comic books.[39]

4. Film review boards. The interception of expressive materials by Customs officials is one example of prior restraint. Film censorship, as exercised by provincial review boards, is another. The film review boards fall under provincial jurisdiction in Canada because the provinces license and regulate the operations of theatres. There are currently six such boards, in the Maritimes, Quebec, Ontario, Manitoba, Alberta, and British Columbia. The Ontario Film Review Board, which has been in operation (under one name or another) since 1911, will serve as a model for the rest. It derives its authority from the Ontario Theatres Act, section 7 of which gives it the power to 'approve, prohibit and regulate the exhibition and distribution of film in Ontario'. Section 1 of the act defines 'film' so as to include not only conventional motion picture film for theatrical projection but also videotape and 'any other medium from which may be produced visual images that may be viewed as moving pictures'. All films for theatrical exhibition in Ontario, as well as all videotapes and digital videodiscs for sale or rental in the province, must therefore be submitted to the board for approval in advance of distribution.

One of the board's functions is classification of films and videos into categories: 'family', 'parental guidance', 'adult accompaniment', 'restricted', and 'adult sex film'. If its powers ended there, it would be playing a merely advisory or informational role for consumers, including parents with younger children.[40] However, as stated above, section 7 of the Theatres Act gives it the power not merely to regulate the distribution of a film or video but also to prohibit it. That power includes the authority, 'when authorized by the person submitting film for approval, to remove from the film any portion that it does not approve of for exhibition or distribution'. In other words, the board can require cuts in a film or video as a condition of its approval for distribution. This power makes it a censor.

The vast majority of the videos submitted to the board for approval every year are pornographic – 'adult sex videos'. In deciding what to allow and what to prohibit, the board is guided by Regulation 1031 of the Theatres Act, section 14 of which directs the board to 'take into account the general character and integrity of the film' and authorizes refusal of approval where it contains depictions of violence, degradation, humiliation, sexual activities involving children, and various other bits of nastiness.[41] For the most part, these types of prohibited content seem to be intended to reflect the statutory/judicial definition of obscenity (as determined by the Supreme Court in *Butler*) as well as the statutory definition of child pornography.[42] The board has also attempted to internalize the reference to community standards that is embedded in the definition of obscenity. The part-time members of the classification panels are intended to reflect a diversity of ages, work histories, ethnic backgrounds, and sexual orientations. Every panel includes both male and female members.[43] The board also consults widely with experts and interest groups in formulating its policies and holds twice-monthly screenings where the opinions of public groups on how a film should be classified can be compared with the panel's decision. To the extent that community standards of tolerance have any operational meaning at all, the board would appear to be in closer touch with them than most judges.[44] Presumably in response to community input, its list of prohibited depictions has shrunk over the past decade or so. Whereas activities such as double penetration, anal penetration with an object (other than a penis), fisting, and ejaculation on the face were once *verboten*, their depiction is now commonplace in videos available for rental in Ontario.[45]

If the board limited its censorship activities to cutting scenes of sexual violence or degradation out of pornographic videos then few citizens of Ontario would be likely to complain.[46] However, from time to time it is moved to demand cuts in mainstream films. Over the years its targets have included such celebrated instances as Louis Malle's *Pretty Baby* (1978), Volker Schlöndorff's *The Tin Drum* (1979), and Bernardo Bertolucci's *Luna* (1980).[47] The common thread linking these films, and the source of the board's objection to them, was their depiction of sexual activity involving, or being witnessed by, a minor. The most recent high-profile case was Catherine Breillat's *Fat Girl* (2001), a coming-of-age film about two teenage sisters (thirteen and fifteen years old) which had been distributed without incident in Europe, the United Kingdom, and the United States. The film was screened at the 2001 Toronto International Film Festival and subsequently approved for distribution by the review boards in Quebec, Manitoba, Alberta, and British Columbia. The Ontario board panel which first viewed *Fat Girl* demanded cuts in scenes depicting adolescent nudity and rape. A second panel then viewed the film and rendered the same verdict, which was in turn upheld on a 3-to-2 vote by an appeal panel. The film's distributors refused to make the required cuts and appealed the board's decision to the courts, as provided by section 54 of the Theatres Act. As part of the appeal they also planned to challenge the act as an unjustifiable infringement of section 2(b) of the Charter. However, before the case could be heard the board agreed to reconsider its decision and approved the film for distribution without cuts, thereby heading off the constitutional challenge to its censorship powers.

5. *Internet regulation.* This final stop on our tour is somewhat of a fraud. For one thing, it does not focus on another regulatory device available to the state; instead, its topic is a particular medium of expression, subject (in principle at least) to all of the forms of regulation we have so far examined. More importantly, its message is that most of the legal controls over content communicated via the Internet remain merely notional rather than real. Given the ever-expanding role of the Internet as a medium of communication – especially of pornography and hate messages – this is a matter of no small practical importance. Currently an estimated 60,000 commercial websites offer sexually explicit content to consumers, in addition to countless bulletin board services and newsgroups.[48] On a much smaller scale, but perhaps more alarming, hundreds of hate groups operate websites by means of which they

disseminate their racist or homophobic convictions.[49] Increasingly, the Internet in one form or another is becoming the medium of choice for the circulation of both pornography and hate propaganda. However, unlike attempts in the United States to impose medium-specific controls over at least some of this content, no legislation exclusively governing the Internet has so far been adopted in Canada.[50]

This is not to say that materials communicated via the Internet are immune to regulation by Canadian law. With the exception of the legislation authorizing the activities of Canada Customs and the various provincial film review boards, which agencies have no jurisdiction over the Internet, every regulatory device we have thus far surveyed applies as much to electronic materials as to print or film or video. Posting sexually explicit material – whether text or image – on a website or in a newsgroup counts as publishing, distributing, or circulating it for the purpose of the obscenity section of the Criminal Code. Likewise, a hate message posted in these ways so as to be accessible to anyone who chooses to view it would count as a communication 'other than in private conversation' for the purpose of the hate propaganda section of the Code.[51] As mentioned earlier, the child pornography statute is distinctive in its criminalization of simple possession as well as distribution. In the case of material accessed via a website, bulletin board service, newsgroup, or filesharing protocol, possession might arguably require downloading to a computer hard drive, disk, or printer. However, in 2002 the government amended the child pornography law so as to require no more than mere viewing of the material, as long as the viewing is intentional. The same amendment also clarified the notion of distribution so as to include 'transmitting' and 'making available' child pornography, in order to ensure that the offence of distribution extends to circulation by electronic means. As far as the Canadian Human Rights Act is concerned, in *Zundel* (2002) the Canadian Human Rights Tribunal asserted its jurisdiction over hate messages posted on Ernst Zundel's website, on the ground that the Internet uses 'the facilities of a telecommunication undertaking within the legislative authority of Parliament'.[52] In case there was any lingering doubt about this jurisdiction, in the fall of 2001 the government amended the act to expressly cover material 'communicated by means of a computer or a group of interconnected or related computers, including the Internet'.[53]

Despite the absence of any medium-specific legislation targeting the Internet, there is no legal vacuum in Canada concerning pornography or hate literature communicated by electronic means. In theory, those responsible for circulating the material (and, in the case of child pornography, those who access it) are susceptible to either criminal or administrative proceedings. In the case of Ernst Zundel, at least, this susceptibility has been more than merely theoretical. However, Zundel also nicely illustrates the distance between theory and practice in this domain. It took the tribunal more than four years to deal with the Zundel case, and by the time it had reached its decision and ordered Zundel to cease and desist from posting hate messages on the Zundelsite he had moved out of its jurisdiction. The tribunal may have succeeded in ridding the country of Zundel, but it did not succeed in shutting down his website, which continues to this day to communicate its message of Holocaust denial. Nor did it succeed in denying access to the site by Canadians. For Internet users in the country it is as though nothing happened. Clearly Zundel is just a special instance of a much wider problem. Just as Canadians import most of their print and video pornography or hate literature, they also import most of their electronic versions of these materials from sites located outside the country. Unless these sites are under the effective control of Canadian residents, they are beyond the jurisdiction of Canadian courts and human rights tribunals. Furthermore, whereas the importation of print or video materials can be regulated by such agencies as Customs and the provincial film review boards, no such controls can be put in place for websites, bulletin board services, or newsgroups located elsewhere and accessed by Canadians. The question, therefore, is not whether there is any law in this domain but whether any of the existing law (with the possible exception of the child pornography statute) can be effectively enforced.[54]

6.2 What Matters

It is obvious from the foregoing that the government has a number of means at its disposal for regulating expression, including both hate propaganda and pornography. Our question, however, is which of these means, if any, can be given a principled justification. What would a public policy concerning freedom of expression look like, if it were to be based on a solid foundation of principle? Which regulatory mechanisms, if any, would be supportable within such a policy? My answer to this question will proceed in two stages. In this section I will outline a number of guidelines or desiderata for policy formation in this area, whose aim will be to distinguish between those concerns which deserve to be at the centre of this process and those which can, and should, be disregarded. These guidelines for policy formation will not dictate a unique outcome, but they will serve as signposts pointing us in the right direction. Then, in the following section, I will suggest the general shape of a justifiable policy.

The first step in this process is the easiest: our normative framework dictates that the case for restricting freedom of expression must be exclusively harm-based. Where a particular form of expression cannot be shown to cause harm then there is no basis for its suppression. Where harm can be demonstrated, on the other hand, it must be balanced against the harm that would be done by the suppression. This fundamental harm-centred orientation in turn yields a number of important corollaries. The first of these is a reminder that harm is not the same as offence. In chapter 2 (sec. 2.4) I argued that moral distress (or offence) cannot be countenanced as harm within the meaning of the Harm Principle, lest the principle provide a justification for shrinking the zone of free expression to the vanishing point. Some people find all pornography (as well as all hate literature) morally offensive and distressing. All right-thinking people (people with the right values, namely yours and mine) find some pornography (as well as all hate literature) morally offensive and distressing. But none of this matters. The fact that a form of expression causes offence or moral distress is never a justification (or any part of a justification) for attempting to suppress it. Only evidence of harm can play this justificatory role.

If offensiveness does not matter, then neither does community intolerance. In chapter 4 (sec. 4.3) I argued that the community standards test for obscenity essentially allows the tolerance level of the majority to determine whether the minority of potential consumers will have access to sexually explicit materials. Since people will tend to be intolerant of whatever they find morally offensive or distressing, reliance on community standards effectively allows offensiveness to count as a justification for suppression. The reluctance of Parliament to provide an adequate working definition of obscenity has led the courts to rely on community standards (whether of decency or tolerance) to draw the line between permissible and impermissible forms of erotic expression. Latterly, since the mid 1980s, community intolerance has been reworked as an indicator of harmfulness (ch. 4, sec. 4.1). Since it is an extremely unreliable indicator, and since harm can in any case be measured by other, more direct, means, the community standards test has become obsolete. If (some or all) pornography is harmful then that is the rationale for its suppression, not whether or not the majority might be prepared to tolerate it. It is time, indeed past time, for the abolition of the test from the field of obscenity legislation and adjudication.

If community intolerance is not an appropriate indicator of harmfulness then we must rely on the best available social-scientific evidence. A further corollary, therefore, is that a harm-based approach to limiting free expression must also be evidence-based. Given the importance of the values, both personal and social, advanced by freedom of expression, the default presumption for any form of expression must be free circulation rather than suppression. Overcoming this presumption will require reliable evidence of harm. How reliable? I noted earlier (ch. 3, sec. 3.3) how the Supreme Court has wrestled with this question in its adjudication of free expression cases. Since section 1 of the Charter requires limits on free expression to be 'demonstrably justified', the court has arguably imposed too low a standard of proof on Parliament by demanding no more than a 'reasonable basis' for the conclusion that a certain category of expressive material imposes a risk of harm where the social-scientific evidence is inconclusive or even entirely wanting. On the other hand, the court does have to decide on the appropriate balance between legislative and judicial authority in a system of division of powers, and a case can be made for some degree of judicial deference. We, however, do not need to take the court's perspective on this question. Whenever legislators set out to restrict our freedom to engage in some activity, whatever it may be, we can and should require them to justify the restriction by providing the evidence of harm. The mere belief in risk of harm – even a reasonable belief – will not suffice, in the absence of the confirming evidence. (Another way of putting this is to say that the belief cannot be truly reasonable in the absence of the confirming evidence.)

The survey undertaken in chapter 5 yielded the conclusion that reliable evidence of harm is relatively scarce. One lesson to be learned is that the evidence is least reliable when the harm in question is most diffuse or generalized. Despite two decades of social-scientific inquiry, for instance, it is difficult to demonstrate any causal relationship between the availability of pornography and the level of either sexual violence against women or the social inequality of women. The case is not appreciably different for the relationship between hate literature and either hate crimes or social discrimination against visible minorities. In both cases we may suspect that (some or all of) the expressive materials in question contribute to a climate of violence or oppression against the target group. But where there are many other factors contributing to the same climate, the marginal contribution made by pornography or hate speech is virtually impossible to measure with any degree of certainty. We can do somewhat better when we can find a more specific causal link between the expressive material and the harm. The best case is that of child pornography, where children are harmed both in the production of the material and in its use by pedophiles in recruiting new victims. Here the pedophile serves as the concrete connection between expression and harm which is difficult to identify when the effects are more diffuse. Hate groups may play the same role for the connection between hate messages and hate crimes, if their dissemination of these messages has the effect of recruiting members who are then motivated to practise their acquired ideology by means of acts of violence against the groups they have been induced to hate.

A further corollary of the harm-centred approach applies exclusively to pornography. As we saw in chapter 5, section 5.1, there is some evidence (far from conclusive) that exposure to violent pornography may have a negative effect on men's attitudes concerning sexual violence against women. If this is indeed the case, we need to ask what it is about the material in question that produces this effect. Is it the sexual content? Is it the explicitness of the sexual content? Or is it the violent content, independently of whether it is sexual (or sexualized)? There is some reason to think that it is the violence that matters in these cases rather than the sex. If so, then the focus of obscenity legislation, which targets sexual content, is entirely wrongheaded. We have seen (ch. 4, sec. 4.2) that the Supreme Court is now permissive concerning explicit sexual content but (to varying degrees) restrictive when that content is either violent or degrading or dehumanizing. This line of thinking may now need to be taken a step further. Perhaps the lesson to be learned is that the sexual content does not matter at all; instead, the risk of harm attaches to forms of expression (whether erotic or not) that either portray women in a degrading way or endorse violence against them. The logical conclusion would then be that we do not need laws specifically targeting erotic content at all. If women need protection against the risk of violence or degradation then that protection should extend to any expressive materials imposing that risk, whether they have sexual content or not.

The only justification for restraints on pornography or hate speech is to reduce the risk of harm to members of vulnerable social groups, such as children, visible minorities, gays, and women. However, we must also keep in mind that any such restraints carry their own risk of harm.

Because freedom of expression itself advances important interests, any limit on that freedom, to the extent that it is enforceable, necessarily impairs those interests. The impairment may take the form of spill-over into the suppression or discouragement of 'legitimate' expression. Where hate speech is concerned, this potential spillover is usually voiced as the 'chilling effect' legal restraints might have on the vigour and robustness of political debate. The concern is not that the restraints might shut down genuine hate speech: the appropriateness of doing that is taken for granted. Rather, the point is that because of inevitable uncertainty concerning what will be regarded as hate speech, the restraints might also stifle the expression of unpopular or unorthodox – but not hateful – political views. Any such chilling effect would significantly narrow the range of acceptable opinions, to the detriment of both political self-expression and democratic discussion. Where pornography is concerned, the same worry is directed at the vagueness of the boundary between the obscene (however that is delineated) and the merely erotic. Laws targeting the former may have the unfortunate side-effect of inhibiting the free circulation of the latter, to the detriment of sexual self-expression.

Possible spillover, however, is not the only concern. Even if the legal definitions of obscenity amd hate propaganda could be carefully crafted so as to eliminate vagueness and uncertainty, and even if the laws were somehow immune to misapplication, they would still impair expressive interests. Whether we sympathize with them or not, pornographers have an interest in producing and distributing their wares, even when they are legally obscene, and members of hate groups have an interest in disseminating their views. Likewise, the consumers of obscene materials have an interest in that consumption – it is a part of their sexual self-expression – and the audience for hate messages has an interest in receiving those messages. Furthermore, there may be a public interest in the circulation of both kinds of material, if only (as Mill pointed out) to serve as a constant challenge to complacent orthodoxy concerning racial and sexual politics. Finally, we need to keep in mind the utterly practical fact that laws with sanctions attached themselves have harmful consequences, in the form of financial penalties or incarceration, for those against whom they are enforced.

These are all real costs, to be weighed against the potential costs to members of vulnerable groups of leaving pornography or hate propaganda unregulated. Consideration of the costs of restraint imposes an effectiveness requirement on any form of legal regulation.[55] If a particu-

lar measure will have no significant protective effect then it is simply a
dead loss. The absence of protective effect could have either of two
sources. On the one hand, the measure might effectively control the circulation of expressive materials which have no demonstrated potential
for harm. This is the problem we considered earlier in requiring evidence of harmfulness. But a regulative measure might also be ineffective in a different way: the material it targets is genuinely harmful, but it
will have no significant effect on its circulation. In this case the measure
is not misdirected, as in the first case, but futile. Laws that are futile are
worse than pointless; because of the serious damage they can do, they
are evil.

Besides effectiveness, the other requirement on a regulative measure
is that it impair expressive interests no more than is necessary in order
to secure protection against harm.[56] Two minimizing strategies are possible. One is to employ means of harm reduction which do not restrain
expression, whenever they will be at least equally effective. This option
may be available in the case of certain of the alleged harms of pornography – namely, harms done to women who participate in the production
of sexually explicit visual materials. If models or performers are subjected to violence, coercion, or exploitation in the production process,
then instead of attempting to address this problem by restraining distribution of the product, a more direct strategy would be to enforce workplace standards concerning harassment, minimum contract conditions,
the ability to organize, and so on.[57] Measures of this sort hold out the
promise of improving the working conditions of women in the industry
while neither denying them employment nor impairing expressive interests.

When other sites of intervention are unavailable, then the goal of
harm reduction may require imposing restraints on the distribution of
expressive materials. Even in that case, however, less costly restraints
are to be preferred, at least where they promise to be equally effective.
Because the consequences of criminal prosecution can be particularly
serious, the use of criminal sanctions requires a particularly strong justification. Interestingly, this is also the Canadian government's view of the
matter: 'Since many acts may be "harmful", and since society has many
other means for controlling or responding to conduct, criminal law
should be used only when the harm caused or threatened is serious, and
when the other, less coercive or less intrusive means do not work or are
inappropriate.'[58] Where controls on pornography or hate speech are
concerned, some of these 'other means' were surveyed in the preceding

section. Human rights law shares two important features with criminal law: it acts as a subsequent restraint on conduct, and its application employs judicial, or quasi-judicial, procedures, with all of the safeguards to the respondent that these entail. The principal point of difference lies in the severity of the penalties it imposes. A conclusion one might therefore draw from the government's dictum is that if human rights law would be as effective as criminal law at limiting the dissemination of hate messages then it is to be preferred on the ground that it is 'less coercive or less intrusive'.

The other alternative regulatory regimes – Customs interception and film board censorship – are both forms of prior restraint. As such, they are certainly milder on the sanction side, since their principal effect is to remove suspect materials from circulation rather than to punish their distribution, or consumption, after the fact. For this very reason, however, they are also arguably more intrusive into expressive interests, since they typically lack the openness, accountability, and challengeability of court or tribunal decisions. As a tradeoff for threatening less serious outcomes, systems of prior restraint offer few of the procedural safeguards that would be available to defendants in court or respondents before a tribunal. They are also particularly frustrating for members of the general public, who are left completely in the dark about the character of the expressive materials they are not being allowed to view or to read.

6.3 An Immodest Proposal

I draw from the foregoing guidelines the conclusion that a defensible policy concerning the regulation of expression must (1) focus on harm to the exclusion of all extraneous considerations, (2) rest on reliable evidence of all alleged harms, (3) balance the harms of expression against those of restraint, (4) employ only measures of harm reduction which promise to be effective, and (5) among equally effective measures prefer those whose costs to expressive interests are lower. Our question now is what such a policy might look like.

My strategy in trying to answer this question will be to work from the 'inside out', beginning with the limits to expressive freedom for which the most compelling justification is available and then applying the lessons learned to the more problematic and ambiguous cases. Our starting point will be the child pornography law (sec. 163.1 of the Criminal Code), whose purpose is to prevent the sexual abuse or exploitation of children.[59] Because children are sexually abused in the making of most child pornography, and also because these materials can be used by pedophiles to recruit children for abuse, the linkage in this case between the expressive material and the harm it does is particularly direct and well verified. Besides its narrower focus and the more reliable evidence of the harm it aims to prevent, the child pornography law has the further advantage over the obscenity statute of working with a content-based definition of the material it is targeting which is free of reliance on community standards. On the other hand, the law intrudes more deeply into expressive freedom by virtue of criminalizing not just the production or distribution of child pornography but also its mere possession. As the Supreme Court recognized in the *Sharpe* case, the possession offence can be justified only if the definition of child pornography is no broader than it needs to be in order to prevent the harms in question. So let us begin by examining that definition more closely.

Because it is rather complicated, it will be useful to work with a simplified catalogue of prohibited materials. Roughly speaking, the child pornography law targets the following kinds of expression:[60]

1 Visual materials (photographs, films, videos, drawings, etc.) which
   (a) graphically depict children engaged in intimate sexual activity, or
   (b) graphically depict adults engaged in intimate sexual activity, wherethe adults are represented as children, or
   (c) depict nudity in children for a sexual purpose, or
   (d) advocate or counsel any sexual offence against children.
2 Written materials (stories, diaries, essays, etc.) which
   (a) depict any sexual offence against a child for a sexual purpose, or
   (b) advocate or counsel any sexual offence against children.

This list makes it clear that the sweep of the law is very wide indeed. The question is whether it is too wide to satisfy the *Oakes* test of minimal impairment. In that light, some of the categories seem particularly problematic. Two of them, 1(d) and 2(b), include purely argumentative materials, such as an essay advocating some form of sexual activity between adults and children. Whatever we might think of such advocacy, it is difficult both to conceptualize it as child pornography and to find a convincing rationale for its prohibition.[61] I am aware of no evidence implicating materials of this sort in actual harm to children, since they involve no children in their production and would be of little use in recruiting children for abuse. Furthermore, any prohibition of the circulation of an idea is a content restriction which makes particularly deep inroads into expressive freedom. If, on the other hand, these clauses are meant to capture (visual or verbal) depictions of child sexual activity which, by virtue of having the function of sexual stimulation, implicitly endorse this activity then they would seem to be redundant, since such depictions are captured elsewhere in the definition.

A broader, and more difficult, question arises from the fact that, even if we delete these two problematic clauses, the definition still includes not only visual materials whose production involves the actual sexual abuse of children but also materials (both visual and verbal) in whose production real children were not implicated, including stories (2(a)), drawings or computer-generated simulations (1(a)), and visual materials depicting adults as children (1(b)). In these latter cases no harms to participants are in question. The rationale for their inclusion must therefore rest entirely on the prevention of more indirect harms to third parties, especially the potential use of such materials to lure children into abusive situations. As far as I am aware, there is no evidence that erotic stories have any such potential, so it is difficult to make out a good case for including any written materials within the purview of the law.

Visual materials in which the depiction is simulated or virtual are a harder case. Category 1(b), for example, prohibits visual representations of sexual activity involving persons who are not actually underage but are depicted as such. This provision is obviously intended to prevent circumvention of the law by using adult models or performers who are dressed or otherwise made to look much younger. Much material of this sort exists; indeed, it is the standard fare on commercial websites claiming to offer explicit sexual images involving 'young' models. However, it is of little interest to collectors of child pornography or to pedophiles hoping to recruit children for abuse. While it could in principle be used for this purpose, there is no reason to think that it would be more successful than other forms of adult pornography which are perfectly legal. In any case, the principal target for law enforcement agencies is material depicting very young (pubescent or pre-pubescent) children for whom there are no plausible adult surrogates.[62] The provision is also inherently difficult to enforce. While producers of sexually explicit materials can be required to document the age of all models or performers (and most are willing to comply, if only to stay on the safe side of the law), how are we to decide when someone over the age of eighteen is being depicted as underage (unless the scenario somehow makes that clear)? It is doubtful, therefore, whether this component of the definition of child pornography has any useful function.

What then of real-looking but computer-generated images of children in sexual scenarios? This question was recently adjudicated by the U.S. Supreme Court in *Ashcroft* (2002a). In the Child Pornography Prevention Act of 1996 Congress expanded the federal prohibition of child pornography so as to include sexually explicit images that appear to depict minors but were produced by means other than using real children (such as computer-imaging technology). In its decision the court struck down this expansion on the ground that 'virtual child pornography' lacked the direct connection to the sexual abuse of children that was involved in 'real' pornography. Moreover, the court concluded, the claim that virtual materials could still be used to groom or seduce children was too speculative to justify a content restriction on expression. The effect of the court's decision was to confine the definition of child pornography to materials whose production involved the use of real children.[63]

Given its decision in *Sharpe*, there is no reason to think that the Canadian court would draw a distinction between real and virtual child pornography. On this issue, therefore, we are offered two diametrically opposed positions: continuing to include visual depictions of child sexual abuse whether or not real children were involved in their production or restricting the definition of child pornography to visual records of actual abuse. The choice between these alternatives is not an easy one. However, especially in light of the possession offence, which trenches particularly deeply on individual freedom, it would be consonant with the evidence-based approach which I have advocated to expand the definition no farther than reliable evidence of harm. That evidence is incontrovertible in the case of materials produced by abusing children. Furthermore, the possession offence has a particularly compelling rationale in this case, since it can be argued that consumer demand for 'real' pornography stimulates the market for more production and therefore more abuse. Where this rationale is absent, it is reasonable to demand reliable evidence of the use of virtual pornography to groom victims. Absent such evidence, the safer route is to limit the definition of child pornography to its narrowest confines.

If we consolidate our results to this point then we are left with categories 1(a) and 1(c), understood in each case to include only materials depicting real children. However, even category 1(a) is not without its defects. Unlike category 1(c), it lacks the condition that the depiction must be 'for a sexual purpose', which the Supreme Court has glossed as meaning that it could be 'reasonably perceived as intended to cause sexual stimulation'.[64] In its present formulation, therefore, it could capture explicit depictions of child sexual activities which had an educational or scientific, rather than a sexual, purpose. In its 1993 version the child pornography law provided an exception for materials with an educational, scientific, or medical purpose.[65] However, the amendments tabled by the government in Bill C-20 would delete this paragraph in favour of a (much vaguer) 'public good' defence.[66] In that case, it becomes imperative that educational or scientific materials, with no stimulative function, not be caught by the definition in the first place. The qualifier 'for a sexual purpose' should therefore be read into the formulation of category 1(a). This has the effect of bringing the materials in this category within the accepted notion of pornography, which requires that their purpose be sexual arousal.[67]

One further difficulty with the definition remains. For the purpose of section 163.1 a child is defined as someone under the age of eighteen. This age limit has the advantage both of being somewhat conservative and of being in line with similar provisions in many other jurisdictions, especially the United States. It is therefore widely recognized and observed by producers and distributors of mainstream pornography.[68] There is a case to be made for Canadian law harmonizing with international standards in this area. However, the use of eighteen as a cut-off point is curiously at odds with the other Criminal Code provisions concerning sexual offences against children (secs 151–153). Simplifying considerably, those provisions absolutely prohibit sexual contact only with children under the age of fourteen (secs 151 and 152). Between the age of fourteen and seventeen, such contact is prohibited only where a relationship of trust, authority, or dependency exists with the child – in other words, where there is reason to suspect exploitation of the child (sec. 153). Now it could be argued that using a child in the production of pornography is tantamount to exploiting such a relationship, but it is difficult to see how this could be made out where the pedophile is a stranger or someone only casually connected to the child. The section as written seems aimed principally at those who have an established relationship with the child (parents, guardians, teachers, coaches, etc.). The amendments introduced by the government in Bill C-20 add an exploitative relationship to the prohibited list in section

153, where the following factors are to be taken into account in determining when a relationship is exploitative: age difference, the evolution of the relationship, and the degree of control or influence over the child. This provision arguably harmonizes better with the child pornography law, since most pedophiles may satisfy the conditions for an exploitative relationship with the children they recruit to appear in visual pornography. However, it is noteworthy that the government elected the foregoing change in the characterization of sexual offences against children instead of raising the age of consent (say, to sixteen). That decision might well have been a sound one, since a rigid age of consent risks criminalizing many forms of innocuous sexual contact with (and between) underage adolescents. However, it does leave the sexual offence provisions (whose age of consent is fourteen) out of step with the child pornography provision (whose age of consent is eighteen). It is difficult to understand why it would be unlawful to depict sexual activity (with a sixteen-year-old, for instance) which is itself perfectly lawful. A case could therefore be made for enforcing a single age of consent for both sexual activities and depictions of such activities, somewhere between fourteen at the lower end and eighteen at the upper.[69] However, a better alternative would be to incorporate sections 151 to 153 into section 163.1 by defining child pornography as any graphic visual depiction, for a sexual purpose, of child nudity or of intimate sexual activity involving children which would itself be a sexual offence.

While in its present form the child pornography law is overbroad, and therefore trenches too deeply on freedom of expression, it is clear that a version of the law which is more narrowly targeted in this way would easily surpass the threshold for criminal legislation. In light of both the similarities and the differences between the child pornography and obscenity laws, it is natural now to ask whether the same case can be made for criminal legislation regulating (at least some) adult pornography. One thing that is clear by now is that the harm done by pornography, whatever it might be, cannot be measured by any appeal to community standards. This implies, at a minimum, that the current obscenity law in Canada, with its obsolete reference to 'undue exploitation of sex', must go.[70] It is the vagueness and unworkability of that definition that led the judiciary to rely on community standards to define the boundary between the obscene and the acceptable. If we are to have an obscenity law at all then, like the child pornography law, it must bite the bullet and provide an operational definition of obscenity in terms of both content and function. In the case of child pornography that project is feasible, since we can specify the objectionable content in terms of sexual images of children. No parallel content-based definition seems possible in the case of obscenity. During the 1980s the government of the day made two attempts to replace section 163 of the Criminal Code with legislation which defined obscenity in terms of a catalogue of prohibited depictions.[71] Both attempts failed, in part because any such catalogue was found to be too inflexible to accommodate evolving standards of sexual morality and tolerance. Whatever its other defects, at least the community standards criterion was capable of moving with the times. But the deeper problem was that 'bad' pornography (for which legal regulation might be appropriate) cannot be distinguished from 'good' pornography simply on the basis of the sexual activities it depicts or the body parts it displays. The same content – the sexual scenario itself – is capable of depiction in 'good' or 'bad', pornographic or non-pornographic, ways.

The *Butler* decision in 1992 went a considerable distance toward resolving the very considerable legal uncertainty throughout the 1980s as to which erotic depictions were to be regarded as obscene. Henceforth, the problematic representations were of sexual violence or degradation; depictions of sexual scenarios free of these features, however explicit they might be, were to fall outside the prohibited area. While this was doubtless a step forward, it did not solve the underlying definitional problem. For one thing, even a very explicit depiction of sexual violence or degradation can be produced for a number of different purposes, only one of which is sexual stimulation or arousal.[72] In order to capture the specifically pornographic the sexual *purpose* must be added to the sexual *content*. But even when that is done it is virtually impossible to contour the definition of 'bad' pornography (the obscene) so as to map onto the harm whose prevention is the sole legitimate rationale of obscenity legislation. Consider, for example, visual depictions of the following two scenarios:

The gang-rape scenario. The repeated rape of a young woman is explicitly depicted in such a way as to be sexually arousing for a male audience. While she is initially shown to be resisting her attackers, she eventually comes to welcome and enjoy the violation.

The BDSM scenario. Two women are shown engaging in consensual sadomasochistic activities in which the 'top' subjects the 'bottom' to bondage and mild forms of torture. While the depiction is clearly meant to

be sexually stimulating, the bottom is shown to be an active participant in the scenario and capable of calling an end to it whenever she
chooses.

In both cases the activity depicted is violent and the depiction has the
purpose of sexual arousal. Both therefore fall within the category of violent pornography. Yet while the first depiction clearly endorses violence
against women by eroticizing it, it is far from clear that the second does
so or that there is any identifiable kind of harm we might expect to flow
from it. (Perhaps it would stimulate other couples – same-sex or otherwise – to experiment with consensual BDSM, but so what?) The difference between the two depictions is that only the first expresses an
attitude of hatred or contempt toward women; in eroticizing forced sexual violence against them it degrades them to the status of objects or
things. This further element – the endorsement of a degraded status for
women – is not picked up by a content-based definition of obscenity,
even when the content is violent and its depiction is for a sexual purpose. It is that element, however, which appears to constitute the potential harm of misogynist pornography and to provide the sole legitimate
rationale for exercising legal control over it.

As we have seen, the strongest rationale for exercising such control
over child pornography is to prevent the sexual abuse of children
involved in its production. However, when we turn to participant harms
in the case of adult pornography, imposing content restrictions on the
product appears to be fundamentally misdirected. Unlike the case of
children, exploitation or abuse of adult women, however frequently it
occurs, is not an essential feature of the production process. Given the
evident demand for pornography, criminalizing its production will succeed only in driving it underground, making the enforcement of fair
employment practices impossible. The preferable route is to regard this
as another problem of working conditions to be dealt with through
enforcement of regulations in the workplace.[73] As the 'adult' film industry goes increasingly mainstream, it should be required to adopt the
normal protections for workers against harassment and duress: standardized contracts, minimum wages, supervision of shoots, the ability to
organize effective associations or unions, and so on. With the constant
risk of sexually transmitted diseases there are potentially serious health
concerns to be dealt with as well, but they are best addressed as workplace health and safety issues.

The harms most frequently associated with pornography are its encouragement of sexual violence against women and its reinforcement of women's inferior social status. As we saw in the previous chapter, the supporting evidence for these effects is, for the most part, inconclusive at best. Given an initial presumption in favour of expressive liberty, inconclusive evidence is insufficient to surmount the threshold for criminal regulation. If the purpose of the obscenity law is to prevent these diffuse and systemic harms, then it must specifically target erotic materials which are misogynist in the attitudes they express toward women. Misogynist attitudes, however, can also be expressed in visual or verbal materials with no erotic content whatever (for instance, in novels or films portraying female characters as brainless). What this suggests is that the focus on the sexual, which is the hallmark of an obscenity law, is fundamentally misdirected. Pornography is problematic when it constitutes hate literature concerning women. But in that case the appropriate vehicle for its legal regulation is legislation targeting not the obscene but the hateful.

The logic of the obscenity law therefore takes us to the hate law. As I conceive it, this is the crux of the matter concerning defensible limits to expressive freedom and the hardest case to decide. Setting aside its details, section 319(2) of the Criminal Code prohibits any public communication intended to promote hatred against an 'identifiable group'. What is most obviously problematic about the statute, and the principal source of civil libertarian objections to it, is that it criminalizes the circulation of hateful opinions whether or not they have any discernible effect on the level of hostility toward their target groups. It is the nature of the views – whether they are hateful or not – that matters for the purpose of the law, not whether they actually succeed in influencing attitudes. As far as the law is concerned, it does not matter whether a hate message evokes nothing but ridicule or repudiation, as long as the intent of the message, as interpreted from its content and the context of its dissemination, was to promote hatred.

The most common argument in favour of regulating hate speech is that it contributes to a general climate of hostility or bigotry directed against target minorities which can in turn encourage or reinforce practices of discrimination or violence. The main problem with this argument, as with the parallel argument concerning pornography and women, is that we have very little hard evidence of this causal relationship. Because the attitudinal effects attributed to hate messages are diffuse and systemic, they are difficult both to measure and to trace to one particular cause. It is undeniable that members of racial and ethnic minorities in Canada have been victims of both discrimination and hate crimes (whether against persons or property). But it is far from clear just how much of this inequality and violence can be attributed to the circulation of hate messages. Because the groups most responsible for these messages operate clandestinely on the margins of Canadian society, they are likely to have little influence on mainstream public opinion. It might well be that the principal consequence of allowing them to voice their views openly and frankly, without codes and subtexts, would be to marginalize and discredit them even further.

The recent episode involving David Ahenakew provides a case in point. Ahenakew has been an influential aboriginal leader, with a long history of achievements in advancing Native rights and interests in Canada in general and Saskatchewan in particular. However, in December 2002, at a meeting of the Federation of Saskatchewan Indian Nations on the subject of health care, he made a number of strongly anti-Semitic remarks, including the suggestion that the Nazis were justified in initiating the Holocaust. Unlike the rantings of obscure white supremacists, these remarks received prominent media attention. They also elicited an overwhelming backlash of condemnation, not only from Jewish groups but also from Native leaders, politicians, the media, and so on. Ahenakew was stripped of every position he occupied as a Native leader and faces expulsion as well from the prestigious Order of Canada. There is no doubt that Ahenakew's remarks constituted hate propaganda, within the meaning of the statute. However, there is little likelihood that they succeeded in promoting any hatred against Jews or strengthening anti-Semitic attitudes in Canada. Six months after the event the Attorney General of Saskatchewan finally decided to proceed with charges against Ahenakew under section 319(2). However, it is difficult to see what the point of the prosecution might be. The overwhelming adverse reaction to his remarks would seem to serve by itself as an adequate deterrent, both to him and to others of like opinion.

The Ahenakew incident illustrates two important points. Recall the condition that criminal sanctions should be employed only 'when the harm caused or threatened is serious, and when the other, less coercive or less intrusive means do not work or are inappropriate'. Both discrimination and hate violence certainly qualify as serious harms. However, there appear to be less intrusive means available of neutralizing any contribution that hate speech might make to these practices. One of these means is precisely the kind of counterspeech elicited by Ahenakew's remarks. By the time the uproar over his comments had subsided and he had been denounced by every influential source of public opinion, the net effect was a forceful reminder of the evils of anti-Semitism. The antiracism cause was arguably better served by having Ahenakew speak his mind and arouse a firestorm of opposition than it would have been had he been intimidated into silence by the fear of prosecution. The other point has to do with an argument commonly used to support the criminalization of hate speech, namely that it serves as a vehicle for society to express its condemnation of racial hatred and bigotry. This purely symbolic function of law is, of course, rejected by a harm-based approach. But in any case the Ahenakew incident is a timely reminder that we don't need courts to voice our repugnance concerning racism when so many other authoritative social institutions can be relied on to do this.

There are further problems with the hate propaganda law in its present form. When it was first enacted in 1970 it may have made sense to restrict the scope of its protection to groups identified by 'colour, race, religion or ethnic origin'. However, subsequent developments in law and public policy have resulted in a longer list of social groups considered to be vulnerable to discrimination and/or violence. The Canadian Human Rights Act, adopted in 1977, currently prohibits discrimination based on 'race, national or ethnic origin, colour, religion, age, sex, sexual orientation, marital status, family status, disability or conviction for an offence for which a pardon has been granted'. Meanwhile, section 15 of the Charter, which came into effect in 1985, excludes discrimination based on 'race, national or ethnic origin, colour, religion, sex, age or mental or physical disability' (sexual orientation has subsequently been 'read in' to this list by the Supreme Court). Even more to the point, section 718.2 of the Criminal Code provides for penalty enhancement in the case of offences motivated by 'bias, prejudice, or hate based on race, national or ethnic origin, language, colour, religion, sex, age, mental or physical disability, sexual orientation or any other similar factor'. In light of all these precedents, the much shorter list of protected groups in section 319(2) seems arbitrary. If the aim of the statute is to prevent hostility toward religious, racial, or ethnic groups then why would this protection not be extended equally to other groups, such as women and gays and lesbians, who have also been, and continue to be, victims of both discrimination and hate-motivated violence?[74] If the statute is defensible at all, simple consistency requires that the scope of its protection be extended.

I have argued above that the sole defensible rationale for the obscenity law would be much better served by expanding the list of protected groups to include women. Others have made the same case on behalf of gays and lesbians,[75] a case that was recently acknowledged by the House of Commons when it passed a private member's bill adding 'sexual orientation' to the definition of an 'identifiable group'.[76] While these expansions are required by the internal logic of section 319(2), they also have the effect of accentuating another problem with the law, namely the inevitable vagueness of the notion of hatred. In *Keegstra* (1990) the Supreme Court interpreted hatred of a group to include only the most intense feelings of antipathy or detestation toward members of the group.[77] While this gloss helps somewhat to focus the concept by excluding the milder forms of dislike or ill-will, it still leaves much room for interpretation. When does the expression of strong feelings of disapproval or condemnation, directed at a group as such, cross the line into promoting hatred toward the group?

Consider the question of sexual orientation. What are we to make of the opinion, frequently voiced in mainstream outlets such as newspapers and academic journals, that any sexual activity between same-sex partners is inherently immoral or evil? During recent public debates in Canada concerning the legal recognition of same-sex marriages, Alphonse de Valk, the editor of a prominent Catholic magazine, published an opinion piece in a major Toronto newspaper claiming that homosexual acts are narcissistic, unnatural, pathological, and 'grave moral aberrations'.[78] Likewise, in an earlier article published in the *Notre Dame Journal of Law, Ethics and Public Policy,* John Finnis, professor of law at Oxford University, argued that gay sex is immoral, evil, and worthless and likened it to prostitution, masturbation, bestiality, and sex between strangers.[79] In saying such things were de Valk and Finnis promoting hatred against gays and lesbians? It is arguable that they contributed to a climate in which members of this 'identifiable group' would be regarded with aversion or contempt, and that this is the effect they intended (or at least should reasonably have foreseen). I am confident, however, that most people would dismiss as ridiculous any attempt to bring criminal sanctions to bear on opinions such as these, however hateful they might be, when they are expressed by respectable figures in a mainstream newspaper or an academic journal. How then could we justify applying the law to the expression of equally intense negative opinions (whether against gays or any other vulnerable minority) by less respectable sources (such as hate groups)? If the notion of promoting hatred is broad enough to apply, at least in principle, to the publication of opinions like those of de Valk and Finnis then it is overly broad.

The root problem with the hate propaganda law lies in the very idea of criminalizing speech on the ground that it might contribute to an atmosphere of hostility toward a particular social group. That problem merely becomes more visible if the roster of protected groups is expanded (as the rationale behind the law surely requires), but it also afflicts the law in its present form. What makes the law particularly difficult to defend is the fact that hate speech (whoever the target group might be) is political speech. Recall that in his defence of 'liberty of discussion', Mill was particularly concerned to safeguard the expression of opinions concerning 'morals, religion, politics, social relations and the business of life'.[80] Criminal regulation of hate speech aims precisely at the expression of opinions in this vital territory – odious opinions, to be sure, but opinions none the less. Because the expressive interests at stake in political speech, broadly defined in this way, are so important, the regulation of such speech requires a particularly strong justification. The argument that hate speech should be criminalized because of its potential contribution to a climate of hostility fails to surpass this justificatory threshold.

This failure is all the more evident when doubts can be raised about the effectiveness of any such regulation. Since most hard-core hate propaganda (the kind generated by hate groups) is now disseminated via the Internet, it may lie beyond the effective reach of Canadian law. The Canadian Human Rights Tribunal proceeding against Ernst Zundel has shown that human rights law can be used against websites which are either situated in Canada or, while situated abroad, are controlled by Canadian residents. There is no reason to think that criminal proceedings could not succeed as well. But what does success accomplish? In Zundel's case the effect of the proceeding was to secure his relocation from Canada to the United States, from where his website remains as accessible to Canadians as it ever was. We might congratulate ourselves at ridding the country of a notorious anti-Semite (even if only temporarily), but how has that accomplishment diminished the electronic circulation of hate messages within our borders? How, indeed, could we ever diminish that circulation by means of law without unacceptable intrusion into the domain of individual liberty?[81] Individual endusers may, of course, choose to block access from their computers to hate sites (or, more frequently, pornography sites) by means of filtering software. But the imposition of such filters by government at the level of, say, ser-

vice providers would stand no chance of surviving constitutional scrutiny.[82] With the notable exception of child pornography, where the
downloading or even mere viewing of images has been defined as an
offence, existing Canadian law appears to be utterly ineffective at preventing the electronic circulation within the country of objectionable
materials.

For all of the foregoing reasons, the principal argument in favour of
the hate propaganda law – that it can play an important part in preventing discrimination or violence against vulnerable groups by reducing
the general level of hostility toward them – appears to be insufficient.
Because this is not the only argument in support of it, it would be pre-
mature to conclude that the law is indefensible. However, the case
against regulating hate speech by means of human rights legislation
appears to be conclusive. The sole purpose of such legislation is to prohibit discriminatory practices against stipulated social groups. Therefore the justification for including the communication of hate messages
as itself a discriminatory practice must be that it will tend to promote
and reinforce other such practices. If that justification is weak then
there is no reason for human rights law to concern itself with the mere
expression of hateful attitudes concerning the protected groups, as
opposed to concrete discriminatory practices reflecting those attitudes.

Two other arguments for the criminalization of hate speech remain
to be considered. One is that hate messages are hurtful to members
of the target minorities when they are directed specifically at them,
whether in the form of verbal abuse, telephone threats, graffiti spraypainted on sacred places, or whatever. In these cases the harm done by
the communication is direct and verifiable. However, in virtually all of
them the means chosen for delivering the message is itself an offence:
criminal harassment, uttering a threat, mischief, and so on. Where there
is evidence that these offences are hate-motivated, which will generally
be provided by the content of the message, then they can be treated as
hate crimes for the purpose of penalty enhancement.[83] In other cases,
such as neo-Nazi rallies in Jewish neighbourhoods, context (time, manner, or circumstance) restrictions should suffice to ensure that the
offending messages are not imposed on an unwilling target audience. In
none of these instances does there seem to be a need to address the
problem by imposing a general content restriction on hate speech.

To this point we have found a sharp contrast between hate propaganda and child pornography: in the latter case, but not the former, the
material subject to legal regulation is implicated in a concrete and verifi-

able way in the causation of a specific kind of harm. However, we still need to consider the possibility that hate groups play a role in the causal nexus of hate violence analogous to the role of the pedophile in the sexual abuse of children. There is little doubt that the functions of hate messages disseminated by such groups include both recruitment of new members and motivation of adherents to commit hate crimes against members of target groups. This function makes for a much more direct causal relationship between the message and the violence, one which is not mediated by shifts in the overall climate of public opinion about minorities. However, it also opens up the possibility of treating the communication of hate messages, under certain circumstances, as incitement to this violence. The circumstances would be the ones cited by Mill in his discussion of the advocacy of tyrannicide, which would qualify as an instigation 'only if an overt act has followed, and at least a probable connexion can be established between the act and the instigation'.[84] In the previous chapter I cited some instances of hate crimes committed by members, or former members, of known hate groups and clearly inspired by the ideology of those groups.[85] In those cases in which the motivation for the crime can be traced back in a reasonably direct way to hate messages communicated by the groups, there seems no reason not to regard the latter as having incited the violence and as being liable to prosecution on that basis.

As far as hate speech is concerned, the focus of our attention has been on section 319(2) of the Criminal Code – the hate propaganda law at stake in the *Keegstra* case. Less attention is usually devoted to section 319(1), which prohibits communications in any public place which incite hatred against an identifiable group 'where such incitement is likely to lead to a breach of the peace'. These two subsections of section 319, together with section 318, which prohibits the advocacy or promotion of genocide, constitute the Criminal Code provisions concerning hate speech. If, as I think, the principal concern about hate speech is its capacity for inciting violence on the part of those who are in its thrall, then a case can be made for deleting section 319(2) as unnecessarily intrusive of expressive interests and instead reworking section 319(1) so as to apply to cases in which the causation of hate crimes can be traced back to the influence of particular hate messages. Where this is the case, the incitement can itself be classified as a hate crime. This approach is compatible with, indeed requires, expansion of the list of protected groups in section 319(1) to include women, as well as gays and lesbians. In that case the producers or distributors of misogynist pornography would be vulnerable to prosecution for incitement if it could be shown that their publications inspired specific acts of sexual violence against women. In this way both the hate propaganda law and the obscenity law could be subsumed in legislation prohibiting the incitement of hate violence.

My conclusion, therefore, is that no law imposing a content restriction on hate speech can be justified.[86] In reaching this conclusion I am acutely conscious that, as a straight white gentile male, I am not a member of any of the groups whose security and equality (an expanded version of) hate propaganda legislation is meant to protect; the view of the matter from within those groups might be very different. None the less, my claim is that legislation of this sort cannot survive an objective cost-benefit analysis: the equality benefits it promises are too tenuous and uncertain to balance the liberty costs which it imposes. Since my conclusion flows from this kind of consequentialist balancing, it has no more certainty than this methodology can bestow upon it. But the same uncertainty would afflict a case in favour of hate speech regulation. Calculations of consequences on a large social scale are always open to doubt, especially when they depend on the evidence available at a particular time. My conclusion is based on the best evidence I have been able to locate; should new evidence come to light, or should the level of racism, sexism, and homophobia in Canada undergo a significant increase then it may need to be rethought. Meanwhile, I advance it with as much confidence as the nature of consequentialist argumentation will permit.

The policy directions defended to this point will also dictate an abolitionist conclusion for the mechanisms of prior restraint: censorship by Customs officials or film review boards. Since they impose content restrictions by means of bureaucratic procedures which provide complainants with few of the protections and safeguards they would enjoy in a court of law, these regulatory regimes have a particularly high justificatory threshold to surmount. Nothing in their history suggests that they are capable of meeting this challenge. The long, sorry episode of the *Little Sisters* case revealed the arbitrariness of Customs censorship, its persistent homophobia, and its stubborn resistance to change for everyone to see. Even the Supreme Court majority that upheld the constitutionality of the enabling legislation went out of its way to chastise the Customs bureaucracy for its administration of its censorship procedures. It is difficult to share the majority's naïve confidence that Customs could be trusted to do better; in its insistence that the fault lay in the legislation, rather than merely in its application, the dissenting minority had much the better of the argument. In any case, as more and more sexually explicit (and hateful) materials enter the country in electronic form, vigilance at the border will become less and less relevant. The time is overdue for Customs to get out of the business of intercepting expressive materials and focus its attention instead on tariffs and duties.

It can be argued that the provincial film review boards do a somewhat better job of applying the *Butler* criteria to pornographic films and videos, allowing the merely sexually explicit through and screening out the violent or degrading. However, deciding what actually constitutes sexual violence or degradation calls for sophisticated judgment, and the boards are still reliant for guidance on (what they perceive as) community standards of tolerance. The very idea that everyone within a board's jurisdiction will be prevented from seeing a film simply because the majority are thought to disapprove of its distribution should be deeply disturbing to anyone who cares about expressive freedom. Furthermore, the boards are still capable of reaching ludicrous decisions about mainstream films, as the Ontario board did in the *Fat Girl* episode. They can play an important educative role by classifying films and videos, thereby alerting potential viewers to their contents. But their power to prohibit distribution outright, or to demand cuts as a condition of distribution, should be removed from them.

The underlying problem with systems of prior restraint – one which applies with equal force to both Customs and the film boards – was articulated nearly a half-century ago by Thomas Emerson: 'The function of the censor is to censor. He has a professional interest in finding things to suppress ... The long history of prior restraint reveals over and over again that the personal and institutional forces inherent in the system nearly always end in a stupid, unnecessary, and extreme suppression.'[87] The alternative to prior restraint is not no restraint, since, where appropriate, expressive materials can be regulated through the procedures of criminal law. The concern is sometimes expressed that removal of the prior restraint mechanisms would overload the court system as cases come to be pursued instead by the police. However, even if the existing hate and obscenity laws were kept in place, the *Keegstra* and *Butler* decisions have gone a considerable way toward clarifying the criteria for the hateful and the obscene. Law enforcement officials could then limit their attention to expressive materials that were obviously pushing the boundaries of the acceptable. In any case, the pressure on the courts would be considerably reduced if those laws were abandoned in favour of a more targeted focus on the incitement of hate violence (sexual or otherwise). There would be far fewer cases in which the incitement charge could be made out, but they are the ones that matter.

6.4 Conclusion

The policy directions outlined in the preceding section can be summed up in four points: (1) *A slimmed down child pornography law*: the possession offence retained within the context of a narrower definition of child pornography; (2) *No (further) content restrictions*: no criminal or human rights legislation prohibiting expressive materials on the basis of obscene or hateful content; (3) *More use of context restrictions*: in particular, an expanded criminal prohibition of expressive materials inciting hate violence; (4) *No prior restraint*: no censorship of expressive materials by Customs officials, film boards, or other bureaucracies. This is the policy which, I contend, results from the consistent application of a principled normative framework – one which is both harm-centred and evidence-based. Because it defines a considerably more expansive right of free expression than the one the Canadian courts have been willing to protect, advocating a policy of this sort places me at odds with every major Supreme Court decision on free expression since 1990, with the exception of the *Zundel* decision in 1992 which struck down the 'spreading false news' section of the Criminal Code. All of the remaining decisions – *Keegstra, Taylor, Butler, Little Sisters*, even *Sharpe* – I am committed to regarding as mistaken. They have all either upheld laws – criminal legislation governing hate propaganda and obscenity, human rights legislation governing hate propaganda, and Customs legislation authorizing censorship of hate and obscenity – which I believe ought to have been struck down, or have failed to deal adequately with a law – legislation governing child pornography – which, while acceptable in principle, remains overbroad in its current form.

The common defect in all of these decisions is the court's attenuation of the requirement that a restriction of expressive freedom be justified by means of credible evidence of the harm done by the form of expression in question. In place of this requirement the court has imposed a much lower justificatory threshold on Parliament by demanding no more than a 'reasonable basis' for the restriction. What has been lost sight of in this process is the section 1 requirement that limits to Charter rights be 'demonstrably justified in a free and democratic society'.

Where no reliable evidence has been presented that expressive materials can significantly impair important interests, such as security or equality, then the case for limiting freedom has not been demonstrated. In showing this degree of deference to the legislature, the court has doubtless been acting on what it regards as its proper function in a system of checks and balances, and a stricter level of scrutiny would certainly have elicited more complaints about 'judicial activism'. For better or worse, however, the court has been assigned the task of interpreting and applying the Charter, and there is nothing objectionably activist in taking seriously the section 1 condition for justifying limits to expressive freedom.

The aim of this book has been to articulate a framework for determining limits to the right of free expression and to apply it to the particular cases of hate propaganda and pornography. This process has eventuated in a blueprint for a society that strikes an appropriate balance between the potentially competing values of liberty and equality. Having sketched the outcome I favour, I will conclude with a note of pessimism about the prospects of ever achieving it. There are only two means available for expanding the range of expressive freedom: politics and law. But there is little likelihood that any political party will assign a high priority to legal reforms which will be seen as privileging the activities of hatemongers and pornographers, neither of whom form or could form a particularly effective lobby. Meanwhile, the Supreme Court has had its way with these issues and has shown no interest in revisiting them. Being neither a politician nor a lawyer, I have no way forward to propose. As a philosopher I must limit myself to mapping the promised land, leaving to others the task of getting us there.

Notes

Chapter 1 A Theory of Free Expression?

1 The analysis which follows is a greatly simplified version of Sumner 1987, ch. 2.
2 Hart 1982, 171–3.
3 I have borrowed the model of the core and periphery of a right from Wellman 1985, ch. 4.
4 See Wellman 1985, ch. 2; Sumner 1987, ch. 2.
5 For a fuller analysis of the normative function of restrictions and prerogatives, see Scheffler 1982; Kagan 1989.
6 None the less, for convenience I will frequently refer in what follows to the right to free expression, or free speech, since these phrases have such an established place in our moral/political/legal lexicon.
7 In analysing the content of the right I will tend to favour 'expression' (the standard term in Canadian jurisprudence) over 'speech' (the established American usage). The terminological divergence stems from the fact that the Canadian Charter of Rights and Freedoms guarantees freedom of expression, while the American Bill of Rights protects freedom of speech. Since I will be focusing primarily on Canadian law and jurisprudence, it seems appropriate to use the terminology in which it is commonly couched. I also prefer 'expression' to 'speech' on the ground that (outside jurisprudential contexts) it is colloquially broader: many media (such as visual images or dance) which it is natural to include as forms of expression can be described as speech only with considerable strain. However, I will not be fussy in this linguistic preference. Because it would be tedious to stick always with the same terminology, from time to time I will help myself to phrases such as 'free speech', 'hate speech', etc. In every context I will treat 'speech' as synonymous with 'expression'.

8 See ch. 3, sec. 3.1.
9 The classic source for the distinction is Berlin 1969.
10 Conflicts of rights will be examined more closely in ch. 3, sec. 3.1.
11 Defamation also figures in the law in the form of the tort (or, sometimes, also the crime) of libel. Although the law of libel can be an important constraint on expression, it lies outside the scope of this inquiry, except for the affinity between hate speech (or pornography) and group defamation (for a brief treatment of which see ch. 5, sec. 5.3).
12 This definition, and its adjudicative implications, will be examined at length in ch. 4.
13 As things stand in Canada right now, most pornography is not legally obscene.
14 Gloria Steinem was possibly the first and certainly the most influential; see Steinem 1980.
15 For definitions of this sort see Longino 1980, 42–5; MacKinnon 1993, 22–3; Cornell 1995, 106.
16 What is one to make, for instance, of consensual bondage and discipline, or dominance and submission? For diametrically opposed analyses, all by self-described feminist writers, see SAMOIS 1982; Linden et al. 1982.
17 For this reason, among others, I will draw no distinction in this work between pornography and erotica. While I will consistently favour the former term, I will feel free to substitute the latter where necessary for expressive variety.
18 To see how long and convoluted it could become, readers should consult Rea 2001.
19 Quoted in Strossen 1995, 53.
20 This similarity of function between (hard-core) pornography and sex aids led Frederick Schauer to deny that pornography counts as expression (or speech) at all (Schauer 1982, 181–4). But this conclusion overlooks the fact that, unlike sex aids, pornographic materials achieve their stimulant effect through their representation of an erotic content. That they represent in this way is sufficient for them to qualify as communication, thus as expression (or speech).
21 My definition of pornography, in terms of a particular content with a particular function, closely resembles that in Williams 1981, 103. Purposive or functional definitions of pornography are sometimes criticized on the ground that the intentions of producers are irrelevant to the nature of the materials they produce (see, for instance, Copp 1983, 18–19; Rea 2001, 132–4). However, this objection misses the point. Artifacts have purposes or functions which can typically be read from their design, the way in which they are

advertised and marketed, and their normal or standard use. To say that pornography has the function of sexual arousal is to say that this is the end that
it is designed, marketed, and typically consumed *for*. This is entirely analogous to saying that the function of a lawnmower is to cut grass or that the
purpose of a fountain pen is to write. In all cases the thing in question may
sometimes be used for other purposes (a pornographic video may be used
for educational or polemical purposes, a lawnmower may be used to drown
out a criminal conversation, a pen may be used to scratch your head), but
this does not prevent us from being perfectly clear what the purpose or function *of the thing* is. Its purpose need not be the purpose or intention of its
maker: the dominant purpose of producers and marketers of pornography,
lawnmowers, and fountain pens is doubtless to make a profit from their
enterprise.

22 There may seem a closer connection in the case of hate literature between
the purpose of the material and the purpose of its producer than there was
for pornography. But the two cases are entirely analogous. Something will
count as hate literature if it is designed so as to arouse hatred and if this is its
standard use by those who distribute or consume it. The intentions of a particular producer may be otherwise (to gain advancement within a political
organization, to become famous or notorious, or whatever) and are quite
irrelevant.

Chapter 2 Mill's Framework

1 See Rawls 1993, especially Lecture IV.
2 Joel Feinberg is a conspicuous exception; see 1984; 1985; 1986; 1988. Unlike
 Mill, however, Feinberg, does not regard harm to others as necessary to justify a limit to liberty.
3 Mill 1977, 217.
4 Mill 1977, 223.
5 See, for example, Ten 1980, chs 2 and 4; Gray 1983, ch. 3; Rees 1985, ch. 5;
 Riley 1998, ch. 5.
6 We will return to the issue of what constitutes harm, for the purposes of the
 Harm Principle, in sec. 2.4 below.
7 Mill 1977, 224.
8 See, for example, Sartorius 1975, ch. 4; Sumner 1987, ch. 6; Johnson 1991.
 Mill's general theory of rights is analysed in Lyons 1977.
9 Mill 1977, 270, 277.
10 Mill 1977, 224. Cf 1981, 169: 'all questions of political institutions are rela-

tive, not absolute, and ... different stages of human progress not only *will* have, but *ought* to have, different institutions.' (emphasis in original)

11 Mill 1977, 217.

12 Mill 1977, 225–6.

13 Mill 1977, 225–6.

14 Mill 1977, 226. Cf 227, where Mill refers to 'the Liberty of Thought: from which it is impossible to separate the cognate liberty of speaking and of writing'.

15 Mill 1977, 276.

16 Mill 1977, 292. Cf 1965, 938: 'Even in those portions of conduct which do affect the interests of others, the onus of making out a case always lies on the defenders of legal prohibitions. It is not a merely constructive or presumptive injury to others, which will justify the interference of law with individual freedom ... Scarcely any degree of utility, short of absolute necessity, will justify a prohibitory regulation, unless it can also be made to recommend itself to the general conscience; unless persons of ordinary good intentions either believe already, or can be induced to believe, that the thing prohibited is a thing which they ought not to wish to do.'

17 Mill 1977, 293.

18 Mill 1977, 293.

19 Mill 1977, 293.

20 Mill 1977, 293; cf 1965, Book V, ch. 11.

21 On the other hand, it is harder to understand why Mill regarded liberty of thought and discussion as 'a single branch' of his 'general thesis' (1977, 227), since thought and discussion belong to two different 'parts of life', the former personal and the latter social, or why he chose liberty of discussion as the 'first instance' to explore after announcing his general principle, since it is not an application of it.

22 Mill 1977, 257.

23 As Richard Vernon has pointed out (Vernon 1996, 622–3).

24 See, for instance, Mill 1977, 227, and the title of ch. 2.

25 Mill 1977, 244–5.

26 Mill 1977, 276.

27 Mill 1977, 279–80.

28 Mill 1969, 250.

29 Mill 1969, 256.

30 Mill 1969, 256.

31 Mill 1984, 261. For a very full account of what this 'perfect equality' entailed for Mill, see Morales 1996.

32 Mill 1977, 55n., 95.

33 Mill 1969, 258: 'All persons are deemed to have a *right* to equality of treatment, except when some recognised social expediency requires the reverse' (emphasis in original).

34 Mill 1977, 260.

35 Mill 1977, 296.

36 Mill 1977, 296.

37 Mill 1977, 228n.

38 A useful discussion of these issues, within the context of Mill's essay, can be found in O'Rourke 2001, ch. 8.

39 It is important to recognize that consequentialism is not the only possible response to the need to balance conflicting values when justifying rights. The distinctively consequentialist idea is that recognition of a right is justified when it maximizes the overall balance of benefits over costs. An alternative approach, endorsed by some deontologists, would be to treat an instrumentally justified right as establishing a high – but not insurmountable – threshold against conflicting values. These issues are explored in greater depth in ch. 3, sec. 3.2. For present purposes it suffices that Mill clearly subscribed to the maximizing, cost-benefit methodology.

40 Mill 1969, 255: 'Justice is a name for certain classes of moral rules, which concern the essentials of human well-being more nearly, and are therefore of more absolute obligation, than any other rules for the guidance of life; and the notion which we have found to be of the essence of the idea of justice, that of a right residing in an individual, implies and testifies to this more binding obligation.'

41 Mill 1969, 210.

42 Voluntary consumers of a product do not count as 'others' for the purpose of the Harm Principle. Restricting access to the product in order to prevent harm to its consumers would be an instance of paternalism.

43 Cf the account of 'moral injury' in Hampton 1992, 1666–85. Hampton, however, does not classify moral injury as a kind of harm.

44 *Hicklin* (1868), 371.

45 *Hicklin* (1868), 372.

46 *Graf* (1909), 248.

47 As Stephen Strager puts it, 'The masturbating man is pornography's target audience' (Strager 2003, 51). While this dictum understates the diversity of pornography, not all of which is aimed at a male audience, it is accurate for the mainstream product.

48 This continuity was important in the *Butler* decision, since in order not to violate the prohibition on 'shifting purpose' the objective of the 1959 obscenity

law had to be interpreted as the prevention of harm. See ch. 4, sec. 4.1, and *Butler* (1992), 491–6.

49 This argument, based on the Harm Principle, will be assessed in ch. 5, sec. 5.1.

50 I have distinguished these approaches at greater length in Sumner 1996, 8ff.

51 As Joel Feinberg has recognized (Feinberg 1984, 32).

52 Of course, it would still have to be shown that the (moral) harm done by pornography outweighed the harm that would be done by its restriction. But at least the consequentialist balancing would be on the agenda, since the Harm Principle would be satisfied.

53 Or not. The willingness of liberals to support (some) paternalistic policies might depend crucially on the fact that the harm to be prevented is non-moral, since in these cases the state is not imposing moral standards on individuals which they do not themselves endorse.

54 Unless, of course, we could make the case that pornography is capable of corrupting those who are exposed to it unwillingly.

55 See Sumner 1996, sec. 1.3.

56 Sumner 1996, sec. 2.3.

57 For a similar critique of the notion of moral harm, see Feinberg 1984, ch. 2, sec. 1.

58 We return to this issue in ch. 5, sec. 5.3.

59 Steinem 1995, 240–1; Longino 1980, 42ff.

60 This is one of the themes, for instance, in MacKinnon 1993 and Russo 1998. However, both also stress the violence and brutalization allegedly suffered by women in the pornography industry; since these are non-moral harms I consider them separately (in ch. 5, sec. 5.1).

61 Hartley 1987; 1993; 1997; Sprinkle 1991.

62 Sumner 1996, sec. 6.2.

63 Nina Hartley and Candida Royalle are the best-known examples. I suppose one could try to make out the case that they have been morally corrupted by pornography, but I know of no feminist who has gone that far. A feminist rejoinder to the brainwashed-by-patriarchy argument can be found in McElroy 1995, 105–9.

64 I borrow this useful label from Waldron 1993, ch. 5.

65 It is therefore an instance of what Judith Thomson has called 'belief-mediated' distress (Thomson 1990, ch. 10). Indeed, moral distress is doubly belief-mediated: it requires the belief that something bad or wrong has occurred, which depends in turn on the subject's moral convictions.

66 See Feinberg 1985, ch. 7.

67 Judith Thomson distinguishes distress (in all its forms) from harm, which

she reserves for damage or impairment (Thomson 1990, 260ff). But this distinction is (at least in part) normatively driven, since she is seeking a conception of harm which will ground claims against others.

68 Hart 1966, 46–7; for a similar argument see Ellis 1984. Also germane here are Feinberg's distinction between harm and offence, and therefore between the Harm Principle and the Offence Principle (Feinberg 1985), and Thomson's distinction between belief-mediated and non–belief-mediated distress (Thomson 1990, ch. 10).

69 I include here the guilt or shame that might be experienced by male users of pornography. Vance 1993 provides a sketch of Larry Madigan, who testified before the 1986 Attorney General's Commission on Pornography as a self-described 'victim of pornography'. Madigan described how finding a deck of hard-core playing cards at the age of twelve launched him on a career of attraction to pornography, from which he was saved only by finding Jesus. Madigan's guilt-induced distress is doubtless genuine, but no basis for public policy.

70 See, for instance, Cornell 1995, 147ff.

71 Williams 1981, 99. For a critique of the committee's argument see Dworkin 1985, ch. 17.

72 Feinberg 1985, ch. 7.

73 Feinberg 1985, 5.

74 Feinberg 1985, 9–10.

75 Feinberg himself, it should be pointed out, does not recognize moral distress as a harm, since he distinguishes harm from offence. For a critique of Feinberg's approach see Ellis 1984.

Chapter 3 The Balancing Act

1 For the classification of types of rights, see ch. 1, sec. 1.1.

2 Section 2: Everyone has the following fundamental freedoms:
... (b) freedom of thought, belief, opinion and expression, including freedom of the press and other media of communication; ...
Section 15: (1) Every individual is equal before and under the law and has the right to the equal protection and equal benefit of the law without discrimination and, in particular, without discrimination based on race, national or ethnic origin, colour, religion, sex, age or mental or physical disability ...

3 Sec. 319(2): Every one who, by communicating statements, other than in private conversation, wilfully promotes hatred against any identifiable group is guilty of

(a) an indictable offence and is liable to imprisonment for a term not exceeding two years;
   or
(b) an offence punishable on summary conviction.

   Strictly speaking, there are three Criminal Code provisions governing hate propaganda: sec. 318, dealing with the advocacy or promotion of genocide, sec. 319(1), governing the incitement of hatred 'where such incitement is likely to lead to a breach of the peace', and sec. 319(2). Since the last has been the primary focus of legal attention, it will serve as the centrepiece of this chapter.

4 For the definition of immunities and powers, see ch. 1, sec. 1.1.

5 Sec. 319(7), carrying over the definition of sec. 318(4). On September 2003 the House of Commons passed a private member's bill (C-250) which had the effect of expanding the definition of an 'identiable group' by adding sexual orientation to the list of distinguishing features. At the time of writing, this bill must still be passed by the Senate before becoming law.

6 Thomson 1986, 37–42. For a fuller treatment of the idea of specifying norms see Richardson 1990.

7 Other limitations on the liberty may of course be imposed by other exception-clauses.

8 *Oakes* (1986), 135ff. Some elements of the *Oakes* tests were later refined in *Dagenais* (1994), 887ff and *Thomson Newspapers* (1998), 967ff.

9 Conversations with Tom Hurka have revealed some intriguing parallels between the *Oakes* tests and the traditional rules for a just war. In both cases the aim is to stipulate the conditions under which a course of action which is normally unjustifiable (the violation of a constitutionally protected right, the waging of war) could be justified. Like the *Oakes* tests, the rules for a just war address separately the two questions of ends and means. The analogue to the 'pressing and substantial objective' test is the requirement that the cause to be pursued by war must be a just one. Three conditions, paralleling the *Oakes* proportionality tests, then apply to the use of war to pursue that cause: there must be a reasonable prospect of success, no other less costly means must be available, and the costs of war must be proportional to its benefits.

10 Thomson 1986, 40, 51.

11 *Irwin Toy* (1989), 969–70, reaffirmed in *Keegstra* (1990), 729–33. In addition to hate speech, the court has held that advertising (*Ford* (1988), *Irwin Toy* (1989), *Rocket* (1990), *RJR-MacDonald* (1995)), picketing (*Dolphin Delivery* (1986)), pornography (*Butler* (1992)), defamation (*Lucas* (1998)), 'spreading false news' (*Zundel* (1992)), and communication for the purpose of prostitution (*Prostitution Reference* (1990)) are all protected forms of expression.

12 *Irwin Toy* (1989), 978: 'If the government has aimed to control attempts to convey a meaning either by directly restricting the content of expression or by restricting a form of expression tied to content, its purpose trenches upon the [section 2(b)] guarantee.' Cf *Keegstra* (1990), 730; *New Brunswick* (1996), 500.

13 *Keegstra* (1990), 714, 797.

14 *Keegstra* (1984).

15 *Keegstra* (1988).

16 Section 27: 'This Charter shall be interpreted in a manner consistent with the preservation and enhancement of the multicultural heritage of Canadians.'

17 Sec. 319(3) provides the following schedule of defences:
No person shall be convicted of an offence under subsection (2)
   (a) if he establishes that the statements communicated were true;
   (b) if, in good faith, he expressed or attempted to establish by argument an opinion upon a religious subject;
   (c) if the statements were relevant to any subject of public interest, the discussion of which was for the public benefit, and if on reasonable grounds he believed them to be true; or
   (d) if, in good faith, he intended to point out, for the purpose of removal, matters producing or tending to produce feelings of hatred towards an identifiable group in Canada.

18 At the time of the *Keegstra* decision there were two vacancies on the court; the result also could have gone the other way had the full roster of nine justices been available.

19 *Keegstra* (1990), 735.

20 *Keegstra* (1990), 845; cf 846, 848, 863–5.

21 Chief Justice Dickson, in *Oakes* (1986), 139: 'Although the nature of the proportionality test will vary depending on the circumstances, in each case courts will be required to balance the interests of society with those of individuals and groups.'

22 Sniderman, Fletcher, Russell, et al. 1996 provide empirical support for the thesis that the 'contestability' of rights (to both liberty and equality) results from commitment to an underlying plurality of conflicting values.

23 See ch. 2, sec. 2.3, above and Mill 1969, 250ff; Sumner 1987, ch. 6.

24 See Mill 1977, ch. 2; Scanlon 1979; Cohen 1993. For a very full account of the values commonly said to be protected or enhanced by freedom of expression, see Schauer 1982, chs 2–6.

25 For a further discussion of this impact, see ch. 5, sec. 5.5.

26 *Keegstra* (1990), 762–4, 863–4.

27 *Keegstra* (1990), 746–8, 812, 847.
28 *Big M Drug Mart* (1985), 344, referring to *Hunter* (1984), 155; emphasis in original.
29 *Oakes* (1986), 136.
30 *Keegstra* (1990), 736: 'The underlying values of a free and democratic society both guarantee the rights in the *Charter* and, in appropriate circumstances, justify limitations upon those rights' (quoting *Slaight* (1989), 1056).
31 It is also possible that the intended benefits must be not only significant but also of the 'right' kind to justify infringing the constitutionally protected right. For example, even if it could be shown that limiting freedom of expression in some respect would increase economic prosperity, that might not count as a 'pressing and substantial' objective, though economic benefits are undeniably significant. Once again there is a parallel here with the conditions for a just war: the cause to be pursued by military means must be not only just but of the 'right' kind (economic benefits alone would not suffice, even if they were very substantial). I owe this point to Tom Hurka.
32 In *Big M Drug Mart* (1985) the court found that the objective of the Lord's Day Act – which was 'to compel the observance of the Christian sabbath' (351) – was not sufficiently important to justify limiting a Charter right. However, the right in question in that case was freedom of conscience and religion (section 2(a)) rather than freedom of expression. In *Zundel* (1992) the court majority was unable to find a pressing and substantial objective for the 'spreading false news' statute, but gave it the benefit of the doubt on that count and struck it down instead on proportionality.
33 *Keegstra* (1990), 786.
34 *Keegstra* (1990), 863.
35 As McLachlin acknowledged in a later case: *Lucas* (1998), 485.
36 *Oakes* (1986), 139–40; cf *Keegstra* (1990), 786.
37 *Keegstra* (1990), 863.
38 *Dagenais* (1994), 887 (emphasis in original). Cf 888: 'it is necessary to measure the actual salutary effects of impugned legislation against its deleterious effects, rather than merely considering the proportionality of the objective itself.'
39 See, for instance, *New Brunswick* (1996), 512; *Thomson Newspapers* (1998), 967–70.
40 Hogg 2000, 757.
41 Cf *Thomson Newspapers* (1998), 968: 'Determining whether there is a pressing and substantial objective behind the provision under scrutiny necessarily occurs in the abstract, before the specific nature of the legislation and its impact on the *Charter* right has [sic] been analysed.'

42 See Cameron 1997, 66.

43 I owe this point to Tom Hurka.

44 *Keegstra* (1990), 845 (derived from Justice Wilson's opinion in *Edmonton Journal* (1989), 1352–6). McLachlin emphasizes the same theme in *Rocket* (1990), 246–7; *RJR-MacDonald* (1995), 330.

45 *Keegstra* (1990), 845.

46 See ch. 2, sec. 2.3.

47 It may be more apt to label the court's methodology as quasi-consequentialist. For one thing, the judges do not explicitly commit themselves to requiring that a legislative measure deliver an optimal balance of benefits over costs. They might instead be willing to tolerate a measure whose cost-benefit balance is good enough, even if not the best achievable, in which case they would be better described as satisficing rather than maximizing. (Note, however, that minimal impairment appears to be a maximizing – or rather minimizing – requirement; for the distinction between maximizing and satisficing see Slote 1989.) Furthermore, the whole balancing process might be working within a limited domain of costs and benefits, excluding some (such as economic ones) which are deemed to be irrelevant (see note 31, above).

48 A lesson which I have urged in Sumner 1987.

49 Useful overviews of American free speech doctrine can be found in Greenawalt 1995, ch. 2 and Weinstein 1999, ch. 3.

50 *Chaplinsky* (1942), 571–2.

51 Greenawalt 1995, ch. 4.

52 St Paul, Minn.Legis.Code § 292.02 (1990).

53 For an extended analysis of the *R.A.V.* decision and its implications for the regulation of hate speech see Newman 2002, 371–80.

54 See, for instance, Greenawalt 1995; Leeper 2000; Newman 2002.

55 In sections 15, 16–23, and 27 of the Charter, respectively.

56 As in Dworkin 1996, ch. 8. Consequentialist and non-consequentialist justifications of free expression are contrasted in Greenawalt 1995, 3–5.

57 *Zundel* (1992), striking down the section of the Criminal Code which prohibited 'spreading false news' (in Zundel's case, Holocaust denial).

58 Unsurprisingly, the composition of the majority and minority were different in the two cases, although one justice did 'switch sides'.

59 This is argued in Fiss 1996, ch. 1.

60 See, for instance, Aleinikoff 1987; Cameron 1990–1, 80ff. Cf Justice Scalia, writing for the majority in *R.A.V.* (1992): 'From 1791 to the present ... our society, like other free but civilized societies, has permitted restrictions upon the content of speech in a few limited areas, which are of such slight social

value as a step to truth that any benefit that may be derived from them is clearly outweighed by the social interest in order and morality' (382–3).

61 See Railton 1984, 152ff; Sumner 1987, sec. 6.2; Shaw 1999, ch. 5.

62 I have argued (ch. 2, sec. 2.1) that Mill's Harm Principle has the same status within his overall consequentialist framework. Mill also seems to regard his liberty of discussion principle in the same way, i.e., as excluding case-by-case utilitarian deliberation concerning restrictions on expression (or at least on the expression of opinions concerning 'morals, religion, politics, social relations, and the business of life'). If so, then his favoured deliberative procedure is closer to the American model than to the Canadian.

63 Special Committee on Hate Propaganda in Canada 1966.

64 McAlpine 1981; Norman, McAlpine, and Weinstein 1984; House of Commons 1984; Law Reform Commission of Canada 1986.

65 The *Keegstra* decision is criticized on this ground in Newman 2002, 387ff.

66 *Butler* (1992), 501, 502. By contrast, in *Sharpe* (2001), 96–101, where the measure under constitutional scrutiny was the child pornography law (section 163.1 of the Criminal Code), the court took the view that there was reliable social science evidence of at least some of the harms to children allegedly caused by child pornography.

67 *RJR-MacDonald* (1995), 353. Compare *Irwin Toy* (1989), in which the court upheld legislation restricting advertising aimed at children, despite admittedly inconclusive evidence of the harm done by it.

68 *RJR-MacDonald* (1995), 328–9 (emphasis in original). The requirement of *demonstration* is a continuing theme in her judgment; see, e.g., 329–32.

69 Chief Justice Dickson encouraged the same expectation in *Oakes* (1986), 138: 'Where evidence is required to prove the constituent elements of a s. 1 inquiry, and this will generally be the case, it should be cogent and persuasive and make clear to the Court the consequences of imposing or not imposing the limit.'

70 *Oakes* (1986), 137; *Irwin Toy* (1989), 992.

71 *RJR-MacDonald* (1995), 333, 339–40.

72 This appearance is reinforced by Dickson's analysis in *Oakes* (1986), where he says that 'the preponderance of probability test must be applied rigorously. Indeed, the phrase "demonstrably justified" in s. 1 of the *Charter* supports this conclusion' (137). Dickson follows Lord Denning in distinguishing different degrees of probability and concludes: 'Having regard to the fact that s. 1 is being invoked for the purpose of justifying a violation of the constitutional rights and freedoms the *Charter* was designed to protect, a very high degree of probability will be, in the words of Lord Denning, "commensurate with the occasion"' (138).

73 *RJR-MacDonald* (1995), 333.

74 *RJR-MacDonald* (1995), 339. Cf *New Brunswick* (1996), 506–7; *Thomson Newspapers* (1998), 913–14, 960.

75 *Butler* (1992), 502.

76 *Butler* (1992), 502. Cf 504, where Sopinka endorses the view that 'Parliament was entitled [on the basis of the available evidence] to have a "reasoned apprehension of harm"'. Cf *Irwin Toy* (1989), 994: 'In the instant case, the Court is called upon to assess competing social science evidence respecting the appropriate means for addressing the problem of children's advertising. The question is whether the government had a reasonable basis, on the evidence tendered, for concluding that the ban on all advertising directed at children impaired freedom of expression as little as possible given the government's pressing and substantial objective.' For the 'reasonable basis' standard see also *Ross* (1996), 881; *Thomson Newspapers* (1998), 916; *Sharpe* (2001), 96, 151.

77 In his dissenting opinion in *RJR-MacDonald* (1995), 290, Justice La Forest treats the 'reasonable basis' standard as weaker than the civil standard. However, the equivalence of the two standards is affirmed by Justice McLachlin (333), writing for the majority.

78 *Keegstra* (1990), 787. Dickson also observed that hate propaganda 'strays some distance from the spirit of s. 2(b)' (766) and that it is 'distant from the core of free expression values' (787).

79 *Keegstra* (1990), 766. Dickson borrowed the quoted phrase from Justice McLachlin's opinion in *Rocket* (1990), where she applied it to dentists' advertisements of their services.

80 *Keegstra* (1990), 767.

81 'To become transfixed with categorization schemes risks losing the advantage associated with this sensitive examination of free expression principles, and I would be loath to sanction such a result' (*Keegstra* (1990), 767).

82 *Keegstra* (1990), 785 and 765, respectively.

83 *Butler* (1992), 509; cf. 500.

84 *New Brunswick* (1996), 512–13. La Forest is drawing here from views expressed in his (dissenting) opinion in *RJR-MacDonald* (1995), 281; in the same case he referred to 'an attenuated level of s. 1 justification' for measures restricting tobacco advertising, since this form of expression was entitled only to 'a very low degree of protection under s. 1' (284, 283). See also *Ross* (1996), 876–7; *Lucas* (1998), 459; *Sharpe* (2001), 143–4.

85 *Keegstra* (1990), 841.

86 *RJR-MacDonald* (1995), 347.

87 *RJR-MacDonald* (1995), 351.

88 *Lucas* (1998), 486–7. McLachlin cites Cameron 1997 in favour of the view
that she is here articulating. However, in that article Cameron ends by
endorsing an American-style, categorical, levels-of-protection approach quite
at odds with McLachlin's idea of a uniform standard in which the distinctions between types of expression turn up as different entries in the cost-benefit balance sheet.
89 *Lucas* (1998), 488.
90 E.g., Justice La Forest in *RJR-MacDonald* (1995), 279.
91 *Irwin Toy* (1989), 993–4.
92 As was pointed out later by Justice McLachlin (*RJR-MacDonald* (1995), 331–2;
cf Justice Bastarache in *Thomson Newspapers* (1998), 942). A similar point is
made by Beatty 1995, 83.
93 *Irwin Toy* (1989), 993.
94 See, e.g., *RJR-MacDonald* (1995), 279, 312; *Little Sisters* (2000), 1235.
95 *RJR-MacDonald* (1995), 332–3. Cf Aleinikoff 1987; Beatty 1995, 91–2.
96 This connection between balancing and deference is drawn in Greenawalt
1995, 14.
97 However, see Aleinikoff 1987, 980–1, on the pressures which can drive the
court toward a more direct procedure: 'New situations present new interests
and different weights for old interests. If these are allowed to re-open the
balancing process, then every case becomes one of an "ad hoc" balance,
establishing a rule for that case only. Balances are "definitional" only if the
Court wants to stop thinking about the question.'

Chapter 4 The Myth of Community Standards

1 Sec. 163(8) of the Criminal Code. The full text of this section reads: 'For the
purposes of this Act, any publication a dominant characteristic of which is
the undue exploitation of sex, or of sex and any one or more of the following subjects, namely, crime, horror, cruelty and violence, shall be deemed to
be obscene.'
2 In modern terms, therefore, the pamphlet was as much hate literature as
pornography.
3 *Hicklin* (1868), 363.
4 *Hicklin* (1868), 371.
5 *Hicklin* (1868), 372.
6 As late as 1957, Justice Laidlaw of the Ontario Court of Appeal could still
interpret the 'tendency to deprave and corrupt' as the tendency to suggest
impure thoughts, influence persons to commit impure acts, or imperil the

prevailing standards of public morals (*American News* (1957), 157). For accounts of the career of the *Hicklin* test in Canada see Charles 1966, 278; McLaren 1991, 122–9.

7 See, for instance, Mackay 1958. Judges seemed to have fewer doubts about the integrity of the test than did academic lawyers. In 1953 Chief Justice Pickup of the Ontario Court of Appeal could confidently declare 'I see nothing wrong with the [*Hicklin*] test' (*National News* (1953), 29). Four years later, Justice Laidlaw of the same court went about the business of applying the test with little evidence of reluctance or doubt in *American News* (1957).

8 'The object of this clause is to make a statutory extension of the definition of obscenity so as to make it perfectly clear that the law of obscenity does apply to a certain type of objectionable material that now appears on the newsstands of Canada and is being sold to the young people of our country with impunity.

'We believe that we have produced a definition which will be capable of application with speed and certainty, by providing a series of simple objective tests in addition to the somewhat vague subjective test which was the only one formerly available. The test will be: "Does the publication complained of deal with sex, or sex and one or more of the other subjects named? If so, is this the dominant characteristic? Again, if so, does it exploit these subjects in an undue manner?"

'We have been careful in working out this definition not to produce a net so wide that it sweeps in borderline cases or cases about which there may be a genuine difference of opinion. In our efforts we have deliberately stopped short of any attempt to outlaw publications concerning which there may be any contention that they have genuine literary, artistic or scientific merit. These works remain to be dealt with under the Hicklin definition, which is not superseded by the new statutory definition' (quoted in Charles 1966, 253–4).

9 *Brodie* (1962), 702.

10 During the 1960s the courts relied exclusively on the statutory definition in at least two other cases involving (arguably) serious literature: John Cleland's *Fanny Hill: Memoirs of a Woman of Pleasure* (*Coles* (1965)) and Hubert Selby's *Last Exit to Brooklyn* (*Duthie Books* (1966)).

11 *Brodie* (1962), 702.

12 *Brodie* (1962), 704–5.

13 *Brodie* (1962), 705.

14 *Close* (1948). Curiously, Judson made no mention of a community standards test of obscenity which was both more recent and much closer to home: the one formulated by Justice Brennan in *Roth* (1956), 489: 'whether to the aver-

age person, applying contemporary community standards, the dominant theme of the material taken as a whole appeals to prurient interest'. Brennan claimed that this was the test which American courts had been using for some years.

15 *Close* (1948), 465.

16 *Close* (1948), 465.

17 *Brodie* (1962), 706.

18 *Dechow* (1977). For nearly a decade before this ruling the courts had been routinely treating the statutory definition as supplanting the *Hicklin* test. As early as 1969, a legal commentator could conclude that 'the statutory definition is exhaustive' (Barnett 1969, 10). Cf Fox 1972, 59–60.

19 *Dominion News* (1963), 116. In adopting Justice Freedman's reasoning, the Supreme Court also endorsed his opinion that the magazines in question (*Dude* and *Escapade*) were not obscene. Since this was the very sort of material which the justice minister had introduced the new statutory definition of obscenity to control, it did not take long for the futility of his efforts to become apparent.

20 *Dominion News* (1963), 117. This reference to contemporary and changing standards was not an innovation. Even courts using the *Hicklin* test prior to 1959 recognized that 'what would tend to corrupt and deprave in one generation may not in another generation' (*National News* (1953), 29; cf *American News* (1957), 160).

21 *Dominion News* (1963), 117. The idea that the relevant community is a national one quickly became judicial orthodoxy; see, for example, *Prairie Schooner* (1970), 265; *Goldberg* (1971), 191; *Times Square* (1971), 700; *Kiverago* (1973), 464. In this respect the community standards test has come to be interpreted differently in Canada and the United States. In the American courts the operative standard was determined to be local rather than national in scope; see *Miller* (1973), 30–4. This difference may reflect the fact that in Canada obscenity legislation, like all criminal law, is a federal responsibility while in the United States it falls within state jurisdiction.

22 One might say that for Fullagar the community's shared standards provide a reliable epistemic indicator of decency (or indecency): if (enough) people regard something as indecent then it must be indecent.

23 *Brodie* (1962), 705.

24 The decency interpretation was assumed by the courts in many cases throughout the 1960s. See, for instance, *Coles* (1965), 317: 'Since any publication which falls to be tested for obscenity within the definition contained in the *Code* must be judged by the contemporary standard of decency and morality the Judge or the jury, as the case may be, must put to himself or

itself the question – how would a reasonable cross-section of the general public regard it, not the prude or the puritanical, not the libertine but the average, well-intentioned, moderate individual? Even excluding the puritan and the libertine who are at opposite ends of the social spectrum society is made up of a complexity of individuals with varying degrees of decency o[r] morality or propriety or call it what you may.' Similar references to standards of decency or morality may be found in *Cameron* (1966), 788, and *Adams* (1966), 63. The uncertainty felt by some courts on this question is reflected in their references to 'the standards of decency and the measure of tolerance' in the Canadian community (*Coles* (1965), 310; *Duthie Books* (1966), 282). As late as 1969 one legal commentator could say that 'there is no doubt that *community standards* now carry the meaning of "standards of modesty and taste"' (Barnett 1969, 19; emphasis in original).

25 *Prairie Schooner* (1970), 254–5.
26 *Prairie Schooner* (1970), 269. Interestingly, this interpetation of the test is close to what Davie Fulton seems to have had in mind in 1959. When asked to explain what 'undue exploitation' amounted to he suggested that it meant 'generally going beyond what men of goodwill and common sense would tolerate' (quoted in Charles 1966).
27 *Great West News* (1970); *Goldberg* (1971); *Times Square* (1971); *Macmillan* (1976); *Sudbury News* (1978); *Penthouse* (1979). Nevertheless, some references to standards of decency or taste stubbornly persisted: see, for instance, *Ariadne Developments* (1974), 54.
28 *Towne Cinema* (1985), 508 (emphasis in original).
29 See, for instance, *American News* (1957), 171.
30 *Dominion News* (1963), 116. At the original trial, testimony about 'girlie' magazines in general was given by Arnold Edinborough, as a result of his experience on the Ontario Committee on Indecent Literature. His testimony was rejected as having little relevance by the majority of the Court of Appeal, the comments of Justice Monnin being typical: 'Whether there is obscenity or not is a question of fact for the trier of the issue. The principal evidentiary material before the Court is the publication itself' (121). However, it was Justice Freedman's dissenting opinion which was later endorsed by the Supreme Court.
31 *Cameron* (1966), 806. Referring to the magistrate's finding that the pictures in question constituted undue exploitation of sex, Justice Laskin delivered a stinging critique: 'This assessment is so completely subjective, so devoid of any advertent consideration to what has been accepted from time to time in Canada, and even in Toronto, that it raises an important question as to whether the Crown has discharged the burden of proof resting upon it to

establish undue exploitation beyond a reasonable doubt. Granted that the Magistrate is entitled to discount the expert evidence for the defence, as he has done in his reasons, this does not, in my view, mean that he may on an entirely subjective appraisal find that the Crown has proved its case beyond a reasonable doubt ... I do not think that a Judge or Magistrate, as sole trier of law and fact, is entitled to supply the evidence that should come from witnesses for the Crown. This is to restore an aspect of the *Hicklin* rule in another guise' (808–9). The qualifier 'and even in Toronto' sheds an interesting light on the city's lingering puritanism in the mid-1960s.

32 *Great West News* (1970), 314. Dickson characterized expert evidence on a publication's literary or scientific merit as 'both admissible and desirable' (316), but still not indispensable.

33 *Prairie Schooner* (1970), 252.

34 *Times Square* (1971); *Ariadne Developments* (1974); *Sudbury News* (1978); *Rankine* (1983). The same development occurred during the same time period in American obscenity jurisprudence; see Scott 1991, 31ff.

35 *Towne Cinema* (1985), 516. It is worth noting, however, that Justices McIntyre and Wilson both dissented on this question. Citing Justice Laskin's dissenting opinion in *Cameron* with approval, Wilson wrote: 'Having regard to the fact that the onus is on the Crown to establish obscenity beyond a reasonable doubt, it seems to me that the onus is on it to establish both what the community standard of acceptability is and that the accused has gone beyond it' (*Towne Cinema* (1985), 529).

36 *Brodie* (1962).

37 *Duthie Books* (1966).

38 *Coles* (1965).

39 *Cameron* (1966).

40 *Odeon Morton* (1974).

41 *Towne Cinema* (1985), 504.

42 *Towne Cinema* (1985), 505. This special notice of degrading or dehumanizing treatment appears to derive from Judge Borins's decision in *Rankine* (1983), 70: 'films which consist substantially or partially of scenes which portray violence and cruelty in conjunction with sex, particularly where the performance of indignities degrade and dehumanize the people upon whom they are performed, exceed the level of community tolerance.' This theme was subsequently picked up in *Ramsingh* (1984), *Wagner* (1985), and *Red Hot Video* (1985).

43 *Towne Cinema* (1985), 523.

44 *Towne Cinema* (1985), 524. Perhaps the best construction of Wilson's view is that the community's standard of tolerance is a reliable epistemic indicator

of harm: if (enough) people refuse to tolerate something then it must be harmful. In that case the standard of tolerance, as interpreted by Wilson, has the same epistemic function as the standard of decency, as interpreted by Fullagar (see note 22, above).

45 *Towne Cinema* (1985), 505. Dickson's point therefore (*contra* Wilson) is that the community's tolerance of something is not a reliable epistemic indicator of its harmlessness. In that case, however, some non–harm-based rationale must be found for the community standards test.

46 *Butler* (1992), 484. Note the echo of Wilson's words: 'through the application of the community standard test, the public is made the arbiter of what is harmful to it and what is not' (*Towne Cinema* (1985), 524).

47 *Butler* (1992), 485.

48 This interpretation was confirmed by the court in *Little Sisters* (2000), 1157ff. By endorsing the first interpretation, Sopinka embraced Justice Wilson's view that community intolerance is a reliable epistemic indicator of harm (see note 44, above).

49 *Butler* (1992), 486. By contrast, in *Sharpe* (2001), 89, the court determined that community standards are not the measure of artistic merit for the purposes of the child pornography statute (sec. 163.1 of the Criminal Code), since the statute defines child pornography independently of the artistic merit defence. In the obscenity statute, on the other hand, 'the meaning of obscenity and the defence of artistic merit are largely judicial creations'.

50 The Criminal Code currently includes the following 'morals offences', besides obscenity:
    (1) publicly exhibiting a disgusting object or indecent show (sec. 163(2)(b))
    (2) presenting or performing in an immoral or indecent theatrical performance (sec. 167)
    (3) using the mails to transmit indecent, immoral, or scurrilous material (sec. 168)
    (4) performing an indecent act (sec. 173)
    (5) being nude in a public place or while exposed to public view (where nudity is defined as being clothed in such a way as to offend against public decency) (sec. 174)
    (6) exposing an indecent exhibition in a public place (sec. 175(1)(b)).

51 See, inter alia, *Johnson* (1975) (immoral theatrical performance); *Priape* (1979) (importing immoral or indecent material); *Pink Triangle* (1979; 1980) (using mails to transmit immoral, indecent, or scurrilous matter); *Popert* (1981) (using mails to transmit immoral, indecent, or scurrilous matter); *Giambalvo* (1982) (public nudity); *Luscher* (1985) (importing immoral or indecent material); *Pelletier* (1985) (publicly exhibiting an indecent show);

Glassman (1986) (exhibiting a disgusting object); *Tremblay* (1993) (keeping a bawdy house for the purpose of the practice of indecent acts); *Ludacka* (1996) (immoral theatrical performance); *Jacob* (1996) (committing indecent act); *Mara* (1997) (indecent theatrical performance).

52 At least since 1970, the courts have had little difficulty in determining when the exploitation of sex was a 'dominant theme' of the work in question, since prosecutions have increasingly targeted materials (magazines, films, videos) with little or no non-erotic content.

53 *Prairie Schooner* (1970), 269.

54 Intervenors before the *Butler* court included the Women's Legal Education and Action Fund and the Group Against Pornography on the one hand, and the Canadian Civil Liberties Association and two provincial civil liberties associations on the other.

55 *Cameron* (1966), 805; cf 804: 'in countries as large and regionally diverse as Canada and the United States it may be fanciful to believe that a literal country-wide measure can be applied ...' For similar early expressions of scepticism see *Coles* (1965), 317; *Adams* (1966), 65.

56 See, for example, *Penthouse* (1979), 114; *Pink Triangle* (1980), 495; *Rankine* (1983), 69–70; *Ramsingh* (1984), 236–7. The same point was made in May 1999 at the annual convention of the Motion Picture Theatres Association of Canada. Theatre owners argued for a standardized, national system of film classification to replace the current system of classification by provincial boards. The proposal was resisted by representatives of the existing boards on the ground that community standards differ across the country and are better reflected at the provincial level ('Theatre Operators Favour National Film Classification,' *Globe and Mail*, 13 May 1999).

57 *Close* (1948), 465.

58 *Penthouse* (1979), 114–15; *Pink Triangle* (1980), 495.

59 See, for instance, *Prairie Schooner* (1970), 266, in which Justice Dickson speaks of 'the state of mind or attitude of a community' as a matter of fact, seeming to imply that it is singular rather than plural.

60 *Dominion News* (1963), 116.

61 *Cameron* (1966), 805; *Macmillan* (1976), 299; *Penthouse* (1979), 116; *Pink Triangle* (1980), 496.

62 *Dominion News* (1963), 116; cf Justice Laskin's remarks in *Cameron* (1966), 805. The goal of finding a reference point somewhere between puritans and libertines also played a role in adjudication under the old *Hicklin* test; see, for instance, *National News* (1953), 30.

63 Judge Ferg in *Ramsingh* (1984), 237.

64 What happens if the moderate view is not the majority view, as might be the

case if opinion on the issue is very polarized? Canadian jurisprudence is, to say the least, silent on this question.

65 But see *Video World* (1985a), 53; *Fringe Product* (1990), 430.

66 However, one such survey (Sniderman, Fletcher, Russell, et al. 1996, 73) found that ordinary Canadians are evenly divided on the question whether films that show sexually explicit acts should be permitted or prohibited. Interestingly, the same study showed a strong majority in favour of tolerance among members of 'legal elites' (lawyers comprising the pool from which judges are selected).

67 *Prairie Schooner* (1970), 266.

68 Some comments by Judge Harris in *Pink Triangle* (1979) came close to challenging this orthodoxy:

> I am of the opinion that all in all the evidence adduced from the majority of both Crown and Defence witnesses establishes nothing which really assists the Court in ascertaining the limits of community tolerance, that is, the community standard, in this area. It would have been more helpful to have had evidence of competently conducted public opinion surveys of community opinion. Such was not proffered, nor was even the evidence of what might have purported to be several or many persons making up a representative sample of the Canadian community demographically speaking ...
>
> Absent such evidence, and absent any suitable alternative I was left with no real assistance on this branch of the case. On the community standard test, then, the Crown has failed to satisfy me beyond a reasonable doubt that [the material in question] taken as a whole is indecent, immoral or scurrilous. (403–4)

As the final sentence indicates, this was a trial on a charge not of obscenity but of using the mails to distribute 'indecent, immoral, or scurrilous' material. However, community standards of tolerance were the accepted test of these attributes, just as they were for obscenity. In any case, Judge Harris's suggestion that the crown might have to introduce survey evidence in order to make its case was repudiated by Judge Ferguson on appeal: 'At this point in time I think it may be safely stated there is no judicial requirement that public opinion surveys on the subject of community standards form part of the evidence before the Court' (*Pink Triangle* (1980), 497–8).

69 *Rankine* (1983), 69–70. Judge Borins's apt phrase concerning the 'pornographic pulse' was borrowed from *Various Articles* (1983), 136.

70 *Butler* (1989), 25.

71 *Butler* (1989), 30–5 (emphasis in original).

72 *Butler* (1990), 362–3.

73 Forms of evidence which courts have deemed admissible include the results of public opinion surveys (*Prairie Schooner* (1970), 266) and testimony by various expert witnesses, including directors of provincial film censor boards (*Great West News* (1970), 314; *Prairie Schooner* (1970), 267; *McFall* (1975), 217–19; *Pereira-Vasquez* (1985), 346).

74 One sociologist found, on the basis of a survey of more than 7,000 adults, that 'the one independent variable that is an excellent predictor of perceived community standards concerning explicit sexual material is the respondent's own personal standard of acceptability of sexual material' (Scott 1991, 42). The author concluded that if jurors were presented with no evidence concerning community standards, then they would tend to rely on their own standards of tolerance. Presumably the same would be true of judges.

75 *Brodie* (1962), 702.

76 See, for instance, *Priape* (1979), 48; *Cinema International* (1982), 48; *Video World* (1985a); 52–3; *Butler* (1989), 30.

77 *Glad Day Bookshop* (1992b), 16–20.

78 Barnett 1969, 27.

79 The conclusions Judge Hayes draws about the particular items are scarcely surprising given his overview of the materials as a whole: 'The text of the material describes in intimate detail the explicit sexual practices, reactions, and feelings of the participants with excessive, lewd, and disgusting detail' (*Glad Day Bookshop* (1992b), 8).

80 The judgment is particularly repugnant for its apparent homophobia. It is far from clear that Judge Hayes would have reached the same conclusions concerning many of the depicted sexual activities had they taken place between heterosexual participants.

81 *Rankine* (1983), 70.

82 Oddly enough, however, he himself concluded that four of the five films did indeed exceed community standards, by virtue either of having violent or degrading content or, lacking such, of being too explicit (*Rankine* (1983), 70).

83 *Rankine* (1983), 59.

84 *Rankine* (1983), 69.

85 Indeed, it is no exaggeration to suggest that, by means of her testimony in this case, June Rowlands initiated the line of interpretation of contemporary community standards which would eventually be confirmed and codified by the Supreme Court in its *Butler* decision.

86 *Glassman* (1986), 173 (citing *Pelletier* (1985), 257).

87 *Prostitution Reference* (1990), 1151.

88 MacDougall 1984, 86–7; Moon 1993, 370; Crerar 1996–7, 383ff.

89 *Nicols* (1984), 67–9.

90 For typical dispositions of the challenge see *Ramsingh* (1984); *Wagner* (1985); *Red Hot Video* (1985); *Fringe Product* (1990). The challenge was supported by Justice Helper of the Manitoba Court of Appeal in a dissenting opinion in *Butler* (1990), 363–5, but rejected by the court majority and, subsequently, given short shrift by the Supreme Court (*Butler* (1992), 490–1).

91 In *Red Hot Video* (1985), Chief Justice Nemetz of the British Columbia Court of Appeal suggested that the decided cases themselves offer 'a national consensus as to the "Canadian standard of tolerance"' (18), a striking instance of the closed evidential circle. Cases decided on the basis of no reliable evidence of this standard thus become their own evidence for it.

92 See, for instance, *Odeon Morton* (1974); *Hawkins* (1993); *Jorgensen* (1995) (provincial review boards); *Macmillan* (1976) (Canada Customs).

93 *Nicols* (1984), 65.

94 *Rankine* (1983), 70; cf *Ramsingh* (1984), 239–40; *Wagner* (1985), 331–2; *Red Hot Video* (1985), 22–3; *Butler* (1989), 46–8; *Butler* (1990), 342. It is only fair to note that Borins had his own limits of tolerance even of materials containing no such scenes; in *Rankine* he found some videos obscene simply on the ground of their 'degree of explicitness' (70).

95 *Pereira-Vasquez* (1985), 344ff. By the time this case reached the British Columbia Court of Appeal in 1988, Justice Esson could pronounce with confidence that the *Rankine* distinction of different types of erotic materials was a judicial 'detour' or 'tributary stream' (*Pereira-Vasquez* (1988), 284–91). Cf *Butler* (1989), 35–6.

96 *Butler* (1992), 484.

97 *Butler* (1992), 485.

98 *Butler* (1992), 485.

99 *Butler* (1992), 485.

100 *Scythes* (1993), 3. For an account of the trial, see Ross 1997.

101 *Little Sisters* (1996). For an account of this trial, see Fuller and Blackley 1996. The discriminatory targeting by Canada Customs of gay and lesbian materials was acknowledged by the Supreme Court in *Little Sisters* (2000), 1182ff.

102 This interpretation is confirmed in *Little Sisters* (2000), 1155, 1161–2, 1207, 1221.

103 *Hawkins* (1993).

104 In the same way, a judge in Montreal ruled recently, with no supporting evidence, that mate-swapping, involving sexual twosomes or threesomes, fell within the community's standards of tolerance but that orgies, involving

larger numbers of participants, did not ('Swinging Is Legal, Orgy Isn't, Judge Says', *Globe and Mail*, 5 July 2003, A4).

105 Sopinka was joined in his opinion by six of his fellow justices. Interestingly, the remaining two justices (L'Heureux-Dubé and Gonthier) dissented on precisely this question, arguing that sexually explicit materials involving no violence or degradation could exceed the community's level of tolerance.

106 As noted in ch. 2, harm to others is a necessary condition of justified restraint, not a sufficient one. Whether legal restrictions on socially harmful activities are justified is to be determined by a cost-benefit balance. However, restrictions on socially harmless activities are always unjustified.

107 Alternatively, the *Hicklin* test might be interpreted as aiming to prevent harm, either to the morals of the consumers of pornography themselves or to public morals. This interpretation, however, requires the legitimacy of the notion of 'moral harm', which was denied in ch. 2, sec. 2.4.

108 *Hicklin* (1868), 371.

109 Just two years before the adoption of the 'undue exploitation' definition which would eventually supplant the *Hicklin* test, Justice Laidlaw could interpret the 'tendency to deprave and corrupt' as the tendency to suggest impure thoughts or 'to influence certain persons to do impure acts; or ... to imperil the prevailing standards of public morals' (*American News* (1957), 157).

110 The earliest influential public statement of this disquiet occurred in Wolfenden 1957: 'We do not think that it is proper for the law to concern itself with what a man does in private unless it can be shown to be so contrary to the public good that the law ought to intervene in its function as the guardian of that public good' (21). The most sustained philosophical critique of legal moralism during this period was Hart 1966.

111 Note Justice Judson's language in *Brodie* (1962), where he could interpret 'undue exploitation' as 'excessive emphasis on the theme [of sex] for a base purpose' and characterize materials guilty of such emphasis as 'dirt for dirt's sake' (704). The same moralistic language persisted in subsequent cases; see, for example, *Duthie Books* (1966), 280; *Great West News* (1970), 309. As recently as 1988, material deemed to fail the community standards test could be dismissed as 'depraved sludge' (*Pereira-Vasquez* (1988), 291). Even after the adoption of a standard of tolerance, courts continued to endorse moralism as a basis for restraint: 'A free society depends for its vitality on a moral foundation. No such society can exist or continue to exist, absent the presence and preservation of a strong moral fibre. This in part is fostered by Parliamentary proscription. I have no doubt that you cannot legislate morality, but it is a legitimate exercise of responsible Gov-

ernment to deter corruption and create a climate in which healthy attitudes are nourished and encouraged within the community. Sexual morality in children and their attitudes in this regard form an important part of the total spectrum of moral integrity' (*Macmillan* (1976), 312).

112 See *supra*, n. 20.

113 *Towne Cinema* (1985), 508.

114 For the charge of conservatism, see Moon 1993, 368–9. The accusation of male bias is made in Mahoney 1991, 152–3, and of heterosexist bias in Wollaston 1992, 257–8.

115 Mill 1977, 220.

116 For the notion of moral distress, and the argument that it should not count as harm for the purposes of the Harm Principle, see ch. 2, sec. 2.4.

117 See ch. 4, above, sec. 4.1.

118 See, for example, Mahoney 1992, 103–5; Busby 1994, 176. The Supreme Court itself now routinely refers to the *Butler* decision as having been 'harm-based' (see, for example, *Little Sisters* (2000), 1154, 1155).

119 *Butler* (1992), 478–86.

120 This subsumption was reaffirmed by the court in *Little Sisters* (2000), 1162–3.

121 Cameron 1997, 65: 'Simply believing that expression is harmful or has a bad influence is not sufficient to justify limits under section 1 of the *Charter.*'

122 These evidentiary issues concerning harm were on prominent display in *RJR-MacDonald* (1995), where the court faced the question of the justifiability of restrictions on the advertising and promotion of tobacco products. While members of the court disagreed over the kind of evidence the government should be expected to provide of the harmfulness of these forms of expression, no one suggested that an opinion poll might suffice. I return to the question of the evidentiary burden on the legislature in ch. 5.

Chapter 5 In Harm's Way?

1 The decisions were, of course, *Keegstra* (1990) (hate speech) and *Butler* (1992) (pornography). The court also dealt with hate speech in *Andrews* (1990) (the hate propaganda statute), *Taylor* (1990) (the Canadian Human Rights Act), and *Zundel* (1992) (the 'spreading false news' statute). It revisited the pornography issue in *Little Sisters* (2000) (customs censorship) and *Sharpe* (2001) (child pornography). None of these decisions disturbed any essential elements of *Keegstra* and *Butler.*

2 The *Butler* decision was criticized by some influential mainstream media (including the *Globe and Mail*), prominent civil libertarians (Borovoy 1999, ch. 1), a significant number of feminist academics (e.g., Cossman et al. 1997), and even Andrea Dworkin (Toobin 1994).

3 Sniderman et al. 1996, ch. 3.

4 Cameron 1997, 63: 'Harm is the key to section 2(b)'s principle of freedom as well as to section 1's concept of justifiable limits: where harm is present, limits are justifiable, and where it is absent, the principle of freedom must prevail.'

5 *Keegstra* (1990), 745–9 (majority), 846–8 (minority).

6 *Butler* (1992), 491–9; cf ch. 4, above, sec. 4.3. The court has since reaffirmed the harm-based approach of *Butler* in *Little Sisters* (2000), 1158ff, and *Sharpe* (2001), 75ff.

7 For instance, in *RJR-MacDonald* (1995) (tobacco advertising) and *Lucas* (1998) (defamation).

8 Cf ch. 2, secs 2.1 and 2.3.

9 In ch. 2, sec. 2.4.

10 It goes without saying that men can also be victims of sexual violence (whether at the hands of other men or of women). However, a link with sexual violence against men has seldom been advanced as an argument for regulating pornography (not even gay male pornography). (For a possible example of such an argument see the remarks of Judge Hayes in *Glad Day Bookshop* (1992b), 16–20.) I deal separately with the case of sexual violence against, and abuse of, children (of both genders) in section 5.4, below. The sexual abuse of animals, which might be thought to be promoted by pornography featuring scenes of bestiality, is outside the scope of this study.

11 See, for instance, MacKinnon 1991, 796ff.

12 MacKinnon 1991, 796; cf 1987, 199; 1993, 17.

13 MacKinnon 1993, 27: 'In mainstream media, violence is done through special effects; in pornography, women shown being beaten and tortured report being beaten and tortured.'

14 MacKinnon 1991, 797: 'In some pornography called "snuff," women or children are tortured to death, murdered to make a sex film.' Cf MacKinnon 1987, 180: 'It certainly seems important to the audiences that the events in the pornography be real. For this reason pornography becomes a motive for murder, as in "snuff" films, in which someone is tortured to death to make a sex film. They exist.'

15 The story of *Snuff* can be found in Williams 1989, 189–95, and Palac 1998, 144–50. The film was dismissed as a fake as early as Williams 1981, 91–2.

16 Scott and Cuvelier 1987; 1993.

17 Rich 2001, 51. Revenues from all pornography sources (including, besides

videos, cable and satellite networks, websites, in-room hotel movies, phone sex, sex toys, and magazines) were estimated for the same year at $10–14 billion; even the low-end estimate of $10 billion would mean that pornography is a bigger business in the United States than professional baseball, football, and basketball taken together.

18 Rich 2001, 52.

19 In Canada, Rogers Communications Inc., which owns (among many other things) the Toronto Blue Jays, delivers pornographic movies and networks through its cable systems.

20 Rich 2001, 53, contrary to the claim in MacKinnon 1991, 796.

21 The increasing consumption of (various forms of) pornography by women – in private, domestic space – is nicely chronicled in Juffer 1998.

22 Quoted in Rich 2001, 51.

23 We will return to the case of child pornography in section 5.4, below. On the incidence of sexual violence in X-rated videos, see Yang and Linz 1990; Jensen and Dines 1998, 82; Monk-Turner and Purcell 1999. These and other empirical studies contradict the claim by the 1986 Attorney General's Commission that materials featuring sexual violence are 'increasingly, the most prevalent forms of pornography' (Attorney General's Commission on Pornography 1986, 39).

24 See, for instance, Califia 1994; Macy 1996, ch. 5; Ross 1997.

25 Hartley 1993, 1997; McElroy 1995, ch. 7; Strossen 1995, ch. 9.

26 Lovelace and McGrady 1980; cf Steinem 1995, 266–76. For MacKinnon's references to Marchiano, see MacKinnon 1987, 180, and 1993, 113, n. 2. A different take on the implications of Marchiano's experience can be found in McClintock 1993, 128–9; McElroy 1995, 175 (quoting Candida Royalle); Strossen 1995, 182–4.

27 Hartley 1993; McElroy 1995, 151–2; Strossen 1995, ch. 9; Macy 1996, 34ff. Some women have reported the experience of being pressured during a shoot into acts (such as anal sex) which they are reluctant to perform; however, this kind of treatment by directors has its analogue in Hollywood films as well.

28 Attorney General's Commission on Pornography 1986, ch. 5.

29 Attorney General's Commission on Pornography 1986, 34 (emphasis in original).

30 Schauer 1987.

31 Schauer 1987, 752. Schauer credits Cartwright 1979 for this formulation. Similar arguments against utilizing a scientific (deterministic) conception of causation in this context can be found in Adams 2000, 2ff. Adams claims that pornography can cause sexual violence by acting as a stimulus to it.

Although he does not acknowledge Schauer's probabilistic conception of causation, I believe that it provides the best way of making sense of this claim.

32 It is possible, for example, that in countries with higher per capita ownership of VCRs more consumers might adopt videos as their medium of choice while their less technologically endowed counterparts in other places might still be dependent on print materials. The difficulty of finding an appropriate indicator is particularly acute for longitudinal studies as patterns of consumption shift over time. During the 1980s one might have collected box office figures for 'adult' cinemas, but these gradually became obsolete during the 1990s as consumers shifted to watching videos in the privacy of their own homes.

33 Baron and Straus 1987; 1989.

34 Gentry 1991. Drucilla Cornell cites the West Village area of New York City as an example of a neighbourhood with a high degree of sexual tolerance (including pornography) and a low rate of sexual violence (Cornell 1995, 153).

35 Kutchinsky 1991; earlier studies of Denmark and the United States can be found in Kutchinsky 1970; 1973; 1978; 1985.

36 Kutchinsky 1991, 62. Similar results were found by Kupperstein and Wilson 1970 for the period 1960–9 in the United States.

37 Diamond and Uchiyama 1999

38 Court 1984; see also 1977.

39 Court 1984, 166.

40 Though Court is clearly tempted by the bold hypothesis that the increasing availability of violent pornography is (at least partly) responsible for the overall increase in violent crime (Court 1984, 166).

41 For that matter, none of the longitudinal studies attempt to correlate the rape rate in a particular country with any quantifiable measure of the rate of circulation of pornographic materials in that country. Instead, they rely on the intuitive judgment of a substantial increase in the latter rate during a period of relaxation of legal restrictions.

42 See, for instance, Cochrane 1978 and Williams 1981, 69–79.

43 The claim that the circulation of violent pornography is associated with a high rate of sexual violence against women also has difficulty with the case of Japan, where an unusually high proportion of pornography features scenes of bondage and torture of girls and women but which has one of the lowest rates of sexual crime in the world (Diamond and Uchiyama 1999).

44 It would also be possible, in principle, to conduct prospective studies of groups of men with varying histories of exposure to pornography to com-

pare their subsequent rates of sexual offences. As far as I am aware, however, no such study has been undertaken, though at least one group of researchers (Donnerstein, Linz, and Penrod 1987, 144) has recognized its desirability. For what it is worth Potter 1999, although not a longitudinal study, found no correlation between men's (self-reported) history of consumption of pornographic materials and negative attitudes toward women.

45 See, for instance, Wyre 1992.
46 See, for instance, the case of Chuck in Beneke 1982, 71ff (quoted in MacKinnon and Dworkin 1997, 248–50); the case of the serial sexual murderer Ted Bundy in Michaud and Aynesworth 1983, 104–5 (quoted in MacKinnon and Dworkin 1997, 230–2); MacKinnon 1993, 18; Dines, Jensen, and Russo 1998, 119ff.
47 Commission on Obscenity and Pornography 1970, 274–85.
48 Attorney General's Commission on Pornography 1986, 263–71.
49 See Langevin et al. 1988; Murrin and Laws 1990; Fisher and Barak 1991, 74–5; Nutter and Kearns 1993.
50 Catharine MacKinnon has acknowledged this result but has used it to advance the intriguing hypothesis that, because only a minority of rapists are reported, apprehended, and convicted, the data may just show that a lot of these 'average adult males' also commit rape – they just don't get caught (MacKinnon 1987, 184–5).
51 For example, the experimental evidence is crucial to Diana Russell's hypotheses concerning the mechanisms by means of which pornography causes rape (Russell 1992). It has also been relied on, along with the narrative evidence, by Catharine MacKinnon (see, for example, MacKinnon 1991, 799–801).
52 Donnerstein 1984, 78; Donnerstein et al. 1987, ch.5; Linz, Penrod, and Donnerstein 1987, 719; Leighton 1988, 31; Linz and Malamuth 1993, 48–50; Boeringer 1994; Allen, D'Alessio, and Brezgel 1995. The 'consensus' is, however, not universally shared; for a contrarian view see Fisher and Barak 1991; Fisher and Grenier 1994.
53 Donnerstein et al 1987, ch. 4; Linz et al. 1987, 723ff.
54 Zillman 1989; Zillman and Weaver 1989. See also Check and Guloien 1989; Allen et al. 1995. Using a different methodology, contrary results were found by Potter 1999.
55 Attorney General's Commission on Pornography 1986, 41ff.
56 Attorney General's Commission on Pornography 1986, 39. The commission reached a similar conclusion about non-violent materials featuring scenes of subordination or degradation, though with less confidence (41–2).
57 The problem has been nicely presented and analysed by Schauer 1987, 765–7.

58 Linz et al. 1987, 719–21; Schauer 1987, 765–6; Donnerstein et al. 1987, ch. 6; Leighton 1988, 41.

59 Schauer 1987, 766.

60 Schauer 1987, 765, n. 62.

61 Linz et al. 1987, 720.

62 Williams 1981, 65–6; Special Committee on Pornography and Prostitution 1985, 100; Brannigan and Goldenberg 1987; Linz et al. 1987, 714, 722; Schauer 1987, 755ff; Leighton 1988, 12–13; Fisher and Barak 1991, 77ff; Segal 1993, 13–15; Allen et al. 1995, 275–6.

63 A further problem with this behavioural measure is that under the specific conditions of the experiment the administration of this 'punishment' is socially sanctioned by the researchers. Furthermore, subjects are not offered any non-aggressive response to the situation. It is unclear how many subjects would respond aggressively in a similar real-life context where such behaviour is a source of disapproval, or where they had the option of just walking away.

64 Since attitudes influence behaviour, we may still wish to conclude that, other factors equal, inducing hostile or antisocial attitudes toward women is likely to increase aggressive (including sexually aggressive) behaviour toward them; cf Schauer 1987, 766–7. While this hypothesis seems entirely reasonable, it cannot itself be tested under laboratory conditions.

65 But see Zillman 1989.

66 *Butler* (1992), 501–2.

67 'Although the Committee was frequently told that research studies clearly demonstrate that harms to society and to individuals were associated with the availability and use of pornography, we have had to conclude, very reluctantly, that the available research is of very limited use in addressing these questions. We want to articulate our position very clearly: the Committee is not prepared to state, *solely on the basis of the evidence and research it has seen,* that pornography is a significant causal factor in the commission of some forms of violent crime ...' (Special Committee on Pornography and Prostitution 1985, 99; emphasis in original).

68 Attorney General's Commission on Pornography 1986, 39–40.

69 See above, ch. 3, sec. 3.3.

70 Schauer 1987, 763–4.

71 These further conclusions gain some confirmation from the seeming absence of a correlation between the increasing availability of violent pornography and increases in the rate of sexual violence.

72 See, for example, Lahey 1991; Jensen 1998, 101ff; Boyle 2000.

73 Russell 1980; Silbert and Pines 1984; Attorney General's Commission on Pornography 1986; Kelly 1988; MacKinnon and Dworkin 1997; Jensen 1998.

74 'we should be more than foolish if we saw the harm ... as residing in the pornographic images themselves ... and not in the men's ... abuse of power. The
   harm, it is important to be clear about, is contained not in the explicitly sexual material, but in the social context which deprives a woman ... of her ...
   ability to reject any unwanted sexual activity – whether with husband, lover,
   parent, relative, friend, acquaintance or stranger' (Segal 1993, 17).

75 Law enforcement agencies have linked Oliver Stone's film *Natural Born Killers* (1994) to at least eight copycat murders (*Globe and Mail*, 27 December
   2002, R9).

76 Nadine Strossen relates the story of one man who petitioned his local school
   board to remove the Bible from school classrooms and libraries in part
   because it endorsed violence against women (Strossen 1995, 258–9).

77 MacKinnon 1993, 20 (emphasis in original); cf MacKinnon 1991, 798. Similar analyses are offered by Attorney General's Commission on Pornography
   1986, 231–2, 242; Dines 1998, 61–3; Russo 1998, 22–9; Campbell 1993.

78 Nina Hartley is the most widely cited example (Hartley 1987; 1993; 1997;
   Stoller and Levine 1993, ch. 11). For other instances see McElroy 1995,
   171ff; Strossen 1995, 187–8; Macy 1996, 33ff; Nagle 1997, ch. 15.

79 See, for instance, Macy 1996; Tracey 1997; Flowers 1998; Albert 2001; Eaves
   2002.

80 Strossen 1995, 193–8.

81 Cowan, Symansky, and Cowan 2000.

82 McElroy 1995, chs 7 and 8.

83 Hartley 1993; Cowan et al. 2000.

84 See, for instance, Dines 1998, 61–3.

85 Nina Hartley, for example, had completed a degree in nursing when she
   decided to do hard-core videos instead, because she found the sex enjoyable
   and thought she was thereby contributing to improving the sex lives of other
   women and couples (Hartley 1993). The indignation felt by sex workers
   when confronted by the allegation that they are non-autonomous dupes of
   patriarchy is a central theme of Bell 1987.

86 Williams 1981, 91.

87 In ch. 2, sec. 2.4.

88 Equality is the basis of the distinction many feminist writers draw between
   pornography and erotica; see, for instance, Steinem 1995, 238ff; Longino
   1980, 42–5.

89 MacKinnon 1987, 172.

90 This intuition receives some scientific confirmation from Baron 1990, which
   found a positive correlation in the fifty U.S. states between gender equality
   and circulation rates for some of the leading 'adult' magazines.

91 Longino 1980, 45–6.
92 MacKinnon 1991, 802.
93 Sec. 298(1).
94 Brown 1994, ch. 4. Cf *Keegstra* (1990), 723: 'Our common law has long seen defamation as a tortious action, but only where a litigant can show that reputation has been damaged by offending statements towards him or her as an individual.'
95 In ch. 2, sec. 2.4.
96 Recent examples include Tisdale 1994; McElroy 1995; Palac 1998.
97 See ch. 4, sec. 4.3.
98 This line of analysis is also suggested by the notion of 'dehumanization', which presumably involves lowering someone to a less than human status.
99 Nussbaum 1995.
100 There is, of course, a trivial sense in which pornography portrays women as objects for the sexual enjoyment of the (male) audience. But in that sense cooking shows portray chefs as objects for the culinary enjoyment of the (male and female) audience. If the charge of objectification is to have some moral bite then it must mean something more specific and serious than this.
101 In my experience, pornographic websites are more likely to cross this boundary than adult videos, possibly because the more fragmented Internet marketplace is less susceptible to regulation.
102 The text of the ordinances is reproduced in MacKinnon and Dworkin 1997, 426ff.
103 MacKinnon 1993, 22.
104 Sec. 16-1(a)(2) of the Indianapolis ordinance (MacKinnon and Dworkin 1997, 439).
105 Austin 1962.
106 For instance, in MacKinnon 1993, 21, and n. 31, 121. MacKinnon's use of speech act theory is subjected to an extended critique in Butler 1997.
107 Langton 1993; Hornsby 1995; Dwyer 1995; Hornsby and Langton 1998; McGowan 2003. For extended critiques of this approach, see Jacobson 1995; 2001.
108 As suggested by Vadas 1987, 506.
109 Drucilla Cornell makes a similar point about pornography's lack of power to define women's sexual identities (Cornell 1995, 143–4).
110 As Jacobson shows, Austin's claim about the necessity of audience uptake is controversial (see Jacobson 1995, 72–4; 2001, 187–8). However, since the silencing argument rests on the uptake claim, and has no chance of success without it, I will not challenge it.

111 In any case, there are much more direct and effective ways for men to disable women's power of refusal. The date-rape drug gamma-hydroxybutyrate (GHB) has the effect of depriving its victim of a sense of will, thus rendering her unable to resist a sexual advance.

112 In Canada it is an offence to touch anyone under the age of fourteen for a sexual purpose; the same offence applies in the case of adolescents between fourteen and eighteen only within the context of a relationship of trust, authority, or dependency (Criminal Code, secs 151–3). Meanwhile, a child is defined for the purposes of the child pornography statute as anyone under the age of eighteen (sec. 163.1).

113 I have loosely adapted this characterization from Committee on Sexual Offences against Children and Youths 1984, 179–80.

114 See, e.g., Committee on Sexual Offences against Children and Youths 1984, ch. 31; Burgess et al. 1984; Cairns 1999; Fergusson and Mullen 1999; Dorais 2002; Burgess et al. 1986.

115 Even that evidence would establish only a correlation between pornography consumption and sexual violence; by itself it would not show that the former was the cause of the latter.

116 Fergusson and Mullen 1999, 45–7.

117 Since I am using the age of fourteen as the cutoff point for childhood, for the purposes of the present discussion, we are therefore talking about pubescent or pre-pubescent children. I do not regard a twenty-something adult with a sexual interest in seventeen-year-olds as a pedophile.

118 Gillespie 2002; Matthews 2002. The involvement may be by way of a previous charge or complaint, or may come to light as a result of subsequent investigation of children whose images were included in the collection seized by police. The 35–40 per cent estimate appears to have been derived from the U.S. Postal Inspection Service's Child Exploitation Investigative Program and the FBI's Innocent Images Project ('"Predator Could Be Anyone"', *Toronto Star* 10 March 2003, E1). However, the estimate must be treated with some scepticism, since 'known collectors' are, by definition, those who have come to the attention of the authorities. Since it is likely that those collectors actively involved in abuse have a higher risk of being apprehended, the percentage of all collectors with such an involvement may be much lower. There is probably no reliable way of estimating what fraction of the total number of collectors are also abusers; see Jenkins 2001, 127–31.

119 Committee on Sexual Offences against Children and Youths 1984, ch. 52; Moyer 1992, 4; Jenkins 2001, ch. 2. Many commercial pornography websites feature (alleged) teenagers, but they are careful to use only models who are eighteen or over.

120 Jenkins 2001, ch. 3.
121 Belanger et al. 1984; Moyer 1992, 4; Matthews 2002. Pedophile rings under investigation in recent years have operated under such names as the Orchid Club (1996: 16 arrests), Pedo University (1998: 13 arrests), and the Wonderland Club (1998: 100 arrests in twelve countries). Law enforcement authorities are fond of saying that these cases represent only the tip of the iceberg, and that the international trade in child pornography, and therefore the abuse that is implicated in it, are reaching epidemic proportions. For a sceptical and deflationary view, see Levine 2002, ch. 2.
122 Hunt and Baird 1990; Tate 1990, chs 1 and 4; Tate 1992; Kelly 1992.
123 Tate 1990; Kelly 1992; Gillespie 2002; Matthews 2002. Participant harm is obviously limited to those types of visual pornography whose production actually involves the sexual exploitation of children. However, third-party harms can potentially be done by other materials, including stories, 'virtual' representations, and adult pornography.
124 For a convenient summary of the research on this issue, see Heins 2001, ch. 10.
125 The most prominent sceptic has been Jonathan Freedman; see Freedman 2002.
126 Levine 2002, 148–9, quoting Marjorie Heins.
127 This view is argued forcefully in Levine 2002; cf Persky and Dixon 2001, 212.
128 For instance, in MacKinnon 1993.
129 For convenience, I will confine myself in this section to minorities defined by race, religion, ethnicity, disability, or sexual orientation. However, I do not deny that women can also be targets of hate propaganda, nor that misogynistic pornography may constitute such propaganda. I consider the relationship between pornography and hate speech in ch. 6, sec. 6.3.
130 Matsuda 1993, 24–5.
131 Calvert 1997; Leets 2002; Nielsen 2002. The emotional distress which hate speech can inflict on its targets is distinct from the moral distress which we earlier excluded as a form of harm within the meaning of the Harm Principle. The impact of insult or abuse on a person's sense of self-worth does not require the mediation of a moral belief, any more than does the similar impact of other blows, such as rejection or abandonment by loved ones.
132 Matsuda 1993, 25–6 (citation omitted).
133 Calvert 1997, 6.
134 See, for instance, Berrill and Herek 1990; Garnets, Herek, and Levey 1990; Levin and McDevitt 1993; Hamm 1994; Barnes and Ephross 1994; Miethe

and McCorkle 1998; Craig 1999; Herek, Gillis, and Cogan 1999; Herek, Cogan, and Gillis 2002.

135 This upshot of hate speech is emphasized in Aronovitch 2002.

136 Toronto Police Service 2002, 4; League for Human Rights of B'nai Brith Canada 2002, section 3.

137 'during opportune times, [hate speech] inflames and recruits persons who can be catalyzed to wreak havoc on outgroups. Discriminatory oratory functions to unify ingroups through a mutually captivating ideology. It distinguishes ingroups from minorities, expresses the superiority of the dominant group, and organizes for collective action against outgroups' (Tsesis 2002, 117).

138 This is especially so with some of the most frequently reported types of hate crime, such as vandalism and harassment, which, because usually anonymous, result in a lower arrest rate.

139 '[I]t is clear that hate groups are not the primary perpetrators of bias-motivated crime. The vast majority is committed – singly or in groups – by people who are not directly connected to any organized form of hate' (Perry 2001, 142). See also Levin and McDevitt 1993; McDevitt, Levin, and Bennett 2002.

140 See, for instance, League for Human Rights of B'nai Brith Canada 1990; Kinsella 1994. Comprehensive accounts of hate groups in the United States can be found in Ridgeway 1995 and Stern 1996; for a briefer overview see Perry 2001, ch. 6.

141 In 1999 Benjamin Smith, an adherent of the World Church of the Creator, killed two people and wounded twelve during a shooting rampage in Indiana and Illinois in which he was targeting blacks, Jews, and Asians. Later that same year Buford Furrow, who had been affiliated with Aryan Nation–Church of Jesus Christ, shot five people in a Jewish community centre in Los Angeles and then killed a Filipino postal worker an hour later.

142 Recall here Mill's conditions for advocacy to constitute instigation: the act follows the advocacy of it and 'at least a probable connection can be established between the act and the instigation' (see ch. 2, sec. 2.2). Where hate violence is practised by members of groups whose rhetoric endorses just such violence, these conditions would appear to be satisfied.

Chapter 6 From Principle to Policy

1 Jenkins 2001, ch. 2

2 *Butler* (1992), 485.
3 The background to this legislation is described in Persky and Dixon 2001, ch. 2.
4 The *Globe and Mail* offered the editorial opinion that the law was 'a loosely drafted, ludicrously broad piece of legislation, and an unnecessary one at that' (26 February 1994). See also Blugerman 1993–5; 1994.
5 Sec. 163.1(1)(a)(i),(ii).
6 Sec. 163.1(1)(b).
7 Sec. 163.1(4).
8 For a full account of the *Sharpe* case at every level from trial to the Supreme Court, see Persky and Dixon 2001, chs 3–5.
9 See, for instance, Blugerman 1994, 26–8.
10 *Sharpe* (2001), 81.
11 *Sharpe* (2001), 82.
12 See ch. 1, sec. 1.2.
13 *Sharpe* (2001), 83–4.
14 Along precisely these lines, in December 2002 the government tabled an amendment to sec. 163.1 (Bill C-20) which would add a third part to the definition of child pornography: 'any written material the dominant characteristic of which is the description, for a sexual purpose, of sexual activity with a person under the age of eighteen years that would be an offence under this Act'. At the time of writing, this amendment has only passed first reading in the House of Commons.
15 The minority in *Sharpe* dissented on this point and would have upheld the statute with its definition of child pornography intact.
16 The exceptions, as formulated by the court, were the following:
   1. Self-created expressive material: i.e., any written material or visual representation created by the accused alone, and held by the accused alone, exclusively for his or her own personal use; and
   2. Private recordings of lawful sexual activity: i.e., any visual recording, created by or depicting the accused, provided it does not depict unlawful sexual activity and is held by the accused exclusively for private use. (*Sharpe* (2001), 111)
17 Gillespie 2002; Matthews 2002.
18 Sec. 163.1(6). The defence applies as well to materials with 'an educational, scientific or medical purpose'. The child pornography statute also imports the 'public good' defence in the obscenity statute (sec. 163(3)).
19 Ch. 4, sec. 4.1.
20 *Sharpe* (2001), 87.
21 Matthews 2002. The government evidently shared this concern. In Decem-

ber 2002 it tabled an amendment to sec. 163.1 (Bill C-20) which would delete the artistic merit (and educational, scientific, or medical purpose) defence and substitute a public good defence modelled on that already existing in sec. 163. At the time of writing, this amendment has only passed first reading in the House of Commons.

22 Sec. 12 also prohibits the public display of notices or symbols that incite others to discriminate.

23 This is about to change, at least where gays are concerned. In September 2003 the House of Commons passed an amendment (Bill C-250) which expands the list of 'identifiable groups' by adding sexual orientation. At the time of writing, this bill still awaits passage through the Senate.

24 *Taylor* (1990).

25 For an outline of the structure and procedures of human rights commissions and tribunals in Canada, see Howe and Johnson 2000, ch. 2.

26 John Ross Taylor himself (the subject of the Supreme Court decision) served a sentence of one year, imposed by a Federal Court for non-compliance with the tribunal order that he cease transmitting tape-recorded hate messages over the telephone.

27 *Taylor* (1990), 933ff.

28 *Zundel* (1992).

29 *Zundel* (2002).

30 In February 2003 Zundel was returned to Canada by the U.S. Immigration and Naturalization Service for having overstayed his visitor's visa. Since he no longer had permanent resident status in Canada, he applied for refugee status. At the time of writing the Canadian government is attempting to deport him to Germany on the ground that he is a national security threat. While his case is being heard he remains in detention.

31 The further subsections of code 9956 cover hate propaganda and materials of a treasonable or seditious character.

32 For a sampling of such materials see Califia 1995.

33 *Luscher* (1985); *Glad Day Bookshop* (1992a) (1992b).

34 *Little Sisters* (1996). The story of the trial can be found in Fuller and Blackley 1996.

35 *Little Sisters* (1998).

36 *Little Sisters* (2000).

37 *Glad Day Bookshop* (1992b); *Scythes* (1993).

38 The majority judgment is subjected to critique in Ryder 2001.

39 Their case is currently scheduled for hearing before the British Columbia Supreme Court in September 2004.

40 The board likes to emphasize this side of its activities. In the responses to

FAQs posted on its website, it states: 'Today, the Board's focus is classification, not censorship. The OFRB is a valued source of information about movies and videos that help viewers make the right entertainment decisions for themselves and for their children' (www.ofrb.gov.on.ca/english/faqs/page2.html – accessed 19/12/02).

41 The need for legislated guidelines, in order to survive sec. 1 scrutiny, was established in *OFAVAS* (1983) and (1984).

42 Though, curiously, sec. 14(2) also lists 'the explicit depiction of sexual activity' and 'undue emphasis on human genital organs' as grounds for prohibition, both of which run counter to *Butler*. If pornographic videos could be required to remove these sorts of content, it is not clear what would be left of them. For the record, videos consisting entirely of depictions of sexual activity with a good deal of emphasis on genital organs are routinely approved for distribution by the board.

43 www.ofrb.gov.on.ca/english/faqs/page5.html (accessed 19/12/02).

44 See ch. 4, sec. 4.2.

45 The board still draws the line at such activities as bestiality, necrophilia, bondage, torture, and urinating or defecating on a person. Recently it amended its guidelines to prohibit fisting in the anus (but not the vagina).

46 However, some would. The prohibition of scenes of cruelty or torture eliminates videos a dominant characteristic of which is the depiction of consensual bondage and discipline or sadomasochism. Because of their consensual nature, many (including members of the lesbian community) would argue that they are not genuinely violent and should be available for viewing by those whose tastes run in that direction.

47 There was a particularly delicious irony in the board's decision that the anti-pornography documentary *Not a Love Story* (1981) could not be released for general theatrical distribution, since it contained a few snippets of nudity as examples of the kind of material it argued exploited women.

48 *New York Times*, 23 October 2000, A1.

49 The Simon Wiesenthal Center identified 3,000 'problematic' websites in 2001(CD-ROM, 'Digital Hate 2001'). The Southern Poverty Law Center's Intelligence Project tracked 676 hate groups known to be active in the United States in 2001 (www.tolerance.org/maps/hate/index.html – accessed 06/01/03). Most of these groups maintain, or participate in, hate websites. Many more groups are, of course, active in other countries.

50 The best-known example of American legislation targeting Internet pornography is the Communications Decency Act (CDA) passed by Congress in 1996 and intended, *inter alia*, to shield children from sexually explicit materials. However, it was struck down by the U.S. Supreme Court in *Reno* (1997)

on grounds of overbreadth. Congress responded by passing the Child Online Protection Act (COPA) (1998) whose judicial prospects seem equally dim (*Ashcroft* (2002b)); at the time of writing it remains under injunction until its constitutional fate is settled. For a recent account of the careers of both the CDA and the COPA, see Alexander 2002.

51 Bill C-36, the Anti-Terrorism Act passed by Parliament in 2001, explicitly extended sec. 320 of the Criminal Code, which authorizes seizure of hate propaganda, to include materials 'stored on and made available to the public through a computer system'. Presumably, an e-mail message intended for receipt and viewing only by a particular addressee would fall outside this provision, and would also qualify as a 'private conversation' for the purpose of sec. 319(2).

52 Canadian Human Rights Act, sec. 13(1).

53 Ibid., sec. 13(2).

54 Even in the case of child pornography, enforcement is no easy matter; see Jenkins 2001, ch. 6.

55 This is, of course, the rational connection requirement in the *Oakes* tests; cf ch. 3, sec. 3.1.

56 This is, of course, the minimal impairment requirement in the *Oakes* tests.

57 This approach is advocated by Cornell 1995, ch. 5; McElroy 1995, ch. 8; Strossen 1995, ch. 9.

58 Government of Canada 1982, 45.

59 This purpose connects sec. 163.1 closely with the provisions in the Criminal Code (secs 151–3) dealing with sexual offences against children. These sections are grouped together in the Code under the general heading of 'Sexual Offences', whereas sec. 163.1 is grouped (along with sec. 163, the obscenity statute) under the heading of 'Offences Tending to Corrupt Morals'. While the association of the child pornography and obscenity sections is understandable (since both deal with pornography), it is also misleading since the purpose of sec. 163.1 is to prevent serious physical and psychological harm to children, not the corruption of anyone's morals.

60 I have incorporated into this catalogue both the glosses on the definition of child pornography offered by the Supreme Court in *Sharpe* and also the provisions in Bill C-20 (on the assumption that the latter will make their way into law).

61 This particular concern about overbreadth is not merely speculative. In 1997 an Ontario judge convicted Narcisse Kuneman under sec. 163.1 for possession, *inter alia*, of a copy of an advocacy piece entitled 'Men Loving Boys Loving Men' originally published in 1977 in the gay magazine *The Body Politic* ('1977 Sex Article Back in Court', *Globe and Mail*, 13 May 2003, A6). Bruce

Ryder has argued that material advocating sexual offences against children should be removed from the definition of child pornography and instead treated as hate propaganda for the purpose of (an expanded version of) sec. 319(2) (Ryder 2003, 114–17). However, it is far from clear that the advocacy of sexual activities which are offences under secs 151–3 necessarily constitutes the wilful promotion of hatred against children, and it seems to me a considerable stretch to treat 'Men Loving Boys Loving Men' as a piece of hate literature. In any case, I consider, below, the case for expanding the range of protected groups in sec. 319(2).

62 Robert Matthews of the Ontario Provincial Police has said that his unit does not bother with any material in which there is the slightest doubt whether the person depicted is under eighteen (Matthews 2002).

63 The same limitation for sec. 163.1 is advocated in Ryder 2003.

64 *Sharpe* (2001), 82.

65 Sec. 163.1(6).

66 This defence will also replace the existing artistic merit defence. Earlier we looked at the Supreme Court's interpretation of 'artistic merit', which appears to have the implication that the defence can be invoked whenever the materials in question can be fitted into some recognizable category of artistic product. The proposed public good defence not only closes this potentially damaging loophole; it also applies both to the materials themselves and to their production, distribution, or possession. It will therefore potentially cover possession of prohibited materials for a legitimate purpose, such as education or research.

67 See ch. 1, sec. 1.2.

68 Many commercial websites contain explicit disclaimers to the effect that all models depicted are eighteen or over. Producers of hard-core videos also tend to be vigilant in enforcing the minimum age, if only to avoid needless legal complications.

69 In this connection it is interesting that the child pornography law was initially intended to define a child as someone under the age of sixteen; see Persky and Dixon 2001, 58ff.

70 In any case, a thorough overhaul of the obscenity statute is long overdue, since it still prohibits the publication or distribution of crime comics, the public exhibition of disgusting objects, and the advertisement of abortifacients and drugs for restoring sexual virility or curing venereal diseases (sec. 163(1)(b), (2)(b)(c)(d)).

71 Bill C-114 received first reading on 10 June 1986, while bill C-54 received first reading on 4 May 1987.

72 Some of the most graphic depictions of rape occur in mainstream films such

as *The Accused* (1988), whose aim was not to glorify rape but to explore some of its legal ramifications, including the complicity of onlookers.

73 This approach is advocated in Cornell 1995, 112ff, and Weinstein 1999, 165–6.

74 I assume here that rape (where the victim is female) is a hate crime directed at women.

75 Cohen 2000.

76 Bill C-250, sponsored by Svend Robinson, passed third reading on 19 September 2003.

77 *Keegstra* (1990), 777–8.

78 'Under False Pretences', *Toronto Star*, 31 August 2003, A17.

79 Finnis 1995.

80 Mill 1977, 244–5.

81 'the current infrastructure of the internet renders the network so difficult to control that the objectives of restrictive state policies in the area of internet speech cannot be achieved without implementing measures inconsistent with the tenets of democracy' (Mailland 2001, 1181–2).

82 Filtering software is notoriously inefficient at blocking access to objectionable Internet content, both because it can be circumvented and also because it inevitably blocks legitimate sites as well. From a constitutional point of view, its imposition would therefore fail both the rational connection and minimal impairment tests. For a critique of Internet filters, see Haselton 2002.

83 I take no stand here on the justifiability of penalty enhancement for hate crimes; for arguments on both sides of the issue see Jacobs and Potter 1998 and Lawrence 1999.

84 Mill 1977, 228n.

85 Ch. 5, sec. 5.5.

86 On this question I am therefore changing my mind yet again; see Sumner 1994.

87 Emerson 1955, 659.

Cases Cited

Little Sisters (2000)   *Little Sisters Book and Art Emporium v. Canada (Minis-*
                                            ter of Justice), (2000) 2 S.C.R. 1120
Lucas (1998)   *R. v. Lucas*, (1998) 1 S.C.R. 439
Ludacka (1996)   *R. v. Ludacka*, (1996) 105 C.C.C. (3d) 565
Luscher (1985)   *Re Luscher and Deputy Minister, Revenue Canada, Cus-*
                                            toms and Excise, (1985) 17 D.L.R. (4th) 503
Macmillan (1976)   *R. v. The Macmillan Company of Canada Ltd.*, (1976)
                                            31 C.C.C. (2d) 286
Mara (1997)   *R. v. Mara*, (1997) 2 S.C.R. 630
Martin Secker Warburg (1954)   *R. v. Martin Secker Warburg, Ltd.*, (1954) 2 All E.R.
                                            683
McFall (1975)   *R. v. McFall*, (1975) 26 C.C.C. (2d) 181
Metro News (1986)   *R. v. Metro News*, (1986) 29 C.C.C. 35
Miller (1973)   *Miller v. California*, (1973) 413 U.S. 15
National News (1953)   *R. v. National News Co. Ltd.*, (1953) 106 C.C.C. 26
New Brunswick (1996)   *Canadian Broadcasting Corp. v. New Brunswick (Attor-*
                                            ney General), (1996) 3 S.C.R. 480
Nicols (1984)   *R. v. Nicols*, (1984) 43 C.R. (3d) 54
Oakes (1986)   *R. v. Oakes*, (1986) 1 S.C.R. 103
Odeon Morton (1974)   *R. v. Odeon Morton Theatres Ltd.*, (1974) 16 C.C.C.
                                            (2d) 185
OFAVAS (1983)   *Re Ontario Film and Video Appreciation Society and*
                                            Ontario Board of Censors, (1983) 147 D.L.R. (3d) 58
OFAVAS (1984)   *Re Ontario Film and Video Appreciation Society and*
                                            Ontario Board of Censors, (1984) 5 D.L.R. (4th) 766
Pelletier (1985)   *Pelletier v. R.*, (1985) 49 C.R. (3d) 253
Penthouse (1979)   *R. v. Penthouse International Ltd.*, (1979) 46 C.C.C.
                                            (2d) 111
Pereira-Vasquez (1985)   *R. v. Pereira-Vasquez*, (1985) 43 C.R. (3d) 336
Pereira-Vasquez (1988)   *R. v. Pereira-Vasquez*, (1988) 26 B.C.L.R. (2d) 273
Pink Triangle (1979)   *R. v. Pink Triangle Press*, (1979) 45 C.C.C. (2d) 385
Pink Triangle (1980)   *R. v. Pink Triangle Press*, (1980) 51 C.C.C. (2d) 485
Popert (1981)   *R. v. Popert*, (1981) 58 C.C.C. 505
Prairie Schooner (1970)   *R. v. Prairie Schooner News Ltd.*, (1970) 1 C.C.C. (2d)
                                            251
Priape (1979)   *Re Priape Enrg. and the Deputy Minister of National*
                                            Revenue, (1979) 52 C.C.C. (2d) 44
Prostitution Reference (1990)   *Reference Re ss. 193 and 195.1(1)(c) of the Criminal*
                                            Code (Man.), (1990) 1 S.C.R. 1123
Quesnel (1979)   *R. v. Quesnel*, (1979) 51 C.C.C. (2d) 270

Ramsingh (1984)	*R. v. Ramsingh*, (1984) 14 C.C.C. (3d) 230
Rankine (1983)	*R. v. Doug Rankine Co. Ltd.*, (1983) 9 C.C.C. (3d) 53
R.A.V. (1992)	*R.A.V. v. City of St. Paul*, (1992) 505 U.S. 377
Red Hot Video (1984)	*R. v. Red Hot Video Ltd.*, (1984) 11 C.C.C. (3d) 389
Red Hot Video (1985)	*R. v. Red Hot Video Ltd.*, (1985) 18 C.C.C. (3d) 1
Reno (1997)	*Reno v. American Civil Liberties Union*, (1997) 117 S. Ct. 2329
RJR-MacDonald (1995)	*RJR-MacDonald Inc. v. Canada (Attorney General)*, (1995) 3 S.C.R. 199
Rocket (1990)	*Rocket v. Royal College of Dental Surgeons of Ontario*, (1990) 2 S.C.R. 232
Ross (1996)	*Ross v. New Brunswick School District No. 15*, (1996) 1 S.C.R. 825
Roth (1956)	*Roth v. United States*, (1956) 354 U.S. 476
Scythes (1993)	*R. v. Scythes*, (1993) O.J. No. 537 (unreported)
Sharpe (2001)	*R. v. Sharpe*, (2001) 1 S.C.R. 45
Slaight (1989)	*Slaight Communications Inc. v. Davidson*, (1989) 1 S.C.R. 1038
St. Pierre (1974)	*R. v. St. Pierre*, (1974) 17 C.C.C. (2d) 489
Sudbury News (1978)	*R. v. Sudbury News Service Limited*, (1978) 39 C.C.C. (2d) 1
Taylor (1990)	*Canada (Human Rights Commission) v. Taylor*, (1990) 3 S.C.R. 892
Thomson Newspapers (1998)	*Thomson Newspapers Co. v. Canada (Attorney General)*, (1998) 1 S.C.R. 877
Times Square (1971)	*R. v. Times Square Cinema Ltd.*, (1971) 3 O.R. 688
Towne Cinema (1985)	*Towne Cinema Theatres Ltd. v. The Queen*, (1985) 1 S.C.R. 494
Tremblay (1993)	*R. v. Tremblay*, (1993) 2 S.C.R. 932
Various Articles (1983)	*U.S. v. Various Articles of Obscene Merchandise*, (1983) 709 F.2d 132
Video World (1985a)	*R. v. Video World Ltd.*, (1985) 32 Man.R. (2d) 41 (Man. Pr. Ct.)
Video World (1985b)	*R. v. Video World Ltd.*, (1985) 36 Man.R. (2d) 68 (Man. C.A.)
Video World (1987)	*R. v. Video World Ltd.*, (1987) 1 S.C.R. 1255
Wagner (1985)	*R. v. Wagner*, (1985) 43 C.R. (3d) 318
Zundel (1992)	*R. v. Zundel*, (1992) 2 S.C.R. 731
Zundel (2002)	*Citron v. Zundel*, (2002) 41 C.H.R.R. D/724 (C.H.R.T.)

Works Cited

Adams, Don. 2000. 'Can Pornography Cause Rape?' *Journal of Social Philosophy* 31(1).

Albert, Alexa. 2001. *Brothel: Mustang Ranch and Its Women.* New York: Random House.

Aleinikoff, Alexander. 1987. 'Constitutional Law in the Age of Balancing.' *Yale Law Journal* 96(5).

Alexander, Mark C. 2002. 'The First Amendment and Problems of Political Viability: The Case of Internet Pornography.' *Harvard Journal of Law and Public Policy* 25(3).

Allen, Mike, Dave D'Alessio, and Keri Brezgel. 1995. 'A Meta-Analysis Summarizing the Effects of Pornography II: Aggression after Exposure.' *Human Communication Research* 22(2).

Aronovitch, Hilliard. 2002. 'The Harm of Hate Propaganda.' In *Citizenship and Participation in the Information Age,* ed. Manjunath Pendakur and Roma Harris. Aurora, ON: Garamond Press.

Attorney General's Commission on Pornography. 1986. *Final Report.* Nashville, TN: Rutledge Hill Press.

Austin, J.L. 1962. *How to Do Things with Words.* Ed. J.O. Urmson. Cambridge, MA: Harvard University Press.

Barnes, Arnold, and Paul H. Ephross. 1994. 'The Impact of Hate Violence on Victims: Emotional and Behavioral Responses to Attacks.' *Social Work* 39(3) (May).

Barnett, C.S. 1969. 'Obscenity and s.150 (8) of the Criminal Code.' *Criminal Law Quarterly* 12(1).

Baron, Larry. 1990. 'Pornography and Gender Equality: An Empirical Analysis.' *Journal of Sex Research* 27(3).

Baron, Larry, and Murray A. Straus. 1987. 'Four Theories of Rape: A Macrosociological Analysis.' *Social Problems* 34(5).

Baron, Larry, and Murray A. Straus. 1989. *Four Theories of Rape in American Society.* New Haven: Yale University Press.

Beatty, David. 1995. *Constitutional Law in Theory and Practice.* Toronto: University of Toronto Press.

Belanger, Albert J., et al. 1984. 'Typology of Sex Rings Exploiting Children.' In *Child Pornography and Sex Rings*, ed. Ann Wolbert Burgess and Marieanne Lindeqvist Clark. Lexington, MA: Lexington Books.

Bell, Laurie. 1987. *Good Girls/Bad Girls: Sex Trade Workers and Feminists Face to Face.* Toronto: Women's Press.

Beneke, Timothy. 1982. *Men on Rape.* New York: St Martin's Press.

Berlin, Isaiah. 1969. 'Two Concepts of Liberty.' In *Four Essays on Liberty*, by Isaiah Berlin. Oxford: Oxford University Press.

Berrill, Kevin T., and Gregory M. Herek. 1990. 'Primary and Secondary Victimization in Anti-Gay Hate Crimes.' *Journal of Interpersonal Violence* 5(3).

Blugerman, Brian M. 1993–5. 'The New Child Pornography Law: Difficulties of Bill C-128.' *Media and Communications Law Review* 4.

Blugerman, Brian M. 1994. 'Beyond Obscenity: Canada's New Child Pornography Law.' *The Entertainment and Sports Lawyer* 11(4).

Boeringer, Scot B. 1994. 'Pornography and Sexual Aggression: Associations of Violent and Nonviolent Depictions with Rape and Rape Proclivity.' *Deviant Behavior* 15(3).

Borovoy, A. Alan. 1999. *The New Anti-Liberals.* Toronto: Canadian Scholars' Press.

Boyle, Karen. 2000. 'The Pornography Debates: Beyond Cause and Effect.' *Women's Studies International Forum* 23(2).

Brannigan, Augustine, and Sheldon Goldenberg. 1987. 'The Study of Aggressive Pornography: The Vicissitudes of Relevance.' *Critical Studies in Mass Communication* 4(3).

Brown, Raymond. 1994. *The Law of Defamation in Canada.* 2nd ed. Scarborough, ON: Carswell.

Burgess, Ann W., Carol R. Hartman, Maureen P. McCausland, and Patricia Powers. 1986. 'Response Patterns in Children and Adolescents Exploited through Sex Rings and Pornography.' *Annual Progress in Child Psychiatry and Child Development.*

Burgess, Ann W., et al. 1984. 'Impact of Child Pornography and Sex Rings on Child Victims and Their Families.' In *Child Pornography and Sex Rings*, ed. Ann Wolbert Burgess and Marieanne Lindeqvist Clark. Lexington, MA: Lexington Books.

Busby, Karen. 1994. 'LEAF and Pornography: Litigating on Equality and Sexual Representations.' *Canadian Journal of Law and Society* 9(1).

Butler, Judith. 1997. *Excitable Speech: A Politics of the Performative.* New York and London: Routledge.

Cairns, Kate. 1999. *Surviving Paedophilia: Traumatic Stress after Organized and Network Child Sexual Abuse.* London: Trentham Books Limited.

Califia, Pat. 1994. 'Feminism and Sadomasochism.' In *Public Sex: The Culture of Radical Sex,* by Pat Califia. Pittsburgh: Cleis Press Inc.

Califia, Pat. 1995. *Forbidden Passages: Writings Banned in Canada.* Pittsburgh: Cleis Press.

Calvert, Clay. 1997. 'Hate Speech and Its Harms: A Communication Theory Perspective.' *Journal of Communication* 47(1).

Cameron, Jamie. 1990–1. 'The First Amendment and Section One of the Charter.' *Media and Communications Law Review* 59.

Cameron, Jamie. 1997. 'The Past, Present, and Future of Expressive Freedom under the Charter.' *Osgoode Hall Law Journal* 35.

Campbell, Bebe Moore. 1993. 'A Portrait of Angel: The Life of a Porn Star.' In *Making Violence Sexy: Feminist Views on Pornography,* ed. Diana E.H. Russell. New York and London: Teachers College Press.

Cartwright, Nancy. 1979. 'Causal Laws and Effective Strategies.' *Nous* 13.

Charles, W.H. 1966. 'Obscene Literature and the Legal Process in Canada.' *Canadian Bar Review* 44.

Check, James V.P., and Ted H. Guloien. 1989. 'Reported Proclivity for Coercive Sex Following Repeated Exposure to Sexually Violent Pornography, Nonviolent Dehumanizing Pornography, and Erotica.' In *Pornography: Research Advances and Policy Considerations,* ed. Dolf Zillman and Jennings Bryant. Hillsdale, NJ: Lawrence Erlbaum Associates.

Cochrane, P. 1978. 'Sex Crimes and Pornography Revisited.' *International Journal of Criminology and Penology* 6.

Cohen, Jonathan. 2000. 'More Censorship or Less Discrimination? Sexual Orientation Hate Propaganda in Multiple Perspectives.' *McGill Law Journal* 46.

Cohen, Joshua. 1993. 'Freedom of Expression.' *Philosophy and Public Affairs* 22(3).

Commission on Obscenity and Pornography. 1970. *Report of the Commission on Obscenity and Pornography.* New York: Bantam Books.

Committee on Sexual Offences against Children and Youths. 1984. *Sexual Offences against Children.* Ottawa: Canadian Government Publishing Centre.

Copp, David. 1983. 'Pornography and Censorship: An Introductory Essay.' In *Pornography and Censorship,* ed. David Copp and Susan Wendell. Buffalo: Prometheus Books.

Cornell, Drucilla. 1995. *The Imaginary Domain: A Discourse on Abortion, Pornogra-*

phy, and Sexual Harassment. New York and London: Routledge, Chapman and Hall.

Cossman, Brenda, Shannon Bell, Lise Gotell, and Becki Ross, eds. 1997. *Bad Attitude/s on Trial: Pornography, Feminism, and the Butler Decision.* Toronto: University of Toronto Press.

Court, John H. 1977. 'Pornography and Sex Crimes: A Re-evaluation in the Light of Recent Trends around the World.' *International Journal of Criminology and Penology* 5.

Court, John H. 1984. 'Sex and Violence: A Ripple Effect.' In *Pornography and Sexual Aggression,* ed. Neil M. Malamuth and Edward Donnerstein. Orlando: Academic Press.

Cowan, Paul, dir., Adam Symansky, and Paul Cowan, prods. 2000. *Give Me Your Soul.* Montreal: National Film Board of Canada.

Craig, Kellina M. 1999. 'Retaliation, Fear, or Rage: An Investigation of African American and White Reactions to Racist Hate Crimes.' *Journal of Interpersonal Violence* 14(2).

Crerar, David A. 1996–7. '"The Darker Corners": The Incoherence of 2(b) Obscenity Jurisprudence after *Butler.*' *Ottawa Law Review* 28(2).

Diamond, Milton, and Ayako Uchiyama. 1999. 'Pornography, Rape, and Other Sex Crimes in Japan.' *International Journal of Law and Psychiatry* 22(1).

Dines, Gail. 1998. 'Dirty Business: Playboy Magazine and the Mainstreaming of Pornography.' In Dines, Jensen, and Russo, eds, *Pornography.*

Dines, Gail, Robert Jensen, and Ann Russo, eds. 1998. *Pornography: The Production and Consumption of Inequality.* New York and London: Routledge.

Donnerstein, Edward. 1984. 'Pornography: Its Effects on Violence against Women.' In *Pornography and Sexual Aggression,* ed. Neil M. Malamuth and Edward Donnerstein. Orlando: Academic Press.

Donnerstein, Edward, Daniel Linz, and Steven Penrod. 1987. *The Question of Pornography.* New York: The Free Press.

Dorais, Michel. 2002. *Don't Tell: The Masculine Experience of Sexual Abuse.* Isabel Denholm Meyer. Montreal: McGill-Queen's University Press.

Dworkin, Ronald. 1985. *A Matter of Principle.* Cambridge, MA: Harvard University Press.

Dworkin, Ronald. 1996. *Freedom's Law: The Moral Reading of the American Constitution.* Cambridge, MA: Harvard University Press.

Dwyer, Susan. 1995. 'Pornography and Speech Acts.' In *The Problem of Pornography,* ed. Susan Dwyer. Belmont, CA: Wadsworth Publishing Company.

Eaves, Elisabeth. 2002. *Bare: On Women, Dancing, Sex, and Power.* New York: Alfred A. Knopf.

Ellis, Anthony. 1984. 'Offense and the Liberal Conception of the Law.' *Philosophy and Public Affairs* 13(1).

Emerson, Thomas I. 1955. 'The Doctrine of Prior Restraint.' *Law and Contemporary Problems* 20.

Feinberg, Joel. 1984. *Harm to Others.* New York and Oxford: Oxford University Press.

Feinberg, Joel. 1985. *Offense to Others.* New York and Oxford: Oxford University Press.

Feinberg, Joel. 1986. *Harm to Self.* New York and Oxford: Oxford University Press.

Feinberg, Joel. 1988. *Harmless Wrongdoing.* New York and Oxford: Oxford University Press.

Fergusson, David M., and Paul E. Mullen. 1999. *Childhood Sexual Abuse: An Evidence Based Perspective.* Thousand Oaks, London, and New Delhi: Sage Publications, Inc.

Finnis, John M. 1995. 'Law, Morality and "Sexual Orientation."' *Notre Dame Journal of Law, Ethics, and Public Policy* 9(1).

Fisher, William A., and Azy Barak. 1991. 'Pornography, Erotica, and Behavior: More Questions Than Answers.' *International Journal of Law and Psychiatry* 14(1–2).

Fisher, William A., and Guy Grenier. 1994. 'Violent Pornography, Anti-Woman Thoughts, and Anti-Woman Acts: In Search of Reliable Effects.' *Journal of Sex Research* 31(1).

Fiss, Owen M. 1996. *The Irony of Free Speech.* Cambridge, MA, and London: Harvard University Press.

Flowers, Amy. 1998. *The Fantasy Factory: An Insider's View of the Phone Sex Industry.* Philadelphia: University of Pennsylvania Press.

Fox, Richard G. 1972. *Obscenity.* Ottawa: Law Reform Commission of Canada.

Freedman, Jonathan L. 2002. *Media Violence and Its Effect on Aggression: Assessing the Scientific Evidence.* Toronto: University of Toronto Press.

Fuller, Janine, and Stuart Blackley. 1996. *Restricted Entry: Censorship on Trial.* Vancouver: Press Gang Publishers.

Garnets, Linda, Gregory M. Herek, and Barrie Levey. 1990. 'Violence and Victimization of Lesbians and Gay Men: Mental Health Consequences.' *Journal of Interpersonal Violence* 5(3).

Gentry, Cynthia S. 1991. 'Pornography and Rape: An Empirical Analysis.' *Deviant Behavior* 12(3).

Gillespie, Paul. 2002. Interview. Toronto, 4 November.

Government of Canada. 1982. *The Criminal Law in Canadian Society.* Ottawa.

Gray, John. 1983. *Mill on Liberty: A Defence*. London: Routledge and Kegan Paul.

Greenawalt, Kent. 1995. *Fighting Words: Individuals, Communities and Liberties of Speech*. Princeton: Princeton University Press.

Hamm, M.S. 1994. 'Conceptualizing Hate Crime in a Global Context.' In *Hate Crime: International Perspectives of Causes and Control*, ed. M.S. Hamm. Cincinnati, OH: Anderson Publishing and Academy of Criminal Justice Sciences.

Hampton, Jean. 1992. 'Correcting Harms versus Righting Wrongs: The Goal of Retribution.' *UCLA Law Review* 39.

Hart, H.L.A. 1966. *Law, Liberty, and Morality*. New York: Vintage Books.

Hart, H.L.A. 1982. *Essays on Bentham: Studies in Jurisprudence and Political Theory*. Oxford: Clarendon Press.

Hartley, Nina. 1987. 'Confessions of a Feminist Porno Star.' In *Sex Work: Writings by Women in the Sex Industry*, ed. Frederique Delacoste and Priscilla Alexander. Pittsburgh: Cleis Press.

Hartley, Nina. 1993. 'Interview.' Radio program segment. Prime Time: Second Look: Women and Pornography. Canadian Broadcasting Corporation.

Hartley, Nina. 1997. 'In the Flesh: A Porn Star's Journey.' In *Whores and Other Feminists*, ed. Jill Nagle. New York and London: Routledge.

Haselton, Bennett. 2002. 'A Critique of Filtering.' In *Technical, Business, and Legal Dimensions of Protecting Children from Pornography on the Internet: Proceedings of a Workshop*, ed. Committee to Study Tools and Strategies for Protecting Kids from Pornography and Their Applicability to Other Inappropriate Internet Content. Washington, DC: National Academy Press.

Heins, Marjorie. 2001. *Not in Front of the Children: 'Indecency,' Censorship, and the Innocence of Youth*. New York: Hill and Wang.

Herek, Gregory M., Jeanine C. Cogan, and J. Roy Gillis. 2002. 'Victim Experiences in Hate Crimes Based on Sexual Orientation.' *Journal of Social Issues* 58(2).

Herek, Gregory M., J. Roy Gillis, and Jeanine C. Cogan. 1999. 'Psychological Sequelae of Hate-Crime Victimization among Lesbian, Gay, and Bisexual Adults.' *Journal of Consulting and Clinical Psychology* 67(6).

Hogg, Peter W. 2000. *Constitutional Law of Canada; 2000 Student Edition*. Scarborough: Carswell.

Hornsby, Jennifer. 1995. 'Speech Acts and Pornography.' In *The Problem of Pornography*, ed. Susan Dwyer. Belmont, CA: Wadsworth Publishing Company.

Hornsby, Jennifer, and Rae Langton. 1998. 'Free Speech and Illocution.' *Legal Theory* 4(1).

House of Commons, Canada. 1984. *Equality Now!* Report of the Special Committee on the Participation of Visible Minorities in Canadian Society. Ottawa: Supply and Services.

Howe, R. Brian, and David Johnson. 2000. *Restraining Equality: Human Rights Commissions in Canada.* Toronto: University of Toronto Press.

Hunt, Patricia, and Margaret Baird. 1990. 'Children of Sex Rings.' *Child Welfare* 69(3).

Jacobs, James B., and Kimberly Potter. 1998. *Hate Crimes: Criminal Law and Identity Politics.* New York: Oxford University Press.

Jacobson, Daniel. 1995. 'Freedom of Speech Acts? A Response to Langton.' *Philosophy and Public Affairs* 24(1).

Jacobson, Daniel. 2001. 'Speech and Action: Replies to Hornsby and Langton.' *Legal Theory* 7.

Jenkins, Philip. 2001. *Beyond Tolerance: Child Pornography on the Internet.* New York and London: New York University Press.

Jensen, Robert. 1998. 'Using Pornography.' In Dines, Jensen, and Russo, eds, *Pornography.*

Jensen, Robert, and Gail Dines. 1998. 'The Content of Mass-Marketed Pornography.' In Dines, Jensen, and Russo, eds, *Pornography.*

Johnson, Conrad D. 1991. *Moral Legislation: A Legal-Political Model for Indirect Consequentialist Reasoning.* Cambridge: Cambridge University Press.

Juffer, Jane. 1998. *At Home with Pornography: Women, Sex, and Everyday Life.* New York: New York University Press.

Kagan, Shelly. 1989. *The Limits of Morality.* Oxford: Clarendon Press.

Kelly, Liz. 1988. *Surviving Sexual Violence.* Minneapolis: University of Minnesota Press.

Kelly, Liz. 1992. 'Pornography and Child Sexual Abuse.' In *Pornography: Women, Violence and Civil Liberties,* ed. Catherine Itzin. Oxford: Oxford University Press.

Kinsella, Warren. 1994. *Web of Hate: Inside Canada's Far-Right Network.* Toronto: HarperCollins.

Kupperstein, L., and W.C. Wilson. 1970. 'Erotica and Anti-Social Behavior: An Analysis of Selected Social Indicator Statistics.' In *Technical Report of the Commission on Obscenity and Pornography.* Vol. 7. Washington, D.C.: Government Printing Office.

Kutchinsky, Berl. 1970. 'Towards an Explanation of the Decrease in Registered Sex Crimes in Copenhagen.' In *Technical Report of the Commission on Obscenity and Pornography.* Vol. 7. Washington, D.C.: Government Printing Office.

Kutchinsky, Berl. 1973. 'The Effect of Easy Availability of Pornography on the Incidence of Sex Crimes: The Danish Experience.' *Journal of Social Issues* 29(3).

Kutchinsky, Berl. 1978. 'Pornography in Denmark – a General Survey.' In *Censorship and Obscenity,* ed. R. Dhavan and C. Davies. London: Martin Robinson.

Kutchinsky, Berl. 1985. 'Pornography and Its Effects in Denmark and the
United States: A Rejoinder and Beyond.' *Comparative Social Research* 8.

Kutchinsky, Berl. 1991. 'Pornography and Rape: Theory and Practice? Evidence
from Crime Data in Four Countries Where Pornography Is Easily Available.'
International Journal of Law and Psychiatry 14(1–2).

Lahey, Kathleen A. 1991. 'Pornography and Harm – Learning to Listen to
Women.' *International Journal of Law and Psychiatry* 14(1–2).

Langevin, Ron, et al. 1988. 'Pornography and Sexual Offences.' *Annals of Sex
Research* 1(3).

Langton, Rae. 1993. 'Speech Acts and Unspeakable Acts.' *Philosophy and Public
Affairs* 22(4).

Law Reform Commission of Canada. 1986. *Hate Propaganda.* Working Paper 50.
Ottawa: Law Reform Commission of Canada.

Lawrence, Frederick M. 1999. *Punishing Hate: Bias Crimes under American Law.*
Cambridge, MA: Harvard University Press.

League for Human Rights of B'nai Brith Canada. 1990. *Skinheads in Canada and
Their Link to the Far Right.* Downsview, ON: B'nai Brith Canada.

League for Human Rights of B'nai Brith Canada. 2002. *2001 Audit of Antisemitic
Incidents.* Downsview, ON: B'nai Brith Canada.

Leeper, Roy. 2000. 'Keegstra and R.A.V.: A Comparative Analysis of the Canadian and U.S. Approaches to Hate Speech Legislation.' *Communication Law
and Policy* 5(3).

Leets, Laura. 2002. 'Experiencing Hate Speech: Perceptions and Responses to
Anti-Semitism and Antigay Speech.' *Journal of Social Issues* 58(2).

Leighton, Barry. 1988. *A Guide to the Social Science Evidence on the Effects of Pornography, Part I.* Ottawa: Department of Justice Canada.

Levin, Jack, and Jack McDevitt. 1993. *Hate Crimes: The Rising Tide of Bigotry and
Bloodshed.* New York: Plenum Press.

Levine, Judith. 2002. *Harmful to Minors: The Perils of Protecting Children from Sex.*
Minneapolis and London: University of Minnesota Press.

Linden, Robin Ruth, Darlene R. Pagano, Diana E.H. Russell, and Susan Leigh
Star. 1982. *Against Sadomasochism: A Radical Feminist Analysis.* East Palo Alto,
CA: Frog in the Wall.

Linz, Daniel, and Neil Malamuth. 1993. *Pornography.* Newbury Park, CA: Sage
Publications.

Linz, Daniel, Steven D. Penrod, and Edward Donnerstein. 1987. 'The Attorney
General's Commission on Pornography: The Gaps Between "Findings" and
Facts.' *American Bar Foundation Research Journal* 4.

Longino, Helen E. 1980. 'Pornography, Oppression, and Freedom: A Closer

Look.' In *Take Back the Night: Women on Pornography*, ed. Laura Lederer. New York: William Morrow and Company.

Lovelace, Linda, and Mike McGrady. 1980. *Ordeal*. New York: Berkeley.

Lyons, David. 1977. 'Human Rights and the General Welfare.' *Philosophy and Public Affairs* 6(2).

MacDougall, Cynthia A. 1984. 'The Community Standards Test of Obscenity.' *University of Toronto Faculty of Law Review* 42(2).

Mackay, R.S. 1958. 'The Hicklin Rule and Judicial Censorship.' *Canadian Bar Review* 36(1).

MacKinnon, Catharine A. 1987. *Feminism Unmodified: Discourses on Life and Law*. Cambridge, MA: Harvard University Press.

MacKinnon, Catharine A. 1991. 'Pornography as Defamation and Discrimination.' *Boston University Law Review* 71(5).

MacKinnon, Catharine A. 1993. *Only Words*. Cambridge, MA: Harvard University Press.

MacKinnon, Catharine A., and Andrea Dworkin, eds. 1997. *In Harm's Way: The Pornography Civil Rights Hearings*. Cambridge, MA: Harvard University Press.

Macy, Marianne. 1996. *Working Sex: An Odyssey into Our Cultural Underground*. New York: Carroll and Graf.

Mahoney, Kathleen E. 1991. 'Canaries in a Coal Mine: Canadian Judges and the Reconstruction of Obscenity Law.' In *Freedom of Expression and the Charter*, ed. David Schneiderman. Np: Thomson Professional Publishing Canada.

Mahoney, Kathleen E. 1992. 'The Canadian Constitutional Approach to Freedom of Expression in Hate Propaganda and Pornography.' *Law and Contemporary Problems* 55(1).

Mailland, Julien. 2001. 'Freedom of Speech, the Internet, and the Costs of Control: The French Example.' *New York University Journal of International Law and Politics* 33(4).

Matsuda, Mari J. 1993. 'Public Response to Racist Speech: Considering the Victim's Story.' In *Words That Wound: Critical Race Theory, Assaultive Speech, and the First Amendment*, ed. Mari J. Matsuda, Charles R. Lawrence, III, Richard Delgado, and Kimberle Williams Crenshaw. Boulder, CO: Westview Press.

Matthews, Robert E. 2002. Interview. Toronto, 6 November.

McAlpine, John D. 1981. *Report Arising out of the Activities of the Ku Klux Klan in British Columbia*. Report to Government of British Columbia.

McClintock, Anne. 1993. 'Gonad the Barbarian and the Venus Flytrap: Portraying the Female and Male Orgasm.' In *Sex Exposed: Sexuality and the Pornography Debate*, ed. Lynne Segal and Mary McIntosh. New Brunswick, NJ: Rutgers University Press.

McDevitt, Jack, Jack Levin, and Susan Bennett. 2002. 'Hate Crime Offenders: An Expanded Typology.' *Journal of Social Issues* 58(2).

McElroy, Wendy. 1995. *XXX: A Woman's Right to Pornography.* New York: St Martin's Press.

McGowan, Mary Kate. 2003. 'Conversational Exercitives and the Force of Pornography.' *Philosophy and Public Affairs* 31(2).

McLaren, John P.S. 1991. '"Now You See It, Now You Don't": The Historical Record and the Elusive Task of Defining the Obscene.' In *Freedom of Expression and the Charter*, ed. David Schneiderman. Np: Thomson Professional Publishing Canada.

Michaud, Steven G., and Hugh Aynesworth. 1983. *The Only Living Witness: A True Account of Homicidal Insanity.* New York: Simon and Schuster.

Miethe, T.D., and R.C. McCorkle. 1998. *Crime Profiles: The Anatomy of Dangerous Persons, Places, and Situations.* Los Angeles: Roxbury Publishing.

Mill, John Stuart. 1965. *Principles of Political Economy.* Ed. J.M. Robson. Collected Works of John Stuart Mill, vol. 2. Toronto: University of Toronto Press.

Mill, John Stuart. 1969. *Utilitarianism.* In *Essays on Ethics, Religion, and Society.* Ed. John M. Robson. Collected Works of John Stuart Mill, vol. 10. Toronto: University of Toronto Press.

Mill, John Stuart. 1977. *On Liberty.* In *Essays on Politics and Society.* Ed. John M. Robson. Collected Works of John Stuart Mill, vol. 18. Toronto: University of Toronto Press.

Mill, John Stuart. 1981. *Autobiography and Literary Essays.* Ed. John M. Robson and Jack Stillinger. Collected Works of John Stuart Mill, vol. 1. Toronto: University of Toronto Press.

Mill, John Stuart. 1984. *Essays on Equality, Law, and Education.* Ed. John M. Robson. Collected Works of John Stuart Mill, vol. 21. Toronto: University of Toronto Press.

Monk-Turner, Elizabeth, and H. Christine Purcell. 1999. 'Sexual Violence in Pornography: How Prevalent Is It?' *Gender Issues* 17(2).

Moon, Richard. 1993. 'R. v. Butler: The Limits of the Supreme Court's Feminist Re-interpretation of Section 163.' *Ottawa Law Review* 25(2).

Morales, Maria H. 1996. *Perfect Equality: John Stuart Mill on Well-constituted Communities.* Lanham: Rowman and Littlefield.

Moyer, Sharon. 1992. *A Preliminary Investigation into Child Pornography in Canada.* Ottawa: Department of Justice.

Murrin, Mary R., and D.R. Laws. 1990. 'The Influence of Pornography on Sexual Crimes.' In *Handbook of Sexual Assault*, ed. W.L. Marshall, D.R. Laws, and H.E. Barbaree. New York: Plenum Press.

Nagle, Jill, ed. 1997. *Whores and Other Feminists.* New York and London: Routledge.

Newman, Stephen L. 2002. 'Liberty, Community, and Censorship: Hate Speech and Freedom of Expression in Canada and the United States.' *American Review of Canadian Studies.*

Nielsen, Laura Beth. 2002. 'Subtle, Pervasive, Harmful: Racist and Sexist Remarks in Public as Hate Speech.' *Journal of Social Issues* 58(2).

Norman, Ken, John D. McAlpine, and Hymie Weinstein. 1984. *Report of the Special Committee on Racial and Religious Hatred.* Np: Canadian Bar Association.

Nussbaum, Martha. 1995. 'Objectification.' *Philosophy and Public Affairs* 24(4).

Nutter, David E., and Mary E. Kearns. 1993. 'Patterns of Exposure to Sexually Explicit Material among Sex Offenders, Child Molesters and Controls.' *Journal of Sex and Marital Therapy* 19(1).

O'Rourke, K.C. 2001. *John Stuart Mill and Freedom of Expression: The Genesis of a Theory.* London and New York: Routledge.

Palac, Lisa. 1998. *The Edge of the Bed: How Dirty Pictures Changed My Life.* Boston: Little, Brown.

Perry, Barbara. 2001. *In the Name of Hate: Understanding Hate Crimes.* New York and London: Routledge.

Persky, Stan, and John Dixon. 2001. *On Kiddie Porn: Sexual Representation, Free Speech, and the Robin Sharpe Case.* Vancouver: New Star Books.

Potter, Roberto Hugh. 1999. 'Long-Term Consumption of "X-Rated" Materials and Attitudes toward Women among Australian Consumers of X-Rated Videos.' In *Sex Work and Sex Workers*, ed. Barry M. Dank and Roberto Refinetti. New Brunswick and London: Transaction Publishers.

Railton, Peter. 1984. 'Alienation, Consequentialism, and the Demands of Morality.' *Philosophy and Public Affairs* 13(2).

Rawls, John. 1993. *Political Liberalism.* New York: Columbia University Press.

Rea, Michael C. 2001. 'What Is Pornography?' *Nous* 35(1).

Rees, John C. 1985. *John Stuart Mill's On Liberty.* Ed. G.L. Williams. Oxford: Clarendon Press.

Rich, Frank. 2001. 'Naked Capitalists.' *New York Times Magazine*, 20 May.

Richardson, Henry S. 1990. 'Specifying Norms as a Way to Resolve Concrete Ethical Problems.' *Philosophy and Public Affairs* 19(4).

Ridgeway, James. 1995. *Blood in the Face.* New York: Thunder's Mouth Press.

Riley, Jonathan. 1998. *Mill on Liberty.* London and New York: Routledge.

Ross, Becki L. 1997. '"It's Merely Designed for Sexual Arousal": Interrogating the Indefensibility of Lesbian Smut.' In Cossman, Bell, Gotell, and Ross, eds, *Bad Attitude/s.*

Russell, Diana E.H. 1980. 'Pornography and Violence: What Does the New Research Say?' In *Take Back the Night: Women on Pornography*, ed. Laura Lederer. New York: William Morrow and Company.

Russell, Diana E.H. 1992. 'Pornography and Rape: A Causal Model.' In *Pornography: Women, Violence and Civil Liberties*, ed. Catherine Itzin. Oxford: Oxford University Press.

Russo, Ann. 1998. 'Feminists Confront Pornography's Subordinating Practices: Politics and Strategies for Change.' In Dines, Jensen, and Russo, eds, *Pornography*.

Ryder, Bruce. 2001. 'The Little Sisters Case, Administrative Censorship, and Obscenity Law.' *Osgoode Hall Law Journal* 39(1).

Ryder, Bruce. 2003. 'The Harms of Child Pornography Law.' *U.B.C. Law Review* 36(1).

SAMOIS, ed. 1982. *Coming to Power: Writings and Graphics on Lesbian S/M*. 2nd ed. Boston: Alyson Publications, Inc.

Sartorius, Rolf E. 1975. *Individual Conduct and Social Norms*. Encino, CA: Dickenson Publishing Company.

Scanlon, T.M. 1979. 'Freedom of Expression and Categories of Expression.' *University of Pittsburgh Law Review* 40(4).

Schauer, Frederick. 1982. *Free Speech: A Philosophical Enquiry*. Cambridge: Cambridge University Press.

Schauer, Frederick. 1987. 'Causation Theory and the Causes of Sexual Violence.' *American Bar Foundation Research Journal* 4.

Scheffler, Samuel. 1982. *The Rejection of Consequentialism: A Philosophical Investigation of the Considerations Underlying Rival Moral Conceptions*. Oxford: Clarendon Press.

Scott, Joseph E. 1991. 'What Is Obscene? Social Science and the Contemporary Community Standard Test of Obscenity.' *International Journal of Law and Psychiatry* 14(1–2).

Scott, Joseph E., and S.J. Cuvelier. 1987. 'Sexual Violence in Playboy Magazine: A Longitudinal Content Analysis.' *Journal of Sex Research* 23.

Scott, Joseph E., and S.J. Cuvelier. 1993. 'Violence and Sexual Violence in Pornography: Is It Really Increasing?' *Archives of Sexual Behavior* 22(4).

Segal, Lynne. 1993. 'Does Pornography Cause Violence? The Search for Evidence.' In *Dirty Looks: Women, Pornography, Power*, Pamela Church Gibson and Roma Gibson. London: BFI Publishing.

Shaw, William H. 1999. *Contemporary Ethics: Taking Account of Utilitarianism*. Malden, MA: Blackwell Publishers.

Silbert, Mimi H., and Ayala M. Pines. 1984. 'Pornography and Sexual Abuse of Women.' *Sex Roles* 10(11/12).

Slote, Michael. 1989. *Beyond Optimizing: A Study of Rational Choice*. Cambridge, MA: Harvard University Press.

Sniderman, Paul M., Joseph F. Fletcher, Peter H. Russell, and Philip E. Tetlock.

1996. *The Clash of Rights: Liberty, Equality, and Legitimacy in Pluralist Democracy.* New Haven: Yale University Press.

Special Committee on Hate Propaganda in Canada. 1966. *Report of the Special Committee on Hate Propaganda in Canada.* Ottawa: Queen's Printer.

Special Committee on Pornography and Prostitution. 1985. *Pornography and Prostitution in Canada: Report of the Special Committee on Pornography and Prostitution.* Ottawa: Minister of Supply and Services Canada.

Sprinkle, Annie. 1991. *Post Porn Modernist.* Amsterdam: Torch.

Steinem, Gloria. 1980. 'Erotica and Pornography: A Clear and Present Difference.' In *Take Back the Night: Women on Pornography,* ed. Laura Lederer. New York: William Morrow and Company.

Steinem, Gloria. 1995. *Outrageous Acts and Everyday Rebellions.* 2nd ed. New York: Henry Holt and Company.

Stern, Kenneth. 1996. *A Force upon the Plain.* New York: Simon and Schuster.

Stoller, Robert J., and I.S. Levine. 1993. *Coming Attractions: The Making of an X-Rated Video.* New Haven: Yale University Press.

Strager, Stephen. 2003. 'What Men Watch When They Watch Pornography.' *Sexuality and Culture* 7(1).

Strossen, Nadine. 1995. *Defending Pornography: Free Speech, Sex, and the Fight for Women's Rights.* New York: Scribner.

Sumner, L.W. 1987. *The Moral Foundation of Rights.* Oxford: Clarendon Press.

Sumner, L.W. 1994. 'Hate Propaganda and Charter Rights.' In *Free Expression: Essays in Law and Philosophy,* ed. W.J. Waluchow. Oxford: Clarendon Press.

Sumner, L.W. 1996. *Welfare, Happiness, and Ethics.* Oxford: Clarendon Press.

Tate, Tim. 1990. *Child Pornography: An Investigation.* London: Methuen.

Tate, Tim. 1992. 'The Child Pornography Industry: International Trade in Child Sexual Abuse.' In *Pornography: Women, Violence and Civil Liberties,* ed. Catherine Itzin. Oxford: Oxford University Press.

Ten, C.L. 1980. *Mill on Liberty.* Oxford: Clarendon Press.

Thomson, Judith. 1986. *Rights, Restitution, and Risk: Essays in Moral Theory.* Cambridge, MA: Harvard University Press.

Thomson, Judith. 1990. *The Realm of Rights.* Cambridge, MA: Harvard University Press.

Tisdale, Sallie. 1994. *Talk Dirty to Me: An Intimate Philosophy of Sex.* New York: Doubleday.

Toobin, Jeffrey. 1994. 'Annals of Law: X-Rated.' *The New Yorker,* 3 October.

Toronto Police Service. 2002. *2001 Hate Bias Crime Statistical Report.* Toronto: Toronto Police Service.

Tracey, Lindalee. 1997. *Growing up Naked: My Years in Bump-and-Grind.* Vancouver and Toronto: Douglas and McIntyre.

Tsesis, Alexander. 2002. *Destructive Messages: How Hate Speech Paves the Way for Harmful Social Movements*. New York and London: New York University Press.

Vadas, Melinda. 1987. 'A First Look at the Pornography/Civil Rights Ordinance: Could Pornography Be the Subordination of Women?' *Journal of Philosophy* 84(9).

Vance, Carole S. 1993. 'Negotiating Sex and Gender in the Attorney General's Commission on Pornography.' In *Sex Exposed: Sexuality and the Pornography Debate*, ed. Lynne Segal and Mary McIntosh. New Brunswick, NJ: Rutgers University Press.

Vernon, Richard. 1996. 'John Stuart Mill and Pornography: Beyond the Harm Principle.' *Ethics* 106(3).

Waldron, Jeremy. 1993. *Liberal Rights*. Cambridge: Cambridge University Press.

Weinstein, James. 1999. *Hate Speech, Pornography, and the Radical Attack on Free Speech Doctrine*. Boulder, CO: Westview Press.

Wellman, Carl. 1985. *A Theory of Rights: Persons under Laws, Institutions, and Morals*. Totawa, NJ: Rowman and Allanheld.

Williams, Bernard, ed. 1981. *Obscenity and Film Censorship: An Abridgement of the Williams Report*. Cambridge: Cambridge University Press.

Williams, Linda. 1989. *Hard Core: Power, Pleasure, and the 'Frenzy of the Visible.'* Berkeley: University of California Press.

Wolfenden, Sir John. 1957. *Report of the Committee on Homosexual Offences and Prostitution*. London: Her Majesty's Stationery Offfice.

Wollaston, Paul. 1992. 'When Will They Ever Get It Right? A Gay Analysis of *R. v. Butler.*' *Dalhousie Journal of Legal Studies*.

Wyre, Ray. 1992. 'Pornography and Sexual Violence: Working with Sex Offenders.' In *Pornography: Women, Violence, and Civil Liberties*, ed. Catherine Itzin. Oxford: Oxford University Press.

Yang, Ni, and Daniel Linz. 1990. 'Movie Ratings and the Content of Adult Videos: The Sex-Violence Ratio.' *Journal of Communication* 40(2).

Zillman, Dolf. 1989. 'Effects of Prolonged Consumption of Pornography.' In *Pornography: Research Advances and Policy Considerations*, ed. Dolf Zillman and Jennings Bryant. Hillsdale, NJ: Lawrence Erlbaum Associates.

Zillman, Dolf, and James B. Weaver. 1989. 'Pornography and Men's Sexual Callousness toward Women.' In *Pornography: Research Advances and Policy Considerations*, ed. Dolf Zillman and Jennings Bryant. Hillsdale, NJ: Lawrence Erlbaum Associates.

Index